D1327376

Women in Politics in
the American City

Women in Politics in the American City

Mirya R. Holman

TEMPLE UNIVERSITY PRESS
Philadelphia   Rome   Tokyo

TEMPLE UNIVERSITY PRESS
Philadelphia, Pennsylvania 19122
www.temple.edu/tempress

Portions of Chapter 5 originally appeared online in Mirya Holman,
"Sex and the City: Female Leaders and Spending on Social Welfare
Programs in U.S. Municipalities," *Journal of Urban Affairs*, October 29,
2013, doi:10.1111/juaf.12066. Copyright © 2013 Urban Affairs
Association. Reproduced with permission of John Wiley & Sons, Inc.

Library of Congress Cataloging-in-Publication Data

Holman, Mirya.
    Women in politics in the American city / Mirya R. Holman.
        pages cm
    Includes bibliographical references and index.
    ISBN 978-1-4399-1170-9 (hardback : alk. paper) —
ISBN 978-1-4399-1172-3 (e-book)   1. Women city council members—
United States.   2. Women legislators—United States.   3. Municipal
government—United States.   4. Women's rights—United States.
5. Social planning—United States.   6. Political planning—United
States.   I. Title.
    HQ1236.5.U6H65 2015
    320.0820973—dc23

                                                            2014017921

Printed in the United States of America

2 4 6 8 9 7 5 3 1

Contents

Acknowledgments

The process of writing a book lends to the accumulation of debts near and far; these are the most prominent. First, to the mayors and city council members who participated in my survey and especially those who consented to be interviewed, I offer heartfelt thanks for opening up their political lives to me. Thanks are also owed to the city clerks and budget officers who answered my (sometimes awkward) questions about funding, budgets, and representatives.

I am greatly indebted to many wonderful mentors who have provided skills and support for this project. My dissertation committee, Jennifer Merolla, Jean Schroedel, Peter Burns, and Annette Steinacker, provided immeasurable assistance during the writing of the dissertation that led to this book.

Jennifer Merolla read draft after draft of my dissertation and book proposal, providing thoughtful and useful feedback at each stage. Her assistance in the design, execution, and completion of both was essential to this project. In addition, her thoughtful and kind advice throughout my work on the dissertation and other projects buoyed me through graduate school and into my career. She taught me how to be a good scholar—and how to be a great person while being a good scholar. I am lucky that I continue to be able to rely on her for advice and assistance.

Peter Burns has served as my mentor for over a decade now and has been my inspiration for how to teach and research with enthusiasm and care. From encouraging me to attend graduate school to serving on my dissertation committee to giving me advice about the book publishing process, he has helped in innumerable ways.

Many friends and colleagues offered support, read drafts, and helped with various aspects of this project over the years. I received responses on portions of this book at a variety of conferences. Thanks go to Karen Kaufmann, who read a chapter at the Midwest Political Science Association, and many others who have offered feedback and advice. Special thanks go to Travis Coan, who offered comments on the construction of various methods of the book and read drafts of chapters. A summer writing group at Florida Atlantic University kept me on track during my initial revisions. The New Research on Gender and Political Psychology group, run by Angie Bos and Monica Schneider, and the writing group that emerged out of it were particularly helpful to me in my writing. The scholars associated with these groups offered much support and encouragement—thanks are owed to all of them. The writing group's feedback on my final edits to the book kept me going when I was not sure if I would ever be done with the project. I owe special thanks to Emily Farris and Erin Cassese for their recommendations and support. Thanks also go to Alex Holzman and the team at Temple University Press for all their work on this book.

Claremont Graduate University's Dissertation Grant and the M. and M. Johnson Scholarship provided funding for my studies and research. Thanks go to the Center for American Women and Politics and the National Association of Latino Elected and Appointed Officials for data. I owe the J. Michael Goodson Law Library at Duke University—and especially Dick Danner and Molly Brownfield—a debt of gratitude for providing me with a job and an office while I was completing the dissertation that led to this book. I completed the majority of the edits to this book at Florida Atlantic University. I thank FAU and my colleagues for their support. In particular, I thank Jeffrey Morton, whose advice about being a professor, completing research, and living life is priceless but offered freely.

I also thank my parents, Kerry Holman and Shel Anderson, for instilling in me a lifelong passion for learning, as well as a good dose of stubbornness. This book would have been impossible without them and their guidance and support throughout the years. In addition, I owe thanks to other members of my family, especially Laurie Prouty and Jessea Mucha, and to my many friends who tolerated discussions of the book over the years. I also benefited greatly from an incredibly supportive community growing up; my thanks go to Terry, Dan, Tracy, Walter, Rick, Luanne, Debbie, Felicity, Sherry, Jack, Steve, Joanne, and all the other teachers, mentors, and friends who encouraged and challenged me.

I dedicate this book to my husband, Zach Danner, who has helped me become the political scientist, writer, researcher, and person I am today. In keeping me grounded and happy, he provided the balance I needed in my life to write my dissertation and this book. Without him, I would not have had the time, resources, or vitality to complete them. He has lived within and around this project for almost a decade and never complained about it. I thank him for his sense of humor, love, and support.

Women in Politics in
the American City

1 /

Urban Government, Democracy, and the Representation of Gender in the United States

Women in American Cities

When a woman leaves her natural sphere,
And without her sex's modesty or fear
Assays the part of man,
She, in her weak attempts to rule,
But makes herself a mark for ridicule,
A laughing-stock and sham.
Article of greatest use is to her then
Something worn distinctively by men—
A pair of pants will do.
Thus she will plainly demonstrate
That Nature made a great mistake
In sexing such a shrew.
—Anonymous letter to Susanna Salter, first
female U.S. mayor, Argonia, Kansas, 1887[1]

When Argonia, Kansas, elected Susanna Salter in 1887, she became the first woman to hold elected office in the United States. Selected largely as a result of electoral maneuvering by a group of men opposed to a slate of male candidates supported by the Women's Christian Temperance Union, Mrs. Salter's election brought attention to Argonia from reporters, supporters, detractors, and women's rights advocates.[2] Fast-forward more than 120 years, and women hold local elected offices throughout the United States. Yet despite the passage of time, the increase in the number of women in office, and extensive research on female leaders at the state and national levels, little is known about how female municipal leaders influence policy making in American cities.[3]

Is it important that women hold local office? Currently, 17 percent of mayors of large cities are women.[4] Is this enough? How important is it that urban governments look like the cities and citizens they represent? This book is a careful analysis of how gender does and does not influence the political and policy behavior of mayors and council members. It draws on city council meeting minutes, surveys of and interviews with mayors and city council members, surveys of community members, and urban fiscal and employment data. Many theories of urban politics suggest that the gender of a mayor or city council member should be irrelevant, because electoral concerns, institutional limitations, informal relationships with business, and a drive for economic growth constrain the function of local representatives and make them interested in growth, regardless of gender. Indeed, despite identifying widespread gender effects at higher levels of office, such that women in office are more interested in funding social welfare programs and support feminist issues, the limited scholarship on gender and local politics largely concludes that women fail to similarly influence politics at the local level.[5] I disagree. Although the local level *resists the incorporation of women's interests*, I found substantial evidence that the involvement of women in local politics *does* matter and has consequences for urban policy and the state of local democracy.

To demonstrate the importance of women's representation in local politics, the research presented here addresses a number of questions about female leaders in urban politics and the effects of gender on urban governance. First, why would gender matter at the local level? Can we identify a *cohesive set of urban women's issues*? From where does this array of issues emerge, and does it differ significantly from women's issues at other levels of government? Second, how does the gender of mayors and council members influence *policy preferences*, or how local representatives think about urban policies and politics? Do female leaders and male leaders express similar levels of support for urban women's issues, such as those relating to children and welfare policies? Do men and women in local office express the same attitudes about representation? Third, does mayoral gender influence the *policy process*, or how cities engage in policy making? What does the election of women mean for the community's engagement in local politics? Fourth, do cities with female leaders make choices different from cities with male leaders about *policy outcomes* and which programs to fund? Finally, do voters make the correct decision for their city when they elect women? Does the presence of women in local office influence the quality of urban democracy and satisfaction with local government? What does the election of women to local office mean for the fiscal health of cities?

To answer these questions, I examine how gender influences (1) policy preferences, (2) policy processes, and (3) policy outcomes. The rest of this chapter presents an overview of three central bodies of knowledge: my conceptualization and operationalization of a set of women's urban issues, the general influence of gender on the behavior of leaders in decision-making bodies, and how urban policy making presents a unique and challenging frame for understanding the influence of women in politics.

Defining Urban Women's Issues

Our City does not ask us to die for her welfare; she asks us to live for her good, and so to act that her government may be pure, her officers honest, and every home within her boundaries be a place fit to grow the best kind of men and women to rule over her.

—MARY MCDOWELL, "YOUNG CITIZEN'S CREED," 1898

Those policies that really help women—low-income housing, children's services, improving the schools, protecting women, that sort of thing—those are women's policies in my city. Those are what women come to me about.

—A FEMALE MAYOR, EXPLAINING HOW SHE WOULD DEFINE WOMEN'S ISSUES OR POLICIES IN HER CITY

Women have a long history of activism in American urban politics, and extensive research documents women's early work on social welfare, education, and public works in cities. However, we know much less about how women in modern urban politics behave or influence policies.[6] Using a political development approach, I argue that women's extensive work in and interactions with particular areas of urban policy produce a set of *urban women's issues,* or areas under the purview of urban governance that reflect a history of women's political activism and disproportionately influence the lives of contemporary women in urban America.[7] I include policies that address children, education, affordable housing, social welfare, and violence against women under this definition. I posit that women in modern urban politics, compared to their male counterparts, privilege this set of issues in policy making.

Urban women's issues are operationalized as including children, education, affordable housing, social welfare, and domestic violence for a variety of reasons, many of which relate to a gendered difference in the conceptualizations of social ills—in American political development and in modern times. First, 78 percent of female leaders I interviewed identified one or more of these as local women's issues (see Figure 1.1).[8] Second, these issues have a strong history of women's political activism, including women's nascent political work in the nineteenth- and early-twentieth-century United States. Third, women receive the lion's share of services related to these issues. Fourth, women in the public and in political office engage in activism in these areas and value government intervention more than their male counterparts do. Fifth, these urban women's issues represent a subset of traditional women's issues—or "public concerns that impinge on the private (especially domestic) sphere of social life, and particularly those values associated with children and nurturance"[9]— but differ from women's issues traditionally handled by the state and federal governments, such as reproductive rights and pay equality.[10] Finally, these issues continue to be associated with local decision making. While the engagement of state and federal governments in these areas has certainly increased in the last century, intervention largely occurs *within and through* local agencies and governments, not through agencies entirely run by a higher level of government. For example, the Department of Housing and Urban Development administers housing aid to local housing authorities; this significantly differs

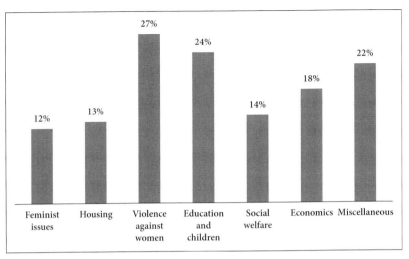

Figure 1.1 **Definition of urban women's issues by female mayors and city council members.** Leaders could name more than one issue, so percentages exceed 100 percent. Feminist issues include sexual discrimination and harassment, equal pay, abortion rights, and reproductive rights; housing includes affordable housing, housing costs, public housing, and renters' rights; violence against women includes rape, domestic violence, sexual assault, and intimate partner violence; education and children includes child care, summer school, foster care, PTA, school quality, and school violence; social welfare includes welfare, food stamps, WIC (the Special Supplemental Nutrition Program for Women, Infants and Children), homeless shelters, job training, and elderly care; economics includes jobs, job creation, wages, property development, and businesses moving to the city; miscellaneous includes cleaning up city hall, fighting corruption, cutting red tape, and eliminating bureaucracy. The data come from interviews with twenty-nine female leaders in the eight case-study cities described in Chapter 3.

from the Social Security Administration, which runs its own agencies in local areas.

I present the case for this array of urban women's issues in three discussions: a brief history of women's political development in activism in these areas in urban America, extant research on use and support of these policies by women and the representation of these policies by women in office, and policy making, particularly in these areas, in urban America. I make the case for a separate subset of *urban women's issues* and for women in city politics to prefer, pursue, and produce policies within this arena.

For women in the United States (and around the world), gender serves as a central component of political identity. Before I proceed, it is necessary to define *gender*. For the purposes of the research here, I define *gender* as the social construction of biological sex, distinguished from sex, which is a biological marker.[11]

Women's Historical Activism in Cities

For the first several decades of U.S. history, society relegated women to the private home and hearth while men acted for themselves and their female relatives in the public political and economic spheres.[12] Eventually, widespread action, particularly in cities and for the right to vote, led to a decline in the separation between the public and private spheres and women's initial engagement in formal political processes.[13] Before women had formal access to politics, they engaged in a variety of informal activities, largely in local politics. Indeed, "voluntary, locally based moral and social reform efforts" represented the majority of women's early political activism.[14]

The concept of republican motherhood often justified political activism of women in the nineteenth century: women held responsibility for the future of the republic in raising their sons to be civic-minded citizens. From the American Revolution through the Progressive Era in the early 1900s, women began to insert themselves into political causes using "the canons of domesticity," in which women framed their public activism in terms of caring and nurturing.[15] Others conceptualize early women's activism as cloaked in Domestic Feminism, in which women employ the ideal traits of a lady—including caring for the home—to justify work in the public sphere. The notion of a "universal womanhood" cultivated by these ideas was at its core essentially class based, constructed by the growing numbers of white middle-class women, often in an attempt to either control women of the lower classes and other races or create a false sense of a single homogenous group of women; by no means did all women participate in these actions.[16] Despite the class- and race-based nature of this early activism, republican motherhood and domestic feminism began to change social roles for wide swaths of American women.[17]

In many circumstances, women's participation in politics occurred through informal means or at the fringes of politics. Voluntary associations, lobbying organizations, and informal groups formed by women allowed political participation from the home without threatening traditional gender roles in society.[18] The work of female urban activists focused on providing services to the poor, hungry, homeless, orphaned, and needy; holding men, including public officials, to high moral standards; and reforming public institutions.[19] Women's work in these causes increased substantially through the women's club movement, first created for literary work but evolved in concern for municipal improvements ("an orgy of philanthropy") and transformed again with the Progressive movement in the early twentieth century.[20]

The women's club movement was particularly important in women's local political activism. After the Civil War, well-to-do women formed self-improvement clubs for women denied college educations. Picking up in popularity in the late 1800s, women's clubs evolved to become loci of women's volunteerism and local civic activism. By the early 1900s, most large municipal areas in the United States saw women's club activities in a wide range of areas, such as education, children, housing, welfare, and the protection of women.[21]

Women's slowly growing political activism eventually attempted to expand the boundaries of the private sphere to frame women as social, public, or "municipal housekeepers,"[22] in which a woman's city became her home, with specific responsibilities because "women's function, like charity, begins at home and then, like charity, goes everywhere."[23] As noted by Rheta Childe Dorr in her 1910 discussion of the women's club movement:

> Woman's place is in the home. This is a platitude which no woman will ever dissent from, provided two words are dropped out of it. Woman's place is Home. Her task is homemaking. Her talents, as a rule, are mainly for homemaking. But Home is not contained within the four walls of an individual home. Home is the community. The city full of people is the Family. The

public school is the real Nursery. And badly do the Home and the Family and the Nursery need their mother.[24]

In the municipal housekeeping movement, "woman's duty and responsibility" became reforming the city where she lived because "the home is but a reflection in miniature of the broader departments of the municipality and the world beyond."[25] Women's work on urban problems also expanded with the settlement house movement, championed by Jane Addams, in which women worked to solve problems in cities *and* address the underlying causes of urban poverty. Because of the Progressive Era, the work of settlement houses eventually led to the first professional social workers.[26]

I concentrate on five areas—children, education, affordable housing, social welfare, and domestic violence—of women's work toward alleviating social ills in cities. I trace women's initial activism in these five areas (as opposed to others) for a variety of reasons: First, these issues persist today as problems or concerns for urban government. For example, a substantial amount of women's political activism in the early 1900s involved the campaign for Prohibition. As this campaign is no longer politically relevant, I do not detail the work here or include alcohol regulation in urban women's issues but instead focus on political areas that still produce substantial activism.[27] Second, urban governments continue to address these issues today, as opposed to those, such as prison reform, that migrated to state and federal control. For instance, women fought vigorously in the late eighteenth and early nineteenth centuries for pure food and milk controls, which the federal government today almost exclusively handles.[28] Third, these urban women's issues initially activated women's political participation in the United States, contributed to early feminist movements, added to women's engagement in suffrage work, and represented specific areas of women's awareness. They represent areas in which women expressed concern and mobilized early on in American history—and men largely did not. The need to address them became particularly important to women in urban areas as social problems mushroomed at the speed of the nation's industrialization.[29]

Children and education: American women's activism in the nineteenth and early twentieth centuries on children and education produced substantial changes in social services and urban education systems, particularly for girls and white children. The maternalists, who argued that women's capacity as mothers extended to an ability to care for society as a whole, made children's welfare a priority and worked through a variety of avenues to improve the lives of women.[30] Girls' education, particularly in trade schools, provided an avenue for women's initial activism in the nineteenth century.[31] Education and children's services were particularly important in urban areas because of influxes of immigrants to cities, the poor state of urban schools (despite "municipal liberty" in school funding), and the unmet need for other children's services like orphanages, Sunday schools, and disease prevention.[32] Urban women's reformers also linked education reform and the protection of children to welfare services: "If [children] were allowed to go to school they would at least be assured of a hot luncheon and the services of the school nurse and doctor."[33]

Through the women's club movement, female urban activists reformed public education by establishing libraries, raising funds to build schools, providing schools (particularly trade schools) for girls, developing home economics courses, and electing women to school boards. Indeed, women ran for school board positions and managed schools well before women won the right to vote. Eventually, pressure from female crusaders and others led to the introduction of compulsory education laws in local areas and states and freely available public education.[34] Women's activism in education produced fundamental changes in the provision of education, views of children as members of society, and the responsibility of urban governments to provide for the needs of young citizens.

Welfare and the elimination of poverty: Early women's activism in the United States focused on benevolent causes, particularly through religious organizations and motivations. The early era of charitable action (which stood out to Alexis de Tocqueville in 1832) often employed a "rhetoric of female benevolence" that encouraged donations to the poor, work for orphans, and other welfare-related activities.[35] The maternalist movement also focused on welfare provision and poverty, particularly among children and mothers. Associations of women provided charity work, often in the form of raw goods (food, tea, or blankets), small amounts of money, spiritual advice, and Bibles.

Later, women's clubs and the municipal housekeeping movement engaged in welfare programs, often arguing for women's particular skill at serving others and "developing the welfare of humanity which man cannot perform."[36] By the early 1900s, women's activism intensified the focus on welfare issues "for the benefit of the poor and the betterment of the city."[37] Women's work on social welfare led to the eventual transformation of American welfare policy at the local, state, and national levels, with women successfully arguing that the government had a responsibility to provide a safety net for the most vulnerable in society.[38] Indeed, by the end of the Progressive Era, "social policy—formerly the province of women's voluntary work—became public policy."[39]

Housing: Problems with housing often attracted women's activism when women identified them as a source for many of the other problems of a city; "to swat disease [women] must swat poor housing."[40] Women's benevolent societies and clubs, settlement houses, and other organizations became actively involved in early work on the regulation of housing for the poor in American cities. Women engaged in a variety of housing-related actions: from lobbying for building codes, regulation of tenement housing, and provision of housing to sending workers to "investigate insanitary conditions of maintenance in tenement houses, and to secure improvements in conditions."[41] Women also often went to the poor to provide services to those in need.[42] Popular accounts of the poor conditions of tenements and urban housing, such as Jacob Riis's *How the Other Half Lives*, inspired women to investigate slums in their hometowns and act on what they found by, for example, instituting housing ordinances.[43] The settlement house movement, largely located in urban slums, exposed the middle- and upper-class residents of the settlement houses to the problems of the urban poor and elevated women's efforts on reforming municipal housing codes and changing urban housing policy. The resulting changes in housing codes combined with rising costs of building materials in the early 1900s to encourage the construction of multiple-unit structures in inner cities, thus dramatically changing the landscape of cities across the country.[44]

Domestic violence, violence against women, and sexual slavery: Early women's activism on violence against women focused on prostitution and sexual slavery, warning young women moving to cities of the temptation and danger of sexuality, with a particular emphasis on the dangers of white slavery, or kidnappings associated with sex trade in cities in the late 1800s.[45] Addams and other contemporaries connected prostitution and sexual slavery to welfare, housing, and class-based characteristics, arguing that prostitution afflicted the poor more heavily than other classes: "The little girls brought into the juvenile court are usually daughters of those poorest immigrant families living in the worst type of city tenement."[46] Evidence of concern about sexual slavery—and women's sexuality as wrong and needing control or camouflage—emerged in the homes for unwed mothers found in many cities. Much of the rhetoric of reformers focused on women's shared experiences as an argument for the protection of women against the perils of sexual slavery and prostitution.[47]

Significantly later, women's activism in American cities again focused on the entrapment of women—this time in abusive marriages. For much of American history, society and government viewed domestic violence, spousal abuse, and intimate partner violence as outside the traditional realm of political action.[48] In 1871, an American court first recognized that husbands do not have a right to abuse their wives physically in *Fulgham v. State*.[49] However, the criminalization of wife battering did not provide women with recourse against abusive husbands until the early 1970s, with the second wave of feminism. Female activists raised public awareness of domestic violence, established shelters and services for victims, and made demands on political actors—starting with local governments—to address the violence.[50] Women sued their local cities for failing to protect them from spousal abuse.[51] These cases and pressure from women's groups contributed to widespread policy changes at the local level.[52]

In each of these areas of reform, women's early activism produced two profound changes: First, women became politically aware and active and to some extent accepted as political beings because of their work in these areas. In this respect, Mary Beard and contemporaries argued for a political place for women precisely because women had demonstrated their ability to reform municipal institutions. Women's work deserved attention "in the hope that more men [would] realize that women have contributions of value to make to public welfare in all its forms and phases, and come to regard the entrance of women into public life with confidence and cordiality."[53] The second change involved urban governments: as women became active in education, children's welfare, social welfare, housing, and violence against women in the late nineteenth and early twentieth centuries, they began to recognize the limits of charity and private work. As women agitated for not just addressing poverty in urban politics but *solving* it, they passed their work on to local government.[54] In many circumstances, ability of women to localize problems meant that the solutions produced by women, "an impressive array of social services and legislative reforms, became a permanent part of what Americans expected from their governments," leading to profound changes for urban governments.[55]

Gender and Attitudes about Women's Urban Issues

Women's activism shaped policy making in education, children, housing, social welfare, and violence against women, and women continue to make these policy areas a priority. In the modern era, women in the general population express high levels of support for government action in these areas and typically support social services more than men do.[56] Generally, the effect of gender on public attitudes is similar to the effect of race or income—that is, a person's gender significantly influences how that person views policies and appropriate government action.[57] Women's support for social welfare programs and government action toward eliminating poverty is evident over time.[58] Table 1.1 displays gender differences in attitudes toward government assistance, social politics, and welfare recipients from 1982 to 2008, using data from the American National Elections Studies.

Women support government assurance of jobs and spending on welfare services at a higher level than men do; similarly, women's attitudes about people on welfare are more positive than those of their male counterparts.[59] Gender differences also appear in other urban women's issue areas, including education, domestic violence, and housing. Men are more willing to cut education spending and less likely to support federal funds going to infrastructure projects, including schools.[60] Women are less likely to blame victims of domestic violence and more likely to believe that government intervention is necessary to address domestic violence.[61] Gender differences also emerge in support for affordable housing: for example, in a Rhode Island survey, 61 percent of women versus 46 percent of men said that the cost of housing was a very or fairly big problem; men and women surveyed in Oregon revealed similar gaps in support for government action in housing.[62]

Gender differences in attitudes also persist when it comes to evaluations of local government action; women express more concern with local social policies (like welfare and crime) and less concern with local economic policies like development.[63] For example, in a study of Lawrence, Kansas, compared with the men, more women opposed large-scale development and supported social service provision by the local government.[64] Women demonstrate an increased willingness to pay for public services relating to social welfare, such as services for the poor and elderly and job training and placement services.[65] The gender differences persist when examining recent data. The second section in Table 1.1 presents gender differences on three questions about support for taxes for health care, schools, and protecting the environment that were in the Kinder Houston Area Survey, which surveys Houston, Texas, residents about a variety of issues, with women supporting local action in women's issue areas but not other areas.[66]

Gender and the Use of Women's Urban Policies

Women often transformed policy making on education, children, affordable housing, social welfare, and violence against women because of the disproportional impact of these services on women, and these services continue to disproportionally serve women today. Women in the United States receive a larger share of services directed at children and the poor, an indication of what scholars have called a "feminization of poverty."[67] Women live in poverty at higher rates; qualify for and receive welfare benefits, food stamps, public housing, and income assistance more frequently; and are much more likely to be struggling single parents.[68]

Women also interact with these services as employees of and service providers to them. As the primary caretakers of children, women seek jobs with flexibility or take time off work to care for children and the elderly, which influences their earning power and employability.

TABLE 1.1   ATTITUDES TOWARD SOCIAL SERVICES AND WELFARE AND THEIR FUNDING, BY GENDER

Attitudes toward social services and welfare

	Government should see to it that every person has a job and a good standard of living (1–7 scale, with higher values indicating more agreement)			Government should provide more/fewer services (1–7 scale, with higher values indicating support for more services)			Feelings about people on welfare (0–50 = unfavorable; 50–100 = favorable)		
	Men	Women	Difference	Men	Women	Difference	Men	Women	Difference
1982	3.58	3.94	0.36*	2.5	2.9	0.49*	—	—	—
1984	3.78	4.15	0.37*	2.8	3.1	0.27	50.7	54.3	3.58*
1986	4.24	4.55	0.32	4.7	5.0	0.24	48.1	50.1	1.94*
1988	3.93	4.29	0.36*	2.5	2.8	0.28	49.6	50.1	0.52
1990	4.09	4.57	0.47*	2.7	3.1	0.43*	48.7	51.6	2.92*
1992	3.88	4.32	0.44*	2.5	2.9	0.44*	49.6	52.1	2.58*
1994	3.38	3.92	0.54*	2.4	3.0	0.55*	44.0	46.7	2.75*
1996	3.67	4.07	0.40*	2.3	2.8	0.50*	50.0	51.9	1.96*
1998	3.99	4.46	0.47*	2.7	3.1	0.39*	—	—	—
2000	2.19	2.34	0.16	4.4	4.7	0.29	50.1	53.1	2.98*
2002	—	—	—	—	—	—	51.9	53.8	1.91
2004	4.32	4.69	0.37*	2.6	3.0	0.37*	53.7	57.6	3.91*
2008	1.97	2.19	0.22	5.0	5.3	0.32*	54.5	58.1	3.61*

Attitudes toward municipal funding

	Percentage "willing to pay higher taxes to improve access to quality health care in the Houston area"	Percentage supporting "raising taxes to make major improvements in the Houston area's quality of life, such as pollution control and park improvements"	Percentage supporting "raising taxes to set aside and protect wetlands, forests, and prairies throughout the Houston area"
Male	47	64	61
Female	52*	55*	57*

Social service use and poverty status

	Male	Female
Children and education		
Percentage of single heads of household with own children under eighteen	6.4	23.5
Percentage of workers employed in educational services	31.5	68.5
Affordable housing		
Percentage of public housing residents	25	75
Owner occupancy percentage, family household, no spouse present	56.9	48.6
Social welfare		
Percentage with income in the past twelve months below poverty level	13.9	16.7
Percentage with income in the past twelve months less than 50% of poverty level	5.2	6.4
Poverty percentage for single heads of household with own children under eighteen	35.1	59.4
Median income for single heads of household with own children under eighteen	$41,441	$29,811
Percentage of Medicaid-eligible recipients	40.7	59.3
Percentage of SNAP participants	43.6	56.4
Domestic violence		
Percentage of victims of domestic violence (1994)	15	85
Percentage of population physically assaulted by a current or former partner in their lifetime	7.4	22.1
Rate experiencing intimate partner violence per 1,000 persons age twelve or older (2010)	1.1	5.9

Note: Data on attitudes about social services come from American National Election Studies, *The ANES Guide to Public Opinion and Electoral Behavior.* Data on attitudes about municipal funding come from Klineberg, *Kinder Houston Area Survey, 1982–2010.* Data on social service use and poverty status come from U.S. Census Bureau, "Own Children under 18 Years by Family Type and Age," 2011; U.S. Census Bureau, "Select Population Profile in the United States," 2010; U.S. Department of Housing and Urban Development, "Picture of Subsidized Households for 2009"; U.S. Census Bureau, "Homeownership Rates by Age of Householder and Household Type," 2010; U.S. Census Bureau, "Industry by Sex," 2011; Centers for Medicare and Medicaid Services, "Medicaid Eligibles Demographics, Selected Fiscal Years," 2010; U.S. Department of Agriculture, Food and Nutrition Service, "Gender and SNAP Benefits of Participants by Selected Demographic Characteristic," 2010; Bureau of Justice Statistics, "Intimate Partner Violence, 1993–2010."

* $p < 0.05$, difference of means tests.

This combines with downstream effects from inequality and continued discrimination to generate "a workforce divided by sex."[69] Women also hold the majority of jobs in education and social services.[70] The final section in Table 1.1 presents data on participation by gender in services for children and education, affordable housing, social welfare, and domestic violence. Generally, the data demonstrate that women, compared to men, are more likely to work in and rely on urban women's issue policies. Because cities make policies in these areas, local governments are actively involved in the perpetuation of particular gender roles and women's entanglement with women's urban issues.[71]

Gender and Political Representation

Why might the election of women to local office matter in the production of policies regarding women's urban issues? Generally, the election of women to local office presents two opportunities to produce change: First, female leaders support policies that women prefer or that help women in their community. This *substantive representation* involves female leaders acting for women. Second, women serve as simple *descriptive representatives* by looking like women and thus providing symbolic value by legitimizing the political process and the governing institution.[72] A significant body of research on the connection between descriptive, substantive, and symbolic representation for women generally finds that "women in office do make a difference" by representing women's interests and providing symbolic value.[73] In particular, gender differences consistently emerge in leaders' preference of issues relating to women's interest.

Gender differences in concern about welfare, children, and the family emerge in political representation behavior. Women in a wide variety of political offices care about, promote, and pass legislation relating to family, children, education, and social welfare at higher rates than their male counterparts. The public often applies gender stereotypes to women in office, such as assuming them to be more caring, more competent on compassion issues like health care and education, and more liberal, further demonstrating the association of women in office with caregiving, compassion, and social welfare.[74]

Scholarship on gender differences at the local level has examined policy attitudes and policy outcomes, often finding conflicting evidence as to whether women in local office are different from their male counterparts in attitudes or actions.[75] All city leaders, regardless of their gender, "cite taxes and development as the most important issues in the community."[76] Many of these studies suggest that women entering local office are not fundamentally different in their attitudes from their male counterparts.

Looking at women in local office and their influence on policy outcomes, the limited existing scholarship finds occasional significant relationships between the gender of local officials and policy outcomes.[77] The presence of a female mayor increases female municipal employment and increases use of Community Development Block Grants for public service.[78] Women in local office in India tend to pursue policies of interest to women living in their villages, and female councilors in Norway positively influence the level of municipal day care provided, with more success when women reach 30 percent of the local council. Similarly, municipalities with 30 percent representation by women established gender-equity committees in Norway.[79] Generally, the effects of gender on local policy appear strongest in areas that directly benefit women in their community.

At the same time, investigations of the experiences of women in local office often find that the existing power structure subjugates women's preferences. In attempting to expand affordable housing, women in local office "find norms are firmly entrenched and local agendas are mostly fixed. Budgets are presented to them, zoning laws are in place, and priorities are already established" and the local policy process seems to represent the interests of men, even with the presence of female leaders.[80]

Representation in Urban Politics

Scholarship on urban politics identifies several reasons why women's representation would *not* matter in urban politics. First, the lack of both authority and control over the movement of people, jobs, and money from city to city means that cities give preference to economic development policies over any form of redistribution. Second, because of these restrictions, cities often collaborate with private actors like businesses to pursue policies, which again gives preference to economic development issues. Third, substantial evidence suggests that efforts to produce policies that conflict with the governing structure often fail, meaning that representatives who do not pursue economic development are stymied in their attempts at other policies. Fourth, although groups of citizens have the potential to influence change in local politics, it is unclear whether they are successful. Furthermore, the diffuse nature of women's residential patterns—that is, that women do not live in a particular area of a city—means that the representation of women's interests is fundamentally different from that of other groups. These four factors suggest that women's interests—not traditionally aligned with economic development—will be subjugated in urban politics.

Urban leaders govern in highly restricted environments. Local and city governments lack autonomy because they are controlled by either Dillon's Rule or Home Rule and because of the constraints put on them by their state and the federal government.[81] Adding to this, cities face significant financial, functional, administrative, and structural limitations, which restrict their ability to do what they want, when they want.[82] Scholars of fiscal federalism also argue that the inability of cities to control the movement of people, jobs, or capital across urban areas requires that city governments focus on specific types of policy making.[83] Because residents can move from one city to another for very little cost, cities have a strong incentive to tailor policies to fit local demand.[84] In particular, the ability of businesses and higher-income residents to choose to move to other locations results in city governments giving preference to the concerns of specific classes of individuals. In addition, local governments are often largely fiscally self-responsible, relying heavily on local taxes for funding.[85] These constraints lead to cities prioritizing the needs of businesses and wealthy residents through bowing to the interests of growth machines, forming coalitions for governing with private actors, and ignoring the concerns of lower-income residents.[86]

Across various types of city governments, in diverse communities and under a variety of mandates from state and federal governments, cities consistently focus on growth (through business attraction and job creation) and basic service provision (such as garbage pickup or street maintenance) and spend less time and money on welfare and redistribution.[87] Paul Peterson and other scholars of urban politics see this as good and caution that cities should avoid pursuing and funding redistributive policies, because the tax rate for higher-income residents and businesses could drive them from the city, creating a downward spiral of demand for welfare services, provision of these services, and exit by higher-income residents.[88] In his work on city policy making, Peterson argues that cities should favor policies that produce more marginal benefits than marginal costs for the average taxpayer, or what Peterson refers to as *developmental policies*. On the other hand, Peterson sees *redistributional policies*, or those with a smaller marginal benefit than marginal cost for the average taxpayer, as bad for the city, because they drive up the tax rate and result in wealthier residents leaving the city. The fiscal federalism stance, as articulated by Peterson and others, is that the funding of social welfare programs is bad for business, and cities should shy away from redistributional activities. Indeed, history has shown that urban leaders who choose to fund such programs often suffer elector consequences, and their cities suffer economic downturns.[89] However, others find Peterson's ideas and fiscal federalism overly simplistic and far too tied to the idea that rational actors govern cities by simply exercising market decisions when making choices about urban policy.[90]

The constraints on cities, particularly from fiscal restrictions, lead to partnerships between local governments and nongovernmental actors, connecting the "popular control of government and the private control of economic resources."[91] The informal arrangement of public and private actors focuses on the production of a public policy agenda that benefits the members of the regime. As a result, urban policy making often reflects the needs and desires of the public and private members of the governing regime.

The private actors in urban regimes can take many forms, but the involvement of the business community is necessary (but not always sufficient) for a successful regime because "business and the resources they control are too important for the enterprises to be left out completely."[92] Yet despite the scholarly focus on the private actors in regimes, public offices continue to play important roles in urban policy making, and the representation of the interests of particular groups often influences policy.[93]

The ability of representatives to produce policies that conflict with the governing structure often fails, particularly at the local level. While some scholars find that electing racial minorities to office can promote substantial policy change, others find that expectations of constituents and precedents set by previous mayors cripple the ability of mayors from minority coalitions to change policy.[94] Other scholars suggest there is a consistent and systemic bias against those seeking outcomes that conflict with the goals of the regime, expand the universe of policies offered, or provide substantial redistributional benefits.[95] Yet female leaders are able to change policy discussions and policy outcomes in urban politics across the United States; one principal reason for the success of female leaders lies in their ability to harness the power of groups in their cities.

Neighborhood and community groups, local organizations, coalitions of voters, minority groups, and business associations all perform a variety of functions for local governments that then lead to the representation of the interests of those groups. While Peterson calls city politics "groupless politics" and many studies of group action find little evidence of the influence of neighborhood groups on city governance, others find that community groups represent diverse interests and serve as a conduit to bring attention of city leaders to the needs of the city.[96] Group action serves a particularly important role in the representation of women's issues in urban politics. Local women's organizations have often been responsible for the representation of women's issues at the local level; for example, the presence (or absence) of women's groups is associated with policy making on domestic and sexual violence.[97] Other research suggests that community groups are particularly successful in using unconventional channels and resources to influence urban politics but that the success of these groups depends on connections to formal representation, the local context, and the resources that the groups can provide to local decision makers.[98]

Extensive research on groups in urban politics demonstrates that they have the *potential* to influence policy but that true incorporation requires connections between formal and informal representation, particularly for marginalized groups. Rufus Browning, Dale Marshall, and David Tabb argue that the representation of the interests of racial minorities requires the formation of active electoral coalitions, success in electoral representation, and membership in liberal governing coalitions.[99] Once minorities meet these formal and informal conditions, descriptive representation and informal action by minorities produce changes in urban government and the representation of minority interests. But what does this mean for women in office?

Local leaders, regardless of where they serve, face roughly equal numbers of men and women in their constituencies. The dispersion of women and men through the population makes the representation of women's interests systematically different from that of many other social groups.[100] In cities, the traditional evaluation of the representation of social groups has focused on racial and ethnic groups or classes of workers, but there is no women's equivalent of a ward of African American or Hispanic voters or neighborhoods of blue-collar workers. In general, the lack of women's segregation in the population suggests that male and female representatives would have equal incentives to represent women's interests. Yet my research demonstrates that women in local office are more interested than men in representing women and women's urban interests and are particularly receptive to demands from women's issue organizations, groups of women, and citizens representing women's urban issues.

Urban Politics and the Subjugation of Women's Interests

What does our understanding of the process of urban politics suggest for the study of women in local government? How might female leaders pursue policies within the set of women's urban issues? The scholarship on urban politics suggests a consistent and systematic bias against those seeking to change the policy agenda, whether the resistance emerges from a preference for growth and development, from a governing coalition, or from the constraints on cities from state and federal governments.[101] At the same time, I have shown that urban political history, women's service provision and use, women's attitudes, and female leaders' actions all suggest that women in local political office will be more likely to support urban women's issue policies and less likely to support business interests and economic development.[102] However, most urban politics scholars suggest that we will see policy making in women's urban issues subjugated to that of development in cities.

The conflict between the dominant understandings of urban policy goals and the priorities of women in politics suggests that the constraints on cities, the centrality of development policies, and a lack of avenues to pursue policies related to women's equality may mean that local politics are the *most resistant* of all levels of government in the United States to the incorporation of women's interests. Yet the power of local groups, women's historical political activism on urban issues, and the basic tenets of representation suggest that women's representation in local office is important and does make a difference. To evaluate this tension, I examine the influence of gender on policy preferences through survey data; policy processes through city council minutes, interviews, and surveys of community groups; and policy outcomes through budget and employment data.

Gender and Policy Preferences, Policy Processes, and Policy Outcomes in Cities

To understand women's representation, it is important to understand the interaction of local political institutions with female mayors and council members, the representation of women's interests, and citizen perception of that representation. To evaluate how the gender of representations influences urban politics, I use a sample of cities in the United States with male and female mayors. Starting with cities in 2007 with a population over thirty thousand and a female mayor,[103] I use a nonparametric matching technique to select one hundred best-matched cities with female and male mayors.[104]

Table 1.2 provides the summary information for the sample as a whole and the male and female mayor subgroups. The sample of cities has a smaller average population than that of all cities in the United States, is relatively similar in racial diversity, has a slightly lower rate of poverty, and has a higher median income. Cities with male mayors

TABLE 1.2   PROFILE OF CITIES IN SAMPLE

	All U.S. cities	Entire sample	Cities with a male mayor	Cities with a female mayor
Average population	102,881	58,508	56,312	61,171
White (%)	64	70	72	68
Black (%)	12	8	9	9
Hispanic (%)	16	11	9	12
Asian (%)	5	6	7	6
Poverty rate (%)	12	10	11	10
Median income ($)	46,147	51,163	50,234	53,541
Median income: men ($)	31,167	34,343	32,637	36,516
Median income: women ($)	20,214	21,336	20,565	22,443
Average number of housing units	41,134	22,410	20,727	23,921
Housing units occupied (%)	94	94	94	94
Cities with a council-manager form of government (%)	63	65	58	71
City council that is female (%)	—	23	24	22

Note: Data on the type of municipal government come from *The Municipal Yearbook 2007*; the countrywide comparison is to cities with a population over twenty-five thousand. I calculate the female percentage of the council by dividing the number of women on the council by the total number of seats, including the mayor. For cities with a female mayor, I subtract the mayor from the number of women, because the purpose is to determine the number of women on the council, regardless of the gender of the mayor. Unfortunately, I cannot compare the average rates of female representation in these cities to that of the United States as a whole, because the level of female representation on city councils throughout the United States is unknown.

and female mayors are very similar; the only differences that approach significance are the size of the Hispanic population (the difference is just outside traditional significance levels) and the percentage of cities with a council-manager form of government (significant to the 0.05 level).[105] For each of these cities, I collected information on the gender of city council members and calculated the percentage of the council that were female—the average rate is just under 23 percent; cities with female mayors had rates of female representation on their councils similar to cities with male mayors.

Within this group of cities, I collected and analyzed a variety of information. First, an Internet survey asked about the leaders' *policy preferences*, goals, attitudes about representation, group membership, and contact with constituents. Chapter 2 uses data from this survey to evaluate the effect of gender on the policy preferences and attitudes of local leaders, revealing a general lack of differences in policy priorities between male and female leaders but the emergence of key differences when specific types of female leaders are evaluated. Chapter 2 also analyzes the effect of women feeling a responsibility to represent women, feminists, and the poor, or preferable descriptive representation,[106] on policy preferences and conceptions of representation using survey data and a case-study approach.

To examine gender and the *policy process*, a year of each city's council minutes was coded and analyzed for content and process; this is supplemented with time-series data and qualitative interview data from leaders and community members. Chapters 3 and 4 examine the effect of the gender of representatives on the policy process and participation in urban decision making. The analyses provide evidence for the wide varieties of ways the gender of a representative can shape and alter the policy-making process at the local level. Chapter 4 also details the effect of a gendered leadership style on the expectations and evaluations of performance of female mayors by community members; in particular, I examine the influence of mayoral gender on group participation in urban politics.

I next examine gender and *policy outcomes* at the local level, including expenditures, employment, borrowing, and grant-seeking behavior of cities with male and female leaders in Chapter 5, finding positive effects of female mayors and female city council members on spending on women's issue programs. This demonstrates that women's representation can change policy outcomes in cities. Chapter 6 evaluates the long-term effects of electing women to local office on urban fiscal health, community, and democracy.

The findings that follow have implications for our understanding of how women influence the policy making of cities in formal and informal ways; the ways that women in office use their political influence to change who has a voice in urban politics; the effect of institutional and informal constraints on the ability of women to transform urban policy; how women in office find new and creative ways to pursue women's urban issues; and the importance of women's representation in urban politics. By evaluating the ways that women can influence urban policy, my research demonstrates that, even in an atmosphere in which formal and informal power structures bias policy making away from urban women's interests, the gender of representatives does influence how leaders think about, craft, and produce policies. The effect of gender on the urban policy process suggests that the quality of democracy in urban politics may suffer until women achieve equal representation in local elected offices.

2 /

She Says, He Says

Gender and Policy Attitudes

Does gender directly influence the policy preferences of male and female representatives in cities? The gender gap in attitudes, that women most use services related to women's issues (children and education, affordable housing, social welfare, and domestic violence), and the traditional association of women's activism with these services would suggest significant differences in policy priorities. However, it may be that the nature of urban governance restricts traditional differences in policy preferences between male and female leaders, and gender differences may emerge only when female leaders conceptualize themselves as leaders of women. If so, descriptive representation will not suffice, and to represent urban women's interests a female leader must meet the criteria of a *preferable descriptive representation*, in which she feels a responsibility to represent women, feminists, and the poor.

In the United States, far fewer women than men hold leadership positions in the political process, regardless of the level of office. Despite the low numbers of female politicians, considerable evidence suggests that women in state and national office work to promote the interests of women in a general sense and express differing values from their male colleagues. In particular, female leaders at the state and national levels value redistributional programs and feminist issues more and small government less than male representatives do. However, these differences often disappear when scholars examine gender differences in attitudes at the local level.[1] At the same time, the majority of women who hold office in the United States serve at the local level,[2] and many women who hold national or state office began their careers in municipal politics.[3] Thus, it is important to understand how the gender of local leaders influences policy preferences about urban women's issues.

Research has well documented the importance of groups in urban politics, particularly for the representation of previously marginalized interests like racial minorities. In particular, local governments respond to women's interests when women pair representation in local politics with informal political action. In bridging the formal-informal political divide, these women educate city leaders, operate as a channel for the use of voice, and connect leaders to community demands.[4] Thus, women's representation may require female leaders to interact with groups in the community, particularly when pursuing policies of importance to women that have been marginalized by the local community.[5]

Suzanne Dovi and other scholars call for more than simple descriptive representation and suggest that true representation comes from preferable descriptive representation.[6] Preferable descriptive representation draws from the idea that women and minorities possess specific, unique interests and that *certain* members of these groups most adequately represent these interests.[7] A representative becomes a preferable descriptive representative when she has a shared history with the group she represents; the common background, combined with collective goals that include "the improvement of the social, economic, and political status of particular historically disadvantaged groups"[8] such as minorities, provides opportunities for substantive representation. These representatives can be identified by "whether [they] reach out (or distance themselves from) historically disadvantaged groups."[9]

Local representation is suited for an evaluation of preferable descriptive representation because local politics is distinguished by the ability of groups to access women in office and the importance of groups in local politics. Gender alone may fail to produce gender differences because of the restraints on urban leaders. However, female leaders who cultivate relationships with groups associated with women's urban interests will prioritize those interests in their attitudes and actions.

Measuring Policy Preferences of Local Leaders

To identify whether gender influences policy preferences at the local level, I sent two e-mail surveys to mayors and city council members: one to the hundred-city group described in detail in Chapter 1 in 2011 and another to a group of three hundred cities randomly selected from the 2000 U.S. census listing of municipalities in 2009. The second survey is used largely for confirmatory analysis. In the remainder of the chapter, where survey data is discussed, it refers to the hundred-city survey unless the three-hundred-city survey is specifically mentioned. These surveys asked questions about general policy preferences to understand the direct relationship between gender and policy preferences. They also contained questions on representation to evaluate how male and female leaders saw themselves as leaders and which groups they viewed as needing representation. Appendixes 2A and 2B provide the full questions and survey details.[10]

For the hundred-city sample, I used city websites and the U.S. Conference of Mayors contact information listing service to gather contact information for 86 mayors and 529 of the 761 city council members. There were 264 respondents to the survey, for a 43 percent response rate.[11] While low, this response rate is in line with surveys of public officials, especially when communication with the respondents is done entirely online.[12] Of the 264 responses received, 97 (35 percent) were from women and 167 (65 percent) from men, 46 percent of the mayoral responses were from women and 54 percent from men, and 29 percent of the responses from city council members were from women and 71 percent from men. Thus, female leaders' response rate exceeds the rates of women's representation in city government but approaches the levels of representation in the sample (see Table 1.2). The higher rate of response by women to the survey could be because women generally respond at higher rates to surveys or female leaders might have identified more with the request for responses or the content of the survey itself.[13]

Leaders identified the city in which they serve, which allowed me to link the leader's responses to socioeconomic, demographic, and crime data for each city. The profiles of the cities for which leaders responded do not differ significantly from the profiles of the one hundred cities given in Chapter 1 as a whole; in other words, the survey responses are representative of the one hundred cities overall. The survey asked leaders about their time in office, age, occupation, and political affiliation and ideology and for their assessment of the ideological identification of their city council as a whole and their constituents. Female representatives were more likely to identify as Democrats and were more liberal (similar to female representatives in higher office) but are otherwise not different in background from their male counterparts.

Gender and Policy Preferences

The effect of gender on representational attitudes was measured through four sets of questions on the hundred-city survey: Two sets asked how important to the respondent and the respondent's community are affordable housing, children, development, domestic violence, education, general government, the local library, public works, parks and recreation, race and ethnicity, public safety, transportation and infrastructure, environment, welfare and health, and women.[14] Another set asked whether the respondent ever worked with other council members on any of the preceding issues. The final set asked how often the city council discussed these issues.[15] For each question, respondents could select "not applicable" if their "city does not address the issue." Given the history of women supporting women's urban issues, female leaders, compared to male leaders, should give preference to women's issues and express a lower level of support for development and other matters.

The issues were aggregated into four general categories:

- Development: economic development, zoning, and transportation and infrastructure
- Quality of life: parks and recreation, culture and the arts, public safety, library, and environmental protection
- General governance: general government and public works

- Urban women's issues: affordable housing, children's welfare, education, social welfare, and domestic violence, as described in Chapter 1

Very few differences emerge between men and women in policy priorities. Both male and female leaders consider issues related to development and general government to be very important, followed by quality of life concerns. They consider women's issues least important. Of the subissues, welfare is least important and public safety the most important. Development presents the only statistically significant difference between male and female leaders; male leaders believe that development is more important to their community than female leaders do.[16]

I also compare male and female council members who serve in cities with male or female mayors.[17] Here, the data are presented to understand whether cities are simply more likely to select mayors who behave in a particular manner, regardless of the person's gender. Evaluating the attitudes of councilors who serve under male or female mayors reveals whether cities have a pattern of feminization or masculinization of their leaders. If they do, councilors of either gender who serve with female mayors should support urban women's issues more (and development issues) less than those who serve with a male mayor. The data in Table 2.1 suggest that this is not the case; councilors who serve with female mayors or male mayors do not differ in their evaluations of the importance of issues or in their perceptions of the community's preference for particular issues.

As an additional measure of gender differences, I identified thirty-six cities in the responses for which pairs—that is, both a male and a female representative from the same city—responded to the survey.[18] These paired responses allow the evaluation of whether female representatives more highly valued urban women's issues, even when controlling for all factors associated with the city. I found no differences in valuation of development, general government, quality of life, or women's issues between male and female leaders serving in the same city.[19]

Some gender differences emerge when respondents reported how frequently the city council discusses an issue (see Figure 2.1).[20] Again, they act most frequently in areas of development and general government and least often on women's issues. City councils discuss public

TABLE 2.1   IMPORTANCE OF ISSUES, BY GENDER OF LEADER SURVEYED

	General government	Development	Quality of life	Women's issues
How important is each of the following to you?				
Male respondents	4.48	4.46	3.92	3.31
Female respondents	4.18	4.55	3.86	3.39
Leaders in cities with male mayors	4.41	4.49	3.89	3.32
Leaders in cities with female mayors	4.21	4.52	4.88	3.39
How important is each of the following in your community?				
Male respondents	4.27	4.27*	3.99	3.42
Female respondents	4.07	4.62	3.88	3.37
Leaders in cities with male mayors	4.16	4.44	3.89	3.31
Leaders in cities with female mayors	4.18	4.39	3.92	3.46

Note: 1 = least important; 5 = most important. Eighteen percent of leaders indicated that their city does not handle one or more issues.

* $p < 0.10$; differences are measured between male and female leaders *or* between leaders in cities with male or female mayors.

safety, public works, and transportation and infrastructure most frequently. Female representatives report working on women's issues and quality of life issues more often. Councilors do not show any differences for gender of mayor.

No gender differences emerged between male and female leaders when they reported on whether they "ever worked with other council members on any of these issues." Again, the rate of working with their colleagues on issues conforms to the general pattern of a stronger emphasis on general government (97 percent of men and 93 percent of women) and development (98 percent of men and 100 percent of women), compared with women's issues (54 percent of men and 53 percent of women).[21] The examination of policy preferences and work at the local level tentatively supports the contemporary wisdom that there are few gender differences at the local level. Women and men consider women's urban issues least important and development to be the primary policy area of interest.

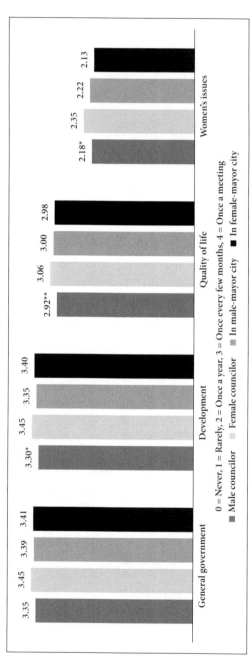

Figure 2.1 How often does the city council discuss the following issues? Responses are from male or female council members serving with either gender of mayor and from either gender of council member under a male mayor or a female mayor.

★ = Difference significant at the 0.10 level; ★★ = Difference significant at the 0.05 level.

Studies of women in political office often find that women are constrained by the institutions in which they serve.[22] Given the realities of urban political governance, women serving at the local level face more constraints than they do at the state and national levels. These institutional constraints could account for some of the lack of basic gender differences in attitudes and work presented thus far. However, gender differences may emerge in leaders' *ideal* policy making.

Large differences emerged when leaders evaluated whether their city "spends too much, the correct amount, or not enough time discussing each of these [issues]." For analysis, responses were coded as 0 if the leader believed the council spent the right amount of time on an area, −1 if the council spent too much time on an issue, or positive 1 if it spent not enough time on an issue.[23] A significant number of male leaders (45 percent) answered that they wanted to spend more time on development issues, compared to only 12 percent of female leaders. Alternatively, 42 percent of female leaders thought that their city did not spend enough time on urban women's issues, compared to 9 percent of men.[24]

Generally, the survey data show that male and female leaders prioritize and work on urban issues in very similar ways. In addition, urban elected officials serving with male or female mayors differ very little in their attitudes about the importance of policies or time that should be spent on them.

Perceptions of Constituent Groups and Representation

After an examination of the general policy priorities and actions of leaders, I turn next to manifestations of preferable descriptive representation and group representation in the respondents. The survey provided each leader a list of groups and asked the respondents if they felt a responsibility to represent any of the groups. Table 2.2 presents the breakdown of the percentage of all leaders and male and female leaders who felt a responsibility to represent a group.[25] Leaders selected Americans in general, business owners, property owners, the middle class, women, and the poor most frequently. Male and female respondents provided very different profiles of the groups they

TABLE 2.2   GROUP REPRESENTATION (PERCENTAGE WHO SELECTED GROUP)

Group	All respondents (%)	Male leaders (%)	Female leaders (%)	Men-women difference (% points)
Whites	8	6	10	−4*
Blacks	16	5	21	−16*
Hispanics	16	6	17	−11*
Asians	10	4	14	−10*
Women	28	0	53	−53**
Men	8	16	0	16*
Liberals	10	4	14	−10**
Conservatives	8	16	0	16*
Independents	11	8	14	−6
Business owners	45	68	10	58*
Developers	16	26	0	26***
Property owners	34	61	7	54**
Feminists	13	1	21	−20**
Middle class	34	36	28	8**
Poor	34	2	48	−46**
Rich	7	6	0	6*
People at your place of worship	8	8	0	8*
People in your neighborhood	45	58	14	44**
People at your place of work	5	5	3	2
Americans in general	61	43	52	−9
Other	34	24	36	−12

Note: Survey question read, "Do you feel a specific responsibility to represent the interests of any of the following groups?"

* $p < 0.10$, ** $p < 0.05$, *** $p < 0.01$.

feel a responsibility to represent. Men felt responsibility to represent business owners, property owners, and people in their neighborhood. Women felt responsibility to represent racial groups, women, and the poor; two-thirds of female respondents felt a responsibility to represent women, making them preferable descriptive representatives. In addition, when development groups (business, developers, property owners, and the rich) and women's issue groups (women, feminists, and the poor) are aggregated, female leaders have much more contact with women's groups and less contact with development groups than the male leaders do, as presented in Figure 2.2.

Using these responses, I turned the focus of analysis to those female representatives who indicated closeness with women or a

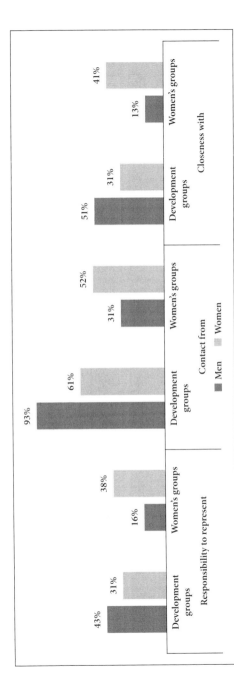

Figure 2.2   Group representation. The survey questions for each category are as follows. Responsibility to represent: Do you feel a specific responsibility to represent the interests of any of the following groups? (See the text for the list of groups.) Contact from: Have members of any of these groups contacted you regarding an issue in your city? Closeness with: Which groups do you feel particularly close to—people who are most like you in their ideas and interests and feelings?

responsibility to represent them. Two key themes emerge from examining the verbatim responses to why these groups needed representation: the representatives either felt camaraderie with other women or concern about women's lack of political power or a voice in politics. The representatives who cited a shared background had responses that varied only slightly: "The other members of my board are all men who tend to represent men's concerns," "I am the only female on the council, and I need to represent women's interests," and "As a woman, I hope to bring a different perspective." These representatives also believed that work by women's groups promoted the connection, saying, for example, " [Members of a women's organization in the community] know that I am sympathetic to their concerns and will listen to them."

Representatives who were concerned about the lack of power for women had explanations like "I don't think that they [women] get a voice in what happens in our city," "They are forgotten a lot of the time," and "I think my job is to be a voice for those who may not have the resources to effectively fight city hall." As with the camaraderie explanation, these female leaders had worked with women's groups. In discussing a project of a group of women to promote a diaper bank for low-income mothers, one leader said, "I know that this isn't something that [the other members of the council] are going push, and I know it is important. So they came to me with the idea that the city could store [the diapers] for free because they knew they wouldn't be heard otherwise. No one else would do anything." Later, the same representative noted that this project was an example of why she believed that women should have more power in their community.

Overall, female representatives revealed significant variety in their attitudes about women's power in their community and society in general. Leaders responded to three questions about the amount of power held by women in their city, government and politics, and their community. For each of these questions, women assess women's power as being low and would prefer women to have more power in politics and in their communities. For example, when asked whether women in the community should have less, the same, or more power, only 15 percent of men thought women should have more power, compared to 36 percent of women and 55 percent of preferable descriptive representatives.

Preferable Descriptive Representation

The responses regarding group representation indicate women who are preferable descriptive representatives of women, feminists, and the poor. These groups represent constituencies in my definition of *urban women's issues*, and feeling a responsibility to represent is included in Dovi's definition of a preferable descriptive representative.[26] This group of representatives consists of 57 percent of the women who responded to the survey. The idea of a responsibility to represent women is consistent with the conceptualization of a strong mutual relationship between the represented and the representative, with qualitative evidence supporting the idea of a shared experience and goals, particularly on policies often ignored by urban governments. As a check of the measure of preferable descriptive representation, Figure 2.3 presents the responses to questions about perceptions of women's power by men, women, and preferred descriptive representatives.

To test whether descriptive characteristics alone or preferable descriptive representation affects the political behavior of representatives, three separate measures that I have discussed—issue priorities, community issue priorities, and frequency of working on issues—and the measure working on issues with others are regressed on gender, leader, and city controls.[27] Theoretically, if gender alone is a driving force behind issue priority, we should see a significant relationship between gender and policy preferences. However, if the representation of women's interests requires bridging the informal-formal representation dichotomy—that is, being a preferable descriptive representative—this rough measure of a preferable descriptive representative should have a positive relationship with preferences for women's issues.

The first set of measures is the individual stated priority for affairs handled by city government: development, general government, quality of life, and women's issues. As Table 2.3 shows, the gender of the representative is an insignificant measure of policy priorities, even though these policies aligned with the issues when the general population's attitudes reflected a gender gap. These findings suggest that gender *alone* does not dictate policy priorities. Instead, Table 2.3 shows that preferable descriptive representatives consider women's issues more important and development issues much less important.

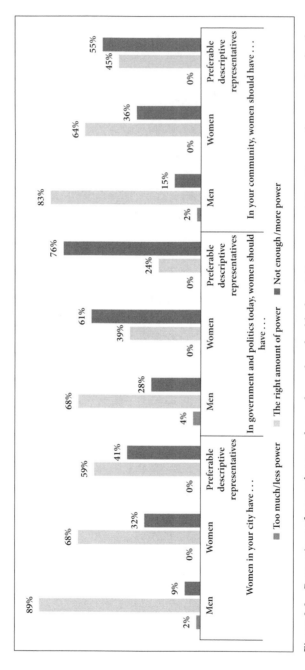

Figure 2.3 **Perceptions of women's power, by gender and preferable descriptive representation.** Bars are for comparison's sake; the group of women overlaps considerably with the group of preferable descriptive representatives—that is, they are not exclusive.

TABLE 2.3   DISCUSSION OF ISSUES AND ISSUE IMPORTANCE TO LEADER

	Discussion of issues		Issue importance to leader	
Variable	Development	Women's issues	Development	Women's issues
Gender	0.13	0.10**	−0.15	−0.01
	(0.126)	(0.04)	(0.21)	(0.14)
Preferable descriptive	0.085	0.47**	−0.25*	0.26**
representative	(0.15)	(0.18)	(0.12)	(0.07)
Party	0.022	−0.10†	0.01	−0.05*
	(0.041)	(0.05)	(0.07)	(0.02)
Ideology	−0.017	0.15†	−0.10	0.04
	(0.06)	(0.08)	(0.11)	(0.07)
Mayor	−0.03	−0.24	1.32*	0.50
	(0.34)	(0.43)	(0.59)	(0.39)
Time in office	−0.01	0.013	−0.01	−0.01
	(0.01)	(0.014)	(0.020)	(0.01)
Constant	3.35**	2.09**	3.33**	2.52**
	(0.42)	(0.53)	(0.73)	(0.48)
N	244	215	247	217
R^2	0.13	0.27	0.18	0.25

Note: "Discussion of issues" shows the leaders' response to "How often does the city council discuss these issues?" Standard errors appear in parentheses. The numbers for N differ because those who indicated that their city did not address the issue are not counted in these analyses.

† $p < 0.10$, * $p < 0.05$, ** $p < 0.01$.

Specifically, preferable descriptive representation has a positive relationship with considering women's issues important. Substantively, preferable descriptive representation has a small to moderate relationship, moving a leader half a point on a five-point scale. The political party the representative belongs to has a relationship with the priorities of almost all these policies; Republicans are coded to represent higher values. These results are consistent with general Republican attitudes toward welfare policies and big government. Policy preferences relating to general government and quality of life are unrelated to the preferable descriptive representation measure or to gender generally.[28]

I next look at evaluations of whether the city spends the right amount of time on the women's urban issues and development. Again, as Table 2.4 shows, the measure of preferable descriptive representation

TABLE 2.4   EVALUATION OF TIME CITY SPENDS ON ISSUE

Variable	Development	Women's issues
Gender	−0.27*	−0.04
	(0.12)	(0.12)
Preferable descriptive	0.17	0.15**
representative	(0.14)	(0.04)
Party	0.07†	−0.12**
	(0.04)	(0.04)
Ideology	−0.03	0.15*
	(0.06)	(0.06)
Mayor	0.33	0.67*
	(0.32)	(0.32)
Time in office	0.01	−0.006
	(0.01)	(0.01)
Constant	−0.57	−0.46
	(0.400)	(0.39)
N	245	212
R^2	0.12	0.12

Note: Dependent variable includes the question "Do you think your city spends too much, the correct amount, or not enough time discussing each of these areas?" While the initial scale is three points (and thus would require ordered logit), each of these is a combination of multiple issues, thus creating a continuous variable for which ordinary least squares regression is an appropriate method of modeling. Standard errors appear in parentheses.

† $p < 0.10$; * $p < 0.05$; ** $p < 0.01$.

has a significant, positive relationship with the discussion of women's issues. Political party affiliation has a negative relationship, and ideology has a positive relationship, conforming to the expectations of partisan and ideological support for these issues. For the first time, gender has a significant albeit substantively weak relationship with the city council's discussions of women's issues, an idea revisited in Chapters 3 and 4.[29]

Finally, I compare the relationship of gender and preferable descriptive representation to respondents' evaluations of whether the city council spends too much, the right amount, or not enough time on development and women's issues. It is important to remember the basic gender differences in terms of perceptions of whether the city council is spending enough time on the issues. Gender alone does not affect perceptions of what the council should do relating to women's issues, but it does increase the likelihood that a female leader will believe the council spends too much time on development. Party affiliation is significant; Republicans are more likely to think that the city does not spend enough time on development. Preferable descriptive representatives are more likely to think that their council does not spend enough time on women's issues.[30]

A Case Study of Descriptive versus Preferable Descriptive Representation

What are the extended consequences of a leader holding or not holding attitudes consistent with being a preferable descriptive representative? The policy attitudes of two leaders are compared to demonstrate the difference between these two types of representatives.[31] The descriptive representative, Diane, is from a medium-sized city.[32] She is a white, liberal, Democratic city council member in a city with a council-manager form of government. She feels a responsibility to represent property owners, people in her neighborhood, and Americans in general. She sometimes feels a sense of pride in the accomplishments of other women, pays some attention to issues that affect women, and thinks that women and businesses have the right amount of power in her community. Diane thinks that if all the elected leaders in her city were female, policies would change, but it would not necessarily be a good thing, stating that she "would want a diversity of opinions."

Susan, the preferable descriptive representative, is also from a medium-sized city and is a white, liberal, strongly Democratic city council member in a council-manager form of government. She feels a responsibility to represent women, the poor, and people in her neighborhood. Susan has a strong sense of pride in the accomplishments of other women and pays a lot of attention to issues that especially affect women as a group. She believes that women should have more power and influence and businesses should have less. If all the elected leaders in her city were female, she believes policies would change: "More people would be represented. Less money [would be spent] on development. More money [would go to] social services. More money [would be spent] on helping hurt/abused/raped/homeless women."

The differences between Diane and Susan are also evident when they are asked what their biggest successes and challenges have been since assuming office. Diane, the descriptive representative, names increased safety of citizens and a ten-year strategic plan as successes. Susan mentions working with community groups to plan for and facilitate the purchase of an affordable housing project, opening a center "for those less fortunate," and fighting for and installing a special-needs-accessible playground with community groups as successes. As for challenges, Diane speaks of time management and dealing with the budget, while Susan talks about dealing with "a mind-set that any controls are business-unfriendly" and that "anyone should be able to do whatever they want to, regardless of how it affects others." In terms of goals for the next year, Diane emphasizes keeping taxes low, bringing in jobs, and protecting the city from state mandates. Susan, on the other hand, wants to pursue more dialogue with citizens, promote responsible economic development, and "institutionaliz[e] a culture of caring for others."

In many ways, Diane is the quintessential *city* leader. She expresses attitudes consistent with what many scholars of urban politics would expect: a dedication to development and public safety and viewing as challenges the enormous fiscal constraints put on cities. Susan, on the other hand, is the typical *female* leader. Susan's support of social services, connection with women's groups, and views on the power of businesses all exemplify what scholars often find when studying women at other levels of government. Elucidating who is a preferable descriptive representative provides additional evidence of the importance of connections across formal and informal boundaries in urban politics to advance the desires of marginalized groups.

Conclusion

The results presented here are consistent with the limited scholarship on female representatives at the local level: gender's effect on policy priorities is very limited. My findings suggest that how a representative understands the relationship between gender, power, and representation is a more important measure of policy priorities. In particular, I find very little evidence that gender has a direct relationship with policy preferences as expressed by local leaders. Instead, how leaders view their community and the groups in their community is more important. In particular, if mayors or city councilmembers believe that they have a responsibility to represent women, children, or the poor in office, they are much more likely to value women's urban issues. Female representatives make up the vast majority of this group of leaders. As a result, gender has an indirect effect on policy preferences through the preferable descriptive representation measure.

Several implications arise from my findings. First, women who serve at the local level may be different from women who serve at higher levels of office. The selection process for state and national offices may result in a larger percentage of women who possess a gender consciousness, so that gender and gender consciousness are easy proxies for each other. Further research on gender consciousness among political leaders at all levels of office is required. Additionally, gender consciousness is a significant predictor of the actions and priorities of municipal leaders, even with controls for party and ideology, suggesting that it is not merely a proxy for liberally minded women holding office. Finally, these results suggest that those seeking to elect female representatives at the local level who will hold attitudes traditionally associated with women may have to be more careful in their selection of a leader.

3 /

Gender, Power, and Policy Making
in American Cities

In a deliberative democracy political representatives with varying opinions on approaches and outcomes to policies engage with each other in a mindful deliberation over policies' merits. The "giving, weighing, acceptance or rejection of reasons" produces policy.[1] The deliberation process requires adequate representation by members of vested groups in society to produce good and legitimate policy.[2]

Descriptive representation by members of historically marginalized groups is of particular importance in the deliberative process when the interests of the groups are unclear, are uncrystalized, or crosscut party lines.[3] In many circumstances, men may provide representation for women in their communities when women express clear policy preferences. However, when the interests of women become complicated, unclear, unknown, or contrary to partisan demands, a descriptive representative may prove to be a better choice.[4]

Cities provide an ideal testing ground for evaluating whether representatives who are members of underrepresented groups better understand group interests. Low levels of information permeate local politics: representatives have little information about constituency opinions, and the public rarely has access to information about representative actions;[5] political parties lack power;[6] political structures are nonpartisan or involve very little control by parties over their members;[7] and issues often fail to correspond with party and ideological positions.[8] In these situations, a female representative may be better equipped to understand the effect that a policy will have on other women or suggest how the political body can address a problem. In one city, during a discussion of whether the city should pass an ordinance criminalizing nudity, a mayor and city council member, both female, objected to the law because it would ostensibly criminalize breastfeeding in public. Female leaders' actions to move urban policy toward recognition of urban women's issues also provide evidence of the expression of women's interests in the policy process. Under a female mayor's oversight, a discussion of the hours that city parks would be open during the summer turned to children, the availability of child care, and working mothers because of the input by female leaders. Thus, female representatives recognized the gendered aspects of an urban action that appeared genderless on its face.

The first section of this chapter evaluates whether cities with female mayors discuss women's urban issues and related matters more frequently than cities with male mayors by examining discussions in city council minutes in the hundred-city data set. The second section introduces two nests of city case studies, one in North Carolina and one in California, to investigate the influence of female mayors over time, with particular focus on domestic violence policy.

The Substance of Urban Policy Making

To examine the effect of gender on the policy-making process at the urban level, I coded for content and process city council minutes from all meetings in 2007 in the hundred cities. In this chapter, I ask: Does the presence of female leaders lead to a change in topic of policy discussions? To evaluate this, the subject matter of each agenda item was categorized into one of the following categories: affordable housing, children, development, domestic violence, education, general government, library, public works, parks and recreation, race and ethnicity, public safety, transportation and infrastructure, environment, welfare and health, women, and zoning.[9] I also ask: Does the change to a female mayor matter? Using data from several cities that changed from male to female mayors, the research presented here evaluates the effect of a change of mayor on a variety of elements. Finally, I ask: Can cities address issues traditionally considered feminist? The research presented here provides information on domestic violence efforts by cities to suggest that, yes, cities do address feminist issues.

In this chapter, the data are presented as comparisons between cities with male and female mayors, with a consideration of the composition of the city council at certain points. I obtained and coded minutes of ninety-two of the hundred-city sample, resulting in 33,450 agenda items.[10] For each city, the information about the discussions is aggregated into count information (how many times the city discussed an issue) and percentage information (the percentage of the cities' total discussions related to an issue). The number of public comments on each agenda item, the number of comments by members of the city council, the number of comments by city staff, the action on the item, and the vote (if applicable) are also tracked. I focus on the percentage measure to eliminate differences between cities in the overall level of discussion of issues.[11] These categories are aggregated into four areas: general government, development, quality of life, and women's issues.[12]

- General government concerns, including hiring and firing employees, raises, promotions, general council business, authorizing purchases, office equipment, office supplies, and legal matters, compose 38 percent of discussions.
- Development policies, including anything relating to economic development, zoning, and transportation and infrastructure, make up 29 percent of the agenda items that cities discuss.
- Quality of life concerns, such as parks and recreation, culture and the arts, public safety, and protecting the environment, make up just under 15 percent of discussions.
- Urban women's issues, including affordable housing, children, domestic violence, education, libraries, welfare, and women, make up 19 percent of the discussions of the city councils.

Some urban politics scholars argue that cities should avoid the trap of redistributional policies and focus on development and allocative interests, but that one-fifth of the discussions of urban policy making relate to urban women's interests is a compelling finding. Again, these findings both confirm and confound the general expectations of the urban politics scholarship that city governments focus on development and allocative policies.

Mayoral Gender and Policy Making

Given the long history of women's activism in urban women's issues and the gender gap on women's issues, the presence of a female mayor should lead to more discussions of urban women's issues. Does the gender of a city's mayor influence the substance of policy-making discussions in cities? Figure 3.1 breaks down discussion of the four general policy areas by mayoral gender. Cities with male mayors discuss development and general government more than cities with female mayors. Cities with female mayors have more discussions of urban women's issues than cities with male mayors do.[13] Indeed, in cities with female mayors, discussions of women's urban issues occurred at more than twice the rate, 26 percent of all discussions, than they did in cities with male mayors, whereas discussions of women's urban issues were 12 percent of discussions.

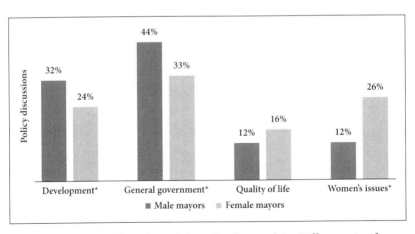

Figure 3.1 Mayoral gender and the topics discussed. * = Difference significant at the 0.05 level.

Examining the difference in discussions under male and female mayors in more detail reveals gender differences on many of the traditional issues in urban government, including development (15 percent of discussions under a male mayor, compared to 7 percent under a female mayor), general government (44 percent vs. 33 percent), and transportation (7 percent vs. 4 percent). Gender differences also appear when urban women's issues are broken down by subtype. As Figure 3.2 shows, cities with female mayors discuss issues relating to children, domestic violence, education, welfare, and women more frequently than cities with male mayors do. Cities with female mayors discuss almost *every* urban women's issue at higher rates than cities with male mayors. The across-the-board increases in discussions of all types of women's issues suggest that female mayors affect policy discussions in many areas.

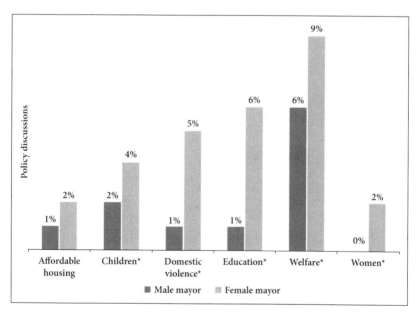

Figure 3.2   Discussion of urban women's issues under male and female mayors. * = Difference significant at the 0.05 level.

City Councils and Discussion of Women's Urban Issues

Mayors do not lead in isolation, and the city council plays an important role in forming policies in cities. Thus, the presence of female city council members should increase discussions of urban women's issues. Studies of the experiences of women in political bodies often focus on how the ratio of the dominant group to the minority group changes the behavior of both groups.[14] Drawing from physics, scholars suggest that women must first reach a critical mass of representation, or "the quantity needed to start a chain reaction, an *irreversible turning point*, a takeoff into a new situation or process" before changing policy outcomes.[15] However, significant disagreements in the literature appear over the cutoff point for mass to become critical or whether a critical mass actually exists.[16] Research on descriptive representation at the local level finds a significant relationship between female mayors and female city council members and between the proportion of women's representation and policy outcomes in other countries.[17] Thus, the presence of women on city councils and the percentage of the city council that are women should have a positive effect on discussions relating to urban women's issues. The variation in female representation on city councils provides an opportunity to test theories of critical mass at the local level.

The percentage of women on the city council has a positive, significant effect on the discussion of women's issues in these cities. Figure 3.3 relates the percentage of women on the city council to the percentage of women's issues covered in the presence of a female or male mayor. On this initial presentation of the data, there seems to be little indication of a critical mass effect—that is, discussions of urban women's issues increase as the level of women's representation increases, but there does not seem to be a threshold that women's representation needs to surpass to become effective.

One possibility is that the root cause of the higher rates of discussions of women's issues is not the presence of a female mayor but the city itself. Women are more likely to be elected from liberal areas with higher levels of education and socioeconomic status.[18] Perhaps the greater discussion of women's issues in cities with female leaders

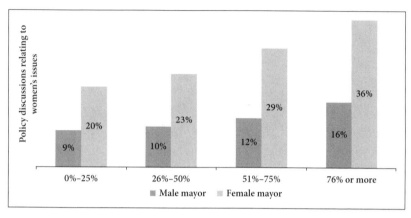

Figure 3.3   Discussion of urban women's issues, by female percentage of council.

simply reflects differences in the communities these women represent. To verify that the differences are caused by mayoral gender and not community characteristics or demand, the mayoral gender, the gender composition of the council, the type of city (mayor-council or council-manager), and demographic controls were regressed against the percentage of city council discussions dedicated to women's issues.[19] Scholars identify an interaction between the form of government and policy making, with mayors exercising more power in mayor-council cities, so I interact the form of city government with the presence of a female mayor and the percentage of women on the council.[20] The results are presented in Table 3.1.

The presence of a female mayor has a positive, significant relationship with the discussion of women's issues in the hundred-city sample, leading to a six-percentage-point increase in the number of discussions of women's issues.[21] In addition, the percentage of women on the council, the interaction between the presence of a female mayor and women on the council and the squared term, and female mayors in mayor-council forms of government all have positive relationships with the discussion of women's urban interests. The continued significant effect of a female mayor on the discussions of issues relating to women's interests demonstrates the importance of women in local leadership and the influence on policy of the mayoral position.[22] The interaction of the

TABLE 3.1   DISCUSSION OF WOMEN'S ISSUES

Variable	Coefficient	Standard error
Female mayor	0.12**	0.01
Percentage female council	0.25**	0.06
Percentage female council, squared	0.95	0.89
Female mayor × % female council	0.75**	0.26
Female mayor × % female council, squared	0.84**	0.08
Mayor-council	0.13	0.79
Female mayor × mayor-council	0.97**	0.30
Percentage female council × mayor-council	0.59	0.81
Median income	−1.0	0.56
Percentage poverty	0.35	0.47
Percentage high school diploma	0.85**	0.39
Percentage public assistance	0.49	0.33
Percentage nonwhite	0.03	0.16
Log of population	1.19	1.40
Ward system	0.69**	0.15
Size of council	−0.24	0.20
Constant	3.11*	1.48
R^2	0.88	
N	96	

* $p < 0.05$, ** $p < 0.01$.

form of government and the presence of a female mayor is also significant, suggesting that female leaders positively influence the discussion of women's urban issues generally and are *more* effective when they govern in a political system that affords them direct power.

The presence of a female mayor also has an indirect relationship with discussions on women's urban issues through the presence of women on the city council, as demonstrated by the significant, positive coefficient on the interaction between mayoral and city council gender. Thus, women on the city council, regardless of their position, increase discussion of women's urban issues, with a strong substantive relationship between women in executive positions (particularly when the position has power) and women's urban issue discussion.

Policy Making over Time

To demonstrate the centrality of the presence of a female mayor to discussions of women's issues, I examine whether changing from a male to a female mayor changes the substance of policy making in cities. The analysis presented here allows consideration of whether gender makes a difference in a city over time. Looking at the subject matter of discussions more generally and discussions of domestic violence more specifically allows more detailed examination of the policy process in cities.

To undertake this examination, ten years of city council minutes were coded from six cities, three each in Southern California and North Carolina, where the mayor had been a white male mayor during the early 1990s and changed to a female mayor during the late 1990s.[23] City council minutes from two cities that elected new male mayors to replace male mayors are also examined as a control group; the six cities of interest and two controls produced twenty-five thousand agenda items over ten years. Details on the cities and new mayors are available in Table 3.2.

The cities in California and North Carolina were chosen because of political characteristics, personal reasons, and city characteristics. In terms of political characteristics, California and North Carolina were two of only four possible states at the time that met all the following six criteria: (a) a set of three female mayors (b) with varying racial and ethnic backgrounds who were (c) elected in the late 1990s in cities (d) with mayor-council forms of government having (e) no instances of corruption or tragedy that either led to the election of the female leaders or resulted in the women leaving office and that had (f) publicly available city council minutes for the entire period. The presence of female minority mayors allowed an evaluation of the intersectional effects of race and gender on the policy process. The states also were convenient because I lived and worked in them.

In terms of city characteristics, the smaller size of the cities with female mayors in Southern California and North Carolina fit my study of women's urban leadership experiences in the typical city, in contrast to the concentration on a single city by many studies of urban politics. The mayor-council form of government provided the opportunity to study women in an executive position with power, compared to mayors in council-manager forms of government, in which the mayor's power is largely ceremonial and the mayoral office is rotational. To this end, all the cities have a strong-mayor, or mayor-council, form of government, in which mayors are selected in an independent election.

TABLE 3.2 DEMOGRAPHIC PROFILES OF CITIES AND NEW MAYOR CHARACTERISTICS

State	New mayor (late 1990s)	Population (rounded)	White (%)	Poverty rate (%)	Median household income ($)	Prior city council member?	Work with women's issue groups?	Ambition for higher office?	Primary support group	Party
CA	Hispanic female	47,000	42	15	53,000	Y	Y	N	Friends	R
CA	Asian female	44,000	61	9	63,000	Y	N	Y	Asian community	R
CA	White female	37,000	59	10	67,000	N	Y	N	Mothers	D
CA	White male	42,000	48	12	55,000	Y	N	Y	Chamber of commerce	D
NC	Black female	69,000	64	18	42,000	Y	Y	N	Neighbors, friends	D
NC	White male	69,000	67	17	42,000	Y	Y	N	Business organizations	R
NC	Hispanic female	77,000	77	22	38,000	N	Y	N	Women friends	D
NC	White female	76,000	81	13	48,000	Y	Y	Y	Church friends	R

Note: City data from the 2000 U.S. Census; mayoral campaign and characteristic information from interviews with the mayors. D = Democratic; R = Republican.

Four cities (including controls) in California and North Carolina that approached similarity in population and demographics were chosen. Because the scholarship on the provision of services at the local level suggests that demographics affect the behavior of leaders, the cities are matched on these variables as much as possible to eliminate socioeconomic factors as the driver for policy making.[24]

The two states have a rich history of women's political activism in the urban arena. In North Carolina, women's activism on education reform, access to higher education, public housing, and social services produced fundamental changes in how cities and the state addressed these policy areas. In California, women's activism on education, children's services, worker's rights, and domestic violence resulted in fundamental changes for policy making in cities there. For example, the activism of women's groups on domestic violence policy (and eventually lawsuits against local governments) resulted in local governments changing how they handled domestic violence incidents. Studying eight cities (including controls) in two states allowed me to evaluate the influence of gender across cities with different racial, ethnic, socioeconomic, economic, and political backgrounds while still controlling for the degree to which states vary in their relationship with cities. California and North Carolina also share institutional structures, including at-large elections and professional managers. Cities in the South adopted many of these measures in efforts to minimize the electoral power of blacks before the civil rights movement. In the West—and California particularly—institutional changes were adopted in the early 1900s in response to the Progressive movement.[25] These reformed structures, by limiting incumbency and local group power, provide additional electoral opportunities for women to seek office at the local level but may inhibit the ability of minority groups to gain true political incorporation, particularly because the move to at-large elections restricts the ability of geographically segregated racial and minority groups to elect representatives from their neighborhoods as they did under ward elections.[26] Thus, these two states make the election of women possible through institutional structures, but those same structures may limit the ability of women to change policy once in office.

The cities in California typify western suburban cities in many ways. The cities range in population from 37,000 to 47,000 and have a median income of just under $60,000. Asians, blacks, and Hispanics make up the majority of the population in two cities, with non-Hispanic whites as the majority in the other two cities. All are within the Los Angeles–Orange County–Riverside Census Metropolitan Statistical Area. Each city exhibits many good-government characteristics, including nonpartisan elections, council members elected at large, and professional staffs of a significant size. Again, all four cities directly elect a mayor with expansive powers of agenda setting, policy creation, and budget control. The cities vary in their organizational capacity, the involvement of the business community in politics, and the strength of local political parties. Two of the three female mayors served as their city's first female mayor; one of the two minority mayors served as her city's first minority mayor.

In North Carolina, the cities range in population from 69,000 to 77,000 and have a median income of $42,750. They are located in the central Triangle-Triad areas or in the southern part of the state. Non-Hispanic whites are the majority in all of the cities, with African Americans representing the substantial majority of nonwhites in three of the four cities; the city with a Hispanic female mayor has a large and growing Hispanic population. All cities use nonpartisan election. Two of the four cities elect council members at large, while the other two use a mix of ward and at-large selections. The cities directly elect their mayor in all four locations and maintain professional staffs. Two of the three female mayors were their city's first female mayor and one of the minority mayors was the city's first minority mayor.

In each city, I obtained ten years of city council minutes: five years before and five years after the change in mayor, which resulted in a time period of roughly 1994 to 2004. The city council minutes from each city were then coded into policy areas, using the same coding scheme used in the hundred-city group. In addition to coding city council minutes, I contacted as many of the leaders from each of the cities as possible for interviews, resulting in interviews with forty-nine, or between five and six leaders in each city; all of the mayors consented to interviews. Women outnumbered men in the interview group, making up 59 percent of the interviewees. The list of interview questions asked of each leader is available in Appendix 3B.

The Experiences of Female Mayors

The female and male mayors possessed a diverse set of political experiences, political ambition, campaign environments, and supporters. Three-quarters of the mayors had held a city council seat before running for mayor, and a quarter of the mayors had lost a previous run for the office. Five of the female mayors, and one male, had some background with urban women's issue groups before becoming mayor.[27] Table 3.3 lists the types of organizations the mayors worked with in their communities. I divide organizational activity into three general categories: women's organizations, women's urban issue organizations, and development organizations. Women's organizations are those that are formed of women but do not include women's urban issues as a core component of their mission. For example, the Junior

TABLE 3.3   MAYORS' ORGANIZATIONAL BACKGROUNDS

Women's organizations	Women's urban issue organizations	Development organizations
American Association of University Women	Children's service organizations	Business associations
		Chamber of commerce
Democratic or Republican Party women's club	Domestic violence shelter board	Downtown development association
	Girl Scouts	
Daughters of the American Revolution	Food banks and hunger awareness organizations	Economic development association
Junior League		Professional associations
League of Women Voters	Mothers Against Drunk Driving	Real estate development league
	Planned Parenthood	Trade organizations
Soroptimist International	Parent teacher organizations	Unions
Women's Leadership Forum	Social service organizations	Young professionals
	YMCA	

Note: Data come from interviews with six female mayors, twenty-nine female leaders (including female mayors), and twenty male leaders (including male mayors).

League promotes volunteerism and the leadership development of women. Its work often overlaps with women's urban issues but not necessarily. Women's urban issue organizations address matters related to children, education, affordable housing, social welfare, or violence against women. Development organizations promote the needs of businesses and economic development. The majority of the female mayors received support from either women's organizations or women's issue organizations in their campaigns.

Female mayors and female city council members had different opinions from male leaders about the power of groups in their city, as demonstrated in Figure 3.4. Women (as either mayors or city council members) listed women's or women's issue organizations as *both* the most and the least powerful groups more frequently than male leaders did. Powerful women's organizations—groups like the Junior League, the League of Women Voters ("They host these meet and greets every year. If you want to be in the running, you go there."), and parent-teacher organizations—provided an opportunity for like-minded people to meet. Weak women's organizations included the neighborhood association of the public housing complex, social service

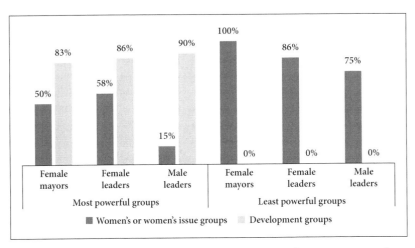

Figure 3.4 **Group power and leader gender.** Data come from interviews with twenty-nine female leaders (including six female mayors), and twenty male leaders (including four male mayors).

organizations, and organizations that serve populations often seen as undeserving. For example, one mayor described the local group that provides drug and alcohol counseling for the homeless in her city as having "no power." She said, "I know [the director], and his job is so hard. So very hard." In many ways, male leaders seemed to be unaware of the women's groups and women's issue organizations in their cities.

All the mayors—male and female—listed general government (such as infrastructure improvements) and development policies as ones they felt pride in passing. Two-thirds of the female mayors specifically mentioned policies on urban women's issues as ones they were proud of, including projects that involved intergovernmental cooperation, like "facilitating the purchase and planning for numerous affordable housing projects, including getting grants from the feds" and "getting the community center to serve food during the summer to kids on free lunch [programs]." The last noted, "We don't even have to pay for it!" Another female mayor, who headed an all-male council, described her success as, "Other than surviving? Passage of the antiharassment ordinance." One of the mayors, in discussing her achievements, pointed to a new bus line in the city: "It might not seem like it is important, but it goes right from the [low-income] housing to the industrial area, so that people can find a job, and they don't need a car. I was able to convince them [the council] that it was good for the city to have it. It took a lot of research, and I met with all the key players." In conversations with the female mayors, the reconstruction of development, quality of life, and general government areas as women's issues emerged as a common theme. The mayor's bus program represents a key example of how female leaders often reframed a subject as a women's issue or understood the nature of a policy that on its face did not relate as a women's issue. Expanding a bus line, for many leaders, is simply transportation, but the female mayor identified the women's issue components in it—such as providing transportation to the residents of low-income housing—and thus framed the issue.

To examine whether female mayors influence the subjects under deliberation and introduce more discussions of urban women's issues, the number of items discussed that relate to women's issues per month in each council was averaged.[28] Figure 3.5 depicts the average number of items discussed per month that related to urban women's

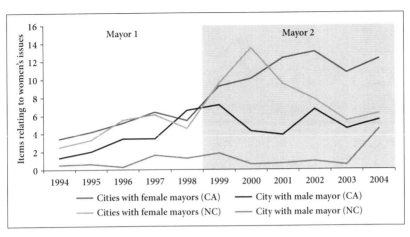

Figure 3.5   Discussions of urban women's issues over time.

issues (children, education, affordable housing, social welfare, domestic violence, and women) by state and mayoral gender. The effect of changing from a male mayor to a female mayor on the discussion of women's issues takes two forms. In the California cities, there is a slow and steady increase in the discussions of these issues, with a maximum difference between the first and second mayor of 8.6 points and a minimum difference of 5.9 points. The California control city, which changed from a male mayor to another male mayor, also experienced a small uptick in the discussion of women's issues after the change. The increase relates largely to two events: the construction of a complex of affordable housing in the city and a crisis with the school district's budget, which required some action of the part of the city.

In North Carolina, however, discussing women's issues takes on a very different pattern. Instead of a slow and steady increase in the discussion of women's issues, there is a dramatic increase (peaking at a difference of 12.95 agenda items) followed by a gradual downturn to result in a rate of discussion similar to that under the previous male mayor; this pattern fits a traditional decay function.[29] The origin of the decay pattern is anecdotally supplied by the city council minutes and interviews with the mayors. Specifically, the female mayors often noted that they pushed a large number of policy changes through shortly after taking office; after those changes, few opportunities emerged for additional action.

Discussing what sets her apart from her predecessor, one female mayor said:

> I'm not just marking off the meeting. We have a meaningful task here to accomplish and lots of good work to be done. These guys want to go home after an hour. They want to just pass the budget without looking at it; they want to say it is okay that our shelter is full of families with kids—they made that choice. That's what [the previous mayor] did. I want to be different. [*Pauses*] I've been reaching out to organizations that do what the city is supposed to be doing and getting them help. Like with the rape crisis line. They do it on their own, but they don't have to. I can help them. *We* can help them.

The majority of female mayors referred to urban women's issues when discussing what set them apart from the previous, male mayor. Five of the female mayors said that attention to "politics forgotten" or "people ignored" marked a departure from the previous administration. In particular, mayors noted their attention to how "*everyone* is doing in the city—we aren't all middle-class real estate agents, you know"—and how they are reaching out to new groups.

Female Mayors and Violence against Women Policy Innovation

A recurring theme among female mayors involves policy work and innovation in the area of violence against women (domestic violence, rape, and sexual assault). In the cities that changed to a female mayor, there was a marked increase in the overall average of discussions of domestic and sexual violence. In California, the change in mayoral gender led to an average increase of discussions from 0.1 items per meeting to 0.7, while the control city increased the discussion from 0.1 items per meeting to 0.2 items. In North Carolina, the change was smaller—an increase from 0.02 to 0.08 items per meeting—but is still significantly larger than the discussions in the control city, in which discussions declined from 0.01 items per meeting to zero.[30] The widely varying substantive effect of changing the gender and race of a mayor largely comes from the opportunities afforded each mayor in discussing issues relating to domestic and sexual violence. For example, in one of the North Carolina cities with a female mayor, a sexual harassment policy for city employees already existed, and a local battered women's shelter pushed through most of the changes in police policy (such as mandatory arrests of domestic violence offenders and training for police in the proper methods of preserving DNA evidence in sexual assault cases). Thus, a quite narrow policy space existed for the mayor. However, in one of the California cities, the female mayor introduced and passed policies relating to the city's financial support of rape kits and issued a formal reprimand of the police chief when a domestic violence incident resulted in the murder of the female victim; the police had been called by the victim multiple times but made no arrest. In an open hearing on the matter, the mayor said to the police chief:

> This isn't something that we want to talk about or even think about. But domestic violence happens, and we failed to protect those that needed protecting. Just as these women have been failed by the man that was supposed to be their number-one protector, so we just restarted the cycle of violence for that woman by not protecting her. And you expect me to just accept that you knew what you were doing? She is dead, and that is on us.

The female mayors often spoke in terms of responsibility and protection on these policies: "It was important for me to support having a [domestic violence] advocate at our local courthouse. Women in our community go there for protection. We should protect them." Another mayor, when she was able to get the city to pay for rape kits and clean clothes for victims, said that she "felt like [she] had to make sure [rape] victims were protected. Nothing else has gone right for them—they should at least be able to get some clean clothes at the hospital." Other women said they pursued policies that related to domestic and sexual violence "over and over again, until [they] got what [they] wanted" or that "no one considered rape to be an important topic." One female mayor said, "I had to bring it up ten times before it was discussed once. And then I had to defend it as something we [the council] should consider." Additional actions included clearing funding for the retesting of rape kits, expressing formal support for a female community member who publicly disclosed her past abuse, and declaring a domestic violence awareness month in the city, which included passing out ribbons, supporting educational events, and funding a speaker for the high school.

Dual Identities and the Role of Race and Gender

Studying subjects with dual identities, such as the minority women in my investigation, provides both challenges and benefits. First, for the four female minority mayors, it is often difficult to separate the effects of gender and race on their behavior, particularly because the extant scholarship points to similar expectations for women and minorities in many circumstances. Second, they may act in a manner that cannot be attributed to their belonging to either a racial or gendered group. Third, the tendency of race and gender to intersect produces unique challenges for minority women.[31] At the same time, these data provide the ability to examine both gender and race, including how the intersection of race and gender might affect a leader's actions in office, and are a new set of information on this often-understudied group of representatives.

In an attempt to separate the effects of race and gender, the gender and race of the mayor were modeled against the discussion of issues relating to domestic and sexual violence and the discussion of issues relating to race and ethnicity. Table 3.4 shows the results of these models.[32] As shown in the second column of Table 3.4, gender is, overall, a significant predictor of the rate of discussion of domestic and sexual violence, but the interaction of race and gender is not a significant predictor, suggesting that gender alone is the important element in influencing such discussions. Looking at the rate of discussion of race and ethnicity in the third column of results, however, suggests the opposite story; here, gender is an insignificant predictor, while the interaction of gender and race is a significant predictor. An obvious limitation of

TABLE 3.4   THE EFFECTS OF GENDER AND RACE ON POLICY DISCUSSIONS

Variable	Domestic and sexual violence		Race and ethnicity	
	Coefficient	Standard error	Coefficient	Standard error
Gender	0.101***	0.029	0.062	0.056
Gender × Race	0.025	0.028	0.360***	0.012
Constant	0.062***	0.001	0.029***	0.002
R^2	0.6847		0.7723	
N	973		973	

*** $p < 0.001$.

my research is the lack of minority male mayors to serve as a comparison group in attempting to separate the effects of race and gender on political behavior.

In the qualitative data, several patterns of interest emerge. First, the female minority mayors see themselves as representatives for the two groups; the dual identity of both woman and minority shapes their actions. Specifically, these representatives feel a responsibility to, as one representative noted, "step in wherever [they are] needed," or serve the needs of women when no one else could or would, and be a voice for minorities when they were underrepresented. Second, the female minority mayors all identified situations in which their dual identity forced them to make a decision between a policy that was good for women and one that was good for their minority group. These choices often involved public safety versus civil rights. For example, in one city, women in the community pushed for the city to provide a database of parolees in their community, so as to identify "dangerous areas" for women in the city. However, the majority of those to be listed were minorities convicted of drug offenses. The female minority mayor had to tread a fine line between the women's groups and the minority groups, eventually proposing that women instead use the sex offender database. However, as the mayor put it, she "lost both fights."

Conclusion

Female mayors exert influence on the deliberative policy-making process at the urban level in the United States. Cities with female mayors spend a significantly larger amount of time on urban women's issues. Similarly, the percentage of the city council that is female has a positive relationship with discussion of women's issues. Qualitative information echoes these findings: female leaders emerge from women's organizations and support women's urban issues more than male leaders. Changing mayoral gender produces changes in the substance of policy making in the United States.

4 /

The More Democratic Sex?

Deliberative Democracy, Gender,
and Urban Governance

> They just come to me. I tell them to come to the meetings.
> I listen to them. They notice. More of them come. Rinse
> and repeat.
> —FEMALE MAYOR, DISCUSSING INTERACTIONS WITH
>   CONSTITUENTS

Among other benefits, participation in local politics increases democratic practices and participation (reinforcing what Benjamin Barber calls a strong democracy) and promotes care for the community and equality.[1] Of primary interest, however, is that public participation may promote government responsiveness to citizen demands and thus reinforce democratic accountability mechanisms. Albert Hirschman calls successfully engaging with government to meet a demand or right a wrong the *effective use of voice.* The use of voice plays a particularly important role in local politics because individuals can choose to exit—leaving the municipality for another city and taking their tax dollars when they leave.[2] By promoting the use of voice (and responding to voice), city leaders encourage tax-paying residents to stay. The key, however, is that the use of voice must be seen as useful and powerful; if not, voice is not seen as effective and does not increase political trust and loyalty.[3]

Examinations of participation in urban politics find some evidence of the benefits of citizen involvement, particularly through groups.[4] Neighborhood groups provide useful political capital and resources

to political leaders seeking to establish consensus or promote deliberation, especially in circumstances with complex policies or unpopular
decisions.[5] Local groups and individuals can also sometimes engage
in agenda setting and problem definition.[6] As discussed in Chapter 3,
feminist groups serve particularly important roles in changing domestic violence policy at the local level, but groups need allies in formal positions of power to be effective. Indeed, connections across the
formal-informal divide truly promote women-friendly policy change.[7]

On the institutional side, scholarship on gender and leadership
often finds that women "speak in a different voice," approach policy
making in a different manner, and have different relationships with
constituents.[8] Female leaders at all levels of office emphasize cooperation and communication in their leadership styles; this results in
female local leaders spending more time with their constituents and
considering constituent demands when making decisions.[9] The mor-
alistic leadership approach taken more often by women lines up with
the transformational leadership style, in which leaders use cooperation, inspiration, and consideration.[10] Through these differing leadership styles, female leaders open up the policy-making process to new
groups, encourage participation of a more diverse group of policy
makers, and often come to alternative conclusions. Female leaders
also promote and discuss women's issues more frequently than male
leaders.[11]

In many ways, cities provide an ideal arena for the application of a
gendered theory of policy making, because constituents need far fewer
resources to enter the policy process, and deliberation occurs in public through city council meetings. Thus, if women in office open up
the policy-making process—if they make urban governments more
democratic—then constituents can easily respond to the invitation to
participate. Furthermore, scholars have demonstrated the importance
of the informal powers of local leaders. In particular, the powers of
mayors "extend far beyond the realm of mere figurehead, regardless of
the urban political structure."[12] One crucial element of this informal
power is the ability to use the ceremonial, spokesperson, and public-
and media-contact elements of the position of mayor to develop and
facilitate interactions among groups and individuals in the community.[13] The idea that the identity of a leader could influence the policy

process is consistent with scholarship on how conceptualizations of legitimacy and fairness (particularly through descriptive representation) produce good public participation processes.[14] The interaction of informal powers, the accessibility of public meetings to citizens, and a gendered conceptualization of power of female mayors increases public participation in the policy-making process.

Urban politics may also present significant obstacles to female leaders changing the deliberation process. Paul Peterson conceptualizes urban politics as groupless politics, and other research echoes the inability of groups to influence local government.[15] Some research on citizen comments on policy fails to find evidence that citizen participation in public hearings has any effect on policy, allowing leaders to continue with predetermined actions while deflecting criticism of nondemocratic policy making.[16] Studies of public participants in city council meetings find large differences between their opinions and the general population's interests on an issue.[17] Finally, many urban theories argue that cities make the majority of important policy decisions behind the scenes and informally, thus rendering public deliberation ineffective in urban politics. Scholars often find that development-oriented individuals and groups, in particular, preempt the deliberation process.[18]

Despite the large body of scholarship on the role, function, and utility of group organization and political participation at the local level, we have no understanding of how the gender of a leader might influence the activity and effectiveness of groups and individuals seeking relief through local political institutions. Female leaders, through informal powers, increase the accessibility of public meetings, work with women's issue groups, and engage in transformational leadership. As a result, these women promote the public use of voice and the engagement of new groups with urban politics.

Measuring Community Participation

To examine community participation in the policy-making process, I return to city council minutes and evaluate the percentage of agenda items with any kind of public participation or comment and the average number of public comments per agenda item.[19] To examine these measures, I use a combination of a year of minutes from the hundred-city sample and data over time from the six cities plus two controls in Southern California and North Carolina (see Chapter 3). These data are supplemented with surveys and qualitative interviews from active community participants in ten cities (described in "Measuring Community Perceptions of Leaders," later in this chapter) and select data from the hundred-city survey of leaders discussed in Chapter 2.

I use these public-participation measures to estimate the overall contribution of the public to policy making at the local level. City council meetings operate in a public manner; any citizen can participate in the policy-making activities in a city by coming to meetings and either initiating a policy in a public comment period or contributing to a policy discussion. Because attending meetings takes time, only those citizens deeply concerned about an issue will comment.[20]

Openness versus Substance versus Controversy

I found that the public tends to comment more in cities with female mayors. In cities with female mayors, 26 percent of agenda items have a public comment, compared to 16 percent with a male mayor. The difference also extends to the average number of comments per item; under female mayors, the average number of comments is 0.95, compared to 0.55 for male mayors.[21] The six cities and two controls support this finding: changing from a male to a female mayor increases the percentage of agenda items with public comments and the average number of comments, but exchanging a male mayor for another male in the control cities did not change public participation in the policy-making process.

Why do more people comment at city council meetings under a female mayor? Competing explanations emerge. First, it is possibly because female leaders in my study change the policy-making process by encouraging the inclusion of new groups in the policy process and engaging in a transformative leadership style. Women may conceptualize the deliberative and policy-making process differently from their male counterparts.[22] Female leaders seem to engage in inclusive leadership actions more often, such as encouraging participation, sharing power and information, enhancing the self-worth of others, energizing others, and leading without formal authority.[23] Gender differences in leadership style include women being motivated by community (rather than personal) concerns, trying harder to reach consensus, and being interested in bringing an "integrative and collaborative dimension to leadership."[24] Emphasizing the complex nature of problems (rather than male leaders' generally more dichotomous view of answers being correct or incorrect), female leaders "stress cooperation rather than conflict, maintaining relationships rather than achieving abstract justice."[25]

A second possibility is that, in changing the *substance* of policy making (Chapter 3), female leaders encourage increased political participation in the policy-making process because a broader sector of the public cares about the policies. Public comments at city and school board meetings can serve several important functions, for example, setting agendas, showing support, shaming, delaying, networking, and providing information. In participating in city meetings, "citizens are free to identify issues that need to be discussed and offer new frameworks for understanding issues already under discussion."[26] Female leaders, by introducing new policies, may activate groups and individuals who care about women's issues. Data presented in Chapter 3 suggest that female leaders more frequently than male leaders know about women's issue groups and topics and recognize them as important in their city. Thus, the content of meetings may inspire citizens to speak out.

A third possibility is that female mayors highlight women's urban issues, and these are simply more contentious than development or quality of life issues. If that is the case, the increase in discussion of women's urban issue policies may be because cities with female mayors are experiencing more conflict over policies, not that female mayors are changing the debate. But if it is that women's urban issues simply inspire more controversy, the gender of the mayor will not have an independent effect on discussion of women's urban issues, and the level of conflict over issues will not increase with female mayors. However, female leaders emphasize cooperation over conflict, which suggests that women in leadership positions may attempt to downplay conflict in their cities.[27]

Citizen Participation by Subject of Agenda Item

Women's issue topics draw more comments from the public, on average, than development or quality of life agenda items.[28] As is evident in Figure 4.1, in cities with male mayors, citizens comment more often on issues related to development, while in cities with female mayors, citizens comment more frequently on women's issues. An example may clarify the nature of deliberation in cities with male and female mayors. Table 4.1 outlines discussions of a development policy in a city with a female mayor versus one with a male mayor. These subjects are similar, but please note that these examples merely illustrate some of the differences between male and female leaders in deliberative practices.[29]

The development policies discussed in the cities involve a tax break as an incentive to get a business to relocate to the community and

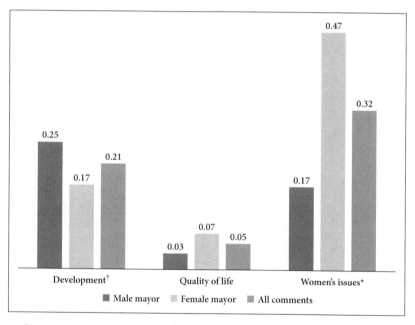

Figure 4.1 **Average number of public comments per agenda item.** Data come from city council minutes and represent the average number of citizen comments per agenda item in that specific issue area. Differences are between cities with a male or female mayor. * = Difference significant at the 0.05 level; † = Difference significant to the 0.10 level.

TABLE 4.1   DISCUSSIONS ON DEVELOPMENT

	Female mayor (tax break for law firm)	Male mayor (tax break for management company)
Number of public comments	3	8
Percentage of comments clearly in favor of the proposal	33	37.5
Total/average lines of comment by public	14/3.5	31/3.9
Number of comments by leaders	4	6
Total/average lines of comment by leaders	28/7	35/5.8

are very similar in their form, function, and outcome. The city with a female mayor offered three years of tax breaks to a law firm considering opening a call center and law office in the city, totaling sixteen professional positions and ten part-time nonprofessional positions. The firm would lease a building in the community. The contract from the city included a clawback provision that required the firm to repay the tax breaks if it left the city within five years of the relocation. The city with a male mayor offered five years of tax breaks (for less money per year) to a management firm considering bringing twenty-one professional jobs to the city. The firm would lease office space currently managed by the Community Redevelopment Agency. The contract from the city contained no clawback provision. The mayors and supporting city council members presented both deals as development opportunities and the right kind of investment for each city to make. The female mayor, before the meeting to discuss and vote on the proposal, produced a substantial report on the proposed deal and made the report available online, which was noted by a citizen, who commented, "Several of my concerns were addressed by the mayor's discussion. I still am concerned about parking for all these employees." The city with the male mayor drew up no report. Citizens with no connections to the law firm deal made the majority of comments in the female mayor's city. Citizen comments divided evenly between positive and negative in tone. One citizen expressed concern, saying,

"Cities should not be in the business of offering citizen money to whoever comes in off the street with a hand out." Business leaders made the majority of comments in the male mayor's city and also divided evenly between positive and negative, with some like the president of the chamber of commerce arguing, "Projects like this will bring the necessary jobs to our city." Others expressed caution. The owner of the parking garage where the employees would park asked, "What does this mean for the city in ten years? In fifteen? What happens if the [company] goes out of business? It seems like the city needs to protect itself. But it is still a good idea."

Differences also emerge between male- and female-governed cities in how the mayor and council comment on policies. Table 4.1 provides summary information on number (far fewer under the female mayor) and length (also far less) of comments by the public on the example development policy. Also shown is information on the mayor's and councilors' comments. While the female mayor and city council members in her city also commented at a lower rate, the difference between leaders' comments in the two cities is not as large as the public's difference. The female mayor's involvement in the discussion, although limited, illustrates a theme I found among female mayors: they overplan, or "prepare for all possible contingencies." One mayor said, "My office manager likes to joke that I have a backup plan for the backup plan." Female mayors, particularly when newly elected or dealing with matters outside their expertise, consider it important to conduct research and equip themselves with information, arming themselves in case of a challenge. At one point in the development discussion, the female mayor, reading a prepared statement, noted, "We are also requesting that [the business move] be done as expeditiously as possible, as we want to be able to address some of these issues before our budget preparations begin. As such, we have prepared and published a forty-six-page document on the proposed tax breaks that citizens can evaluate."

Very few male mayors indicated engaging in similar background work. In the development example, the female mayor's preparation for the council meeting far exceeded that of the male mayor, who said that he was "unsure of the long-term nature of the relationship with [the company]; additional research will need to be conducted to determine if all . . . questions have been answered." Instead of consideration of the future consequences of the tax break proposal, the emphasis in discussions in the male mayor's city was on what the project could do for the city at that point in time. As a city council member said, "What we need is jobs in the city, and this deal will do that for us." Survey and interview data confirm the findings of the development example: women report spending a higher average of time working on issues than men, with no differences by issue area.

Discussions about an urban women's issue in two paired cities (Table 4.2) depart significantly from the development discussion. In this discussion, the city with a female mayor voted to fund and build its first homeless shelter and social service support center. The city with a male mayor supported moving a homeless shelter from an existing location and merging it with a private service-provision center. The city would go from directly running the shelter to contracting the services to a private organization.[30] The construction of the shelter in the city with a female mayor generated a large number of positive and negative comments from the community, with 64 percent of those commenting in clear support. Reflecting the sentiments of many, a staff member of Catholic Charities said, "There is no perfect place for a shelter, in proposal, location, setup, or idea. Everything is flawed, but waiting to act is even more flawed, especially as we let our homeless children, parents, families, veterans, and others live and die on the streets." A resident in the neighborhood of the proposed location had a more negative view: "I am worried about the neighborhood. What is going to happen? There's a lot of children in the neighborhood, women joggers, and that kind of thing, kids going to school. What if the homeless hassle them?"

TABLE 4.2   DISCUSSIONS ON WOMEN'S ISSUES

	Female mayor (shelter construction)	Male mayor (shelter relocation)
Number of public comments	22	9
Percentage of comments clearly in favor of the city action	63.6	77.7
Total/average lines of comment by public	106/4.8	34/3.9
Number of comments by leaders	12	4
Total/average lines of comment by leaders	61/5.1	19/4.8

The move of the shelter in the male mayor's city received largely positive comments from the public (78 percent of the comments were clearly positive). The director of the local organization that took over management of the shelter for the city said, "I am honored to be able to bring our expertise to [the city] and look forward to working with the local officials and the community to continue to make [it] a great place to live for all." The president of a business association in the neighborhood where the shelter was currently located noted his support: "The move is good news and starts to address the problems we have been living with for the past several years." Residents near the proposed location were not as supportive but not outright negative: "We're taking a wait-and-see approach at this point. We obviously are concerned about what might happen if they [the homeless] start being a problem."

The rhetoric of the mayors and council members discussing the two proposals clearly differed as well. The female mayor and the councilors in her city discussed the project in terms of the needs of the homeless and protecting citizens, helping "women and children find their way back to safe and affordable housing," and offered stories of people who became homeless because of circumstances beyond their control. The female mayor said, "This shelter will provide social services, mental health care, and food and housing. It will take people off the streets and will protect our citizens that need it the most." She added, "[The shelter] is an important first step toward helping homeless women and children find their way back to safe and affordable housing." Here, as with many other women's issues, the female mayors and council members speak of caring and connect policies to the welfare of women. The leaders discuss homelessness and poverty as the central problems and frame the homeless as deserving assistance and care. At one point, the female mayor noted the large number of homeless veterans. A council member provided an example of a family whose home burned: "Last winter, a family in [the city] lost their house in a fire, and they had nowhere to go, no place to even spend one night." In comparison, the male mayor and council members in his city refer to the homeless themselves as the problem and frame the issue as business concerns: the mayor said, "It is our sincere hope that by moving emergency services out of [its current location] for transient homeless people, we will be removing any attraction or magnet that may be drawing these individuals to [that location in the city] and . . . revitaliz[ing] the businesses in the area." A city council member expressed concern that the city would ensure "that the proper zoning is in place for the shelter," while another wanted to make sure that businesses in the area where the shelter used to be were alerted to its move. In addition, as the debate went back and forth between citizens and leaders, it became clear that both mayors had discussed the shelters before the meeting with supporters of the move; the key difference in the mayors' discussions was that the female mayor had held hers with organizations involved in urban women's issues, while the male mayor had held his with businesses and development organizations. Other female mayors I interviewed mentioned much behind-the-scenes work they did with community members to ensure consistent messages, "that [they] were all on the same page and knew what to expect," and smooth passage of important legislation.

These examples demonstrate the patterns found in summary data on the relationship between subject matter, the gender of leaders, and citizen comments. I evaluated citizen comments while controlling for a variety of city characteristics. Citizen participation accelerates in three situations: when cities discuss women's urban issues (regardless of the gender of the mayor), when the city has a female mayor (regardless of the topic of discussion), and when cities with female mayors discuss women's urban issues. The number of citizen comments per agenda item relates to the topic area: comments occur more frequently on women's issues and development (albeit not reaching statistical significance) than on quality of life issues. In addition, the presence of a female mayor (but not the percentage of female council members) has a positive, significant relationship with the number of public comments, increasing the average number of public comments on an agenda item by 0.40. The gender of the mayor does not influence the number of comments on development issues; the interaction between the two is insignificant. In cities with female mayors, more citizens comment on women's issue items (an average of 4.3 citizen comments). These findings suggest that female mayors increase citizen participation through a variety of mechanisms.

Women also reveal gendered leadership when discussing interactions with the community. Male leaders, when queried about what kinds of citizen complaints they get, discussed primarily problems with business leaders, development, "jobs, jobs, and jobs," and standard urban issues like noise, crime, and traffic. Female leaders, in addition to making comments similar to those of male leaders on standard urban issues, discussed a wide variety of issues and groups. As one female mayor said, "People approach me about everything." The female leaders emphasized connections with groups and interests relating to women's issues, often because of a shared background. One mayor, in discussing groups, said, "[I] work with the PTA, with the schools, so they [members of those groups] come to me. They know I am a sympathetic ear." Others mentioned that their background in the Junior League, Soroptimist International, child development and advocacy organizations, or social service organizations had promoted a shared relationship with women's issue organizations. Many female leaders also downplayed their gender, instead emphasizing their leadership style as accessible. One said, "People come to me because of how I go about being a mayor, [knowing] that I will talk to them and really listen, that I will work with them to help them get what they need, not [because] I am a woman. What does that have to do with anything?" Yet despite these denials, the leadership style described by many female leaders fits well with a feminine conceptualization of how to lead, such as what James Burns labels a transformational leader or what Lyn Kathlene calls a contextual leader.[31]

Several female leaders specifically mentioned how they thought their leadership style produced changes: "We [women] tend to discuss topics more readily, find compromises, and share feelings, not just ideas or agendas. This helps get citizens out: they think we will listen to them." Another leader noted that citizens would come out in large numbers if the city elected more women: "Discussions and outcomes would be different. So would the tone of things." A female leader also commented on her and her peers' "proactive work to encourage groups to participate," because she believed that "certain issues have been just left out of the equation in [the city]." Women in local office often recognize the need to expand the scope of discussion, introduce context, and empower others to engage in leadership.[32]

Measuring Community Perceptions of Leaders

Given that female leaders want to expand participation by community groups and given the higher rate of public participation in cities with female mayors, what does the community think about interacting with male and female leaders? To understand how the gender of local leaders influences community participation in government, I surveyed community members in a subset of ten cities from the hundred-city sample: five cities randomly chosen from the group with female mayors and five from the group with male mayors. The cities do not differ dramatically in the socioeconomic status of their communities. Three of the five cities in each set (six total) operate under a mayor-council form of government, and two of each set (four total) govern through a council-manager form of government. Omitting the female mayors, the number of women on the city councils is similar (14.5 percent for cities with female mayors and 15.7 percent for cities with male mayors).

For each of the ten cities, I compiled a list of organizations and individuals active in the community through a combination of observation of city council meetings and inquiry of city leaders. Any organization with community representation (i.e., one that was specifically mentioned by a citizen representing it) at a city council meeting and any individual who spoke at more than one meeting was included. I asked the mayor and city council members to each provide a list of active organizations and individuals in their communities. The methods used to develop the list of individuals are common to the literature on urban governance.[33] This process produced contact information for 79 people in the cities with female mayors and 55 people in cities with male mayors.[34] Of the 134 names contacted, 64 percent, or 86 individuals, responded. The response rate was similar for cities with female (65 percent) and male (61 percent) mayors. Appendix 4A provides more details on the types and numbers of groups and numbers of individuals contacted; the group representatives and individuals from the community overlapped a great deal, but the lists did produce unique individuals.

The survey asked these community members to identify issues facing the city, to describe their efforts toward influencing public policy, whether local officials were responsive to their interests, whether they supported the mayor, about their organization's goals, and whether the city and mayor were responsive to their organization's interests. The full survey is available in Appendix 4B.

A diverse set of organization heads and members responded to the survey. They are classified into types on the basis of the organizations they worked for, belonged to, or represented. Table 4.3 lists the organizations and their categories. The groups and individuals active in the cities fall into four general categories: development, quality of life, women's issues, and miscellaneous. Organizations and individuals ranged from the chamber of commerce and property developers to social service organizations and women's services to people with no clear organizational affiliation.

TABLE 4.3   GROUPS BY ISSUE AREA

Development	Quality of life	Women's issues	Miscellaneous
Specific organization			
Chamber of commerce	Clean Parks	Women's Leadership Council	American Legion
	Citizens for Bike Paths		Citizens for an Open Government
Rotary		NARAL Pro-Choice America	
Cultivating Business Leaders in [City]		Citizens for Better Schools	
The Downtown Development Group		Food Bank of [County]	
		Junior League	
Type of organization			
Trade groups (e.g., manufacturers)	Art associations	Social service organizations	Local chapters of national organizations (e.g., AARP, NRA)
Tourism groups (e.g., hotels groups)	Culture associations	Children's service organizations	Individual citizens with no clear organizational affiliation
Owners of businesses	Historical societies	School representatives	
Property developers	Neighborhood associations	Domestic violence organizations	

Note: NRA = National Rifle Association; AARP = American Association of Retired Persons.

Cities with female mayors see more activity from women's issue organizations than cities with male mayors do. In cities with female mayors, the mayor and city council named community organizations active in women's issues more often than leaders in cities with male mayors did, and these groups participate in city council meetings more frequently. In cities with a male mayor, the mayor and council members listed organizations active in economic development and business more frequently. In addition, female council members (regardless of the gender of the mayor) referred me to members of women's issue community organizations more frequently than male city council members did: female mayors and city council members were 26 percent more likely to name a member of a women's issue organization compared to their male counterparts. Female community members more frequently appeared on lists from female leaders and in the cities with female mayors, a not surprising result, given that women make up the majority of workers and volunteers in women's issue organizations.

The connections between female mayors and community members associated with urban women's issues demonstrate the behind-the-scenes ways that female mayors influence urban policy making. Discussions with female leaders confirmed the connections between female leaders and women's urban issue organizations: for example, in the six case-study cities described in Chapter 3, five female mayors noted support from a women's issue organization for their campaign, and half the mayors had these organizations as their primary support. These findings also support the finding that elite women in urban politics construct their own networks of organizations and individuals to support their candidacy and policy agendas.[35]

Members of women's issue organizations perceive a higher degree of responsiveness from female mayors. Of community members asked whether the mayor was responsive to their interests, 80 percent in cities with female mayors answered in the affirmative, compared to 60 percent in the cities with male mayors (Figure 4.2).[36] Removing the members of women's issue organizations from the group of respondents drops the rate to that of cities with a male mayor. Thus, it is only those community groups active on women's issues that view the female mayor as more responsive. I also asked those community members who were a part of an organization if they thought that local

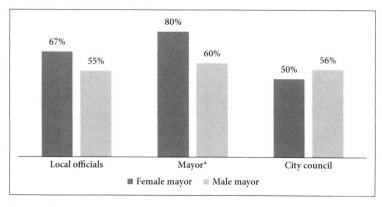

Figure 4.2   Community perception of leader (mayor or city council member) responsiveness. Data come from responses to the community survey question "Do you think that [local officials/mayor/council] are responsive to your interests?" Percentages are yes answers. * = Difference significant at the 0.05 level.

officials were responsive to their organization's interests. Members of women's issue organizations believe that female mayors are responsive to the needs of their organization. Sixty-three percent of members of organizations in cities with a female mayor agree with the statement, compared to just less than half those in cities with a male mayor. Again, members of women's issue organizations drive the higher level of perceived responsiveness: when they are removed from the sample, male and female mayors receive near-identical evaluations of responsiveness to organizational interests.

Formal and Informal Activism by Community Members

The survey also asked community members to report their attendance at and participation in city council meetings. Those who had not attended a meeting but *had* contacted a leader were asked why they chose that route. Few differences emerge between male- and female-governed cities in terms of the percentage of community members who attended and commented in meetings. Given the earlier findings that the number of public comments increases under female mayors, the similarity between male- and female-governed cities in community member attendance and participation in city council meetings is surprising. However, the percentage of public comments on city council agenda items that do not come from organization members is much higher in cities with a female mayor.[37] This suggests that female mayors engage in contextual and transactional leadership by altering the *participants* of the policy process, thus demonstrating that female mayors at the local level engage in behavior similar to that of female leaders at the state and national level.

One concern of scholars revolves around strategic, behind-the-scenes agenda setting by businesses and developers. These groups can influence policies before the public expresses preferences.[38] Some, however, point to informal engagement between citizens and city leaders as a key tool for the representation of marginalized interests. Indeed, when leaders reach out to marginalized groups substantive representation increases.[39] Thus, informal channels of activism can promote a variety of interests. To find the extent that community groups and individuals work behind the scenes, I examined the percentage of organization members who said that they contacted a city leader without attending a city council meeting and their explanations for choosing this path. In the cities with female mayors, just under 40 percent had contacted a public official but had not attended a meeting; the rate is slightly lower (32 percent) in cities with male mayors.

As shown in Figure 4.3, community members contacted officials in cities with female mayors more about women's issues and less about development issues than they did in cities with male mayors. In cities with male mayors, people interested in development compose more than 60 percent of the group who contacted a public official without going to a meeting, compared to just 25 percent in cities with female mayors. Although a very rough measure, this suggests that the business community finds male mayors more receptive to the informal expression of interests than female mayors.[40]

Controversy in City Policy Making

In encouraging political participation in governance, cities also invite controversy. City council meetings are often the site of heated

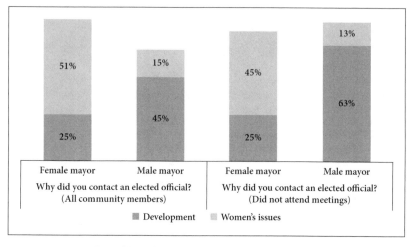

Figure 4.3   Why public officials were contacted, by mayoral gender. Data come from the community survey and do not include quality of life, general government, and miscellaneous reasons for contact.

dialogue between community members and leaders and city staff. The following two exchanges are examples from the hundred-city council minutes coded for analysis.

CITIZEN: The city doesn't know what it is doing, and it is going to drag us all down with them.

CITY CLERK: Mr. [name], please restrain yourself.

MALE MAYOR: No, let's hear. I want to know how I am going to ruin everything.

CITIZEN: Everyone in city government can go to hell. I don't have to deal with your attitude.

CITIZEN: This policy is outrageous and a clear attempt to take over the city for her interests! I demand that someone else look at this.

FEMALE MAYOR: Mr. [name], someone else is looking at it. You were here when I ordered the audit.

CITIZEN: I don't trust you, and I don't trust them.

Women's urban issues cover a variety of contentious policies, including those related to homeless shelters, food kitchens, public housing, public welfare, and domestic violence acts by employees of the city. These policies and the discord related to women's urban issues, not the gender of the mayor, lead to an increase in public participation. To examine this further, the deliberations in the ten cities where community members were surveyed are coded by tone: negative, positive, and neutral. Negative comments were defined as those in which the speaker clearly opposed the agenda item, while positive comments were defined as those clearly in support of the item.[41] Negative comments could be that the city action "is not the thing to do," "is the wrong action," or "clearly is a poor choice," while positive comments expressed "strong support," were "urging to approve," or declared "standing with" a decision. Neutral comments were those expressing no clear preference or containing only information. Only agenda items with public comments are coded.

The proportion of negative and positive comments does not differ in cities with male and female mayors; indeed, it is remarkably uniform, as displayed in Figure 4.4. Indeed, the proportion of neutral, negative, and positive comments is almost identical in cities with male

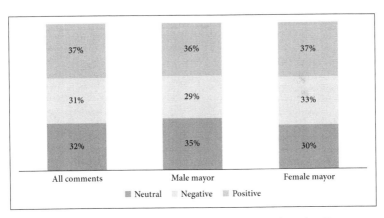

Figure 4.4 **Negative and positive comments, by mayoral gender.** Data come from coding city council minutes for tone in the ten cities where community members were surveyed. There are no significant differences between male and female mayors.

and female mayors. However, given that the public comments more frequently in cities with female mayors, these results demonstrate that although the proportion of negative to positive comments remains the same across mayoral gender, the *total number* of negative and positive comments increases in cities with female mayors. For example, while the percentage of negative comments for male mayors (29 percent) and female mayors (33 percent) is nearly equal, the average number of negative comments per meeting for male mayors (0.9) and that for female mayors (2.0) are very different. Similarly, male mayors and female mayors have very different average numbers of positive comments per meeting, at 1.2 and 2.3, respectively. Female mayors said in interviews that they garnered support for their policies through background work, informal politics, and "rallying the supporters."

Leader Perceptions of Community Groups

Do leaders perceive differences in the amount of community contact? Given that female leaders generally express more interest in constituency service and contextual, or transactional, leadership, compared to male leaders, they should have more contact with community groups, a more diverse group of community contacts, and more interactions with groups associated with women's issues. Using data from the hundred-city survey presented in Chapter 2, I evaluate how leaders report contact from groups in their communities.[42] Keep in mind that here, as opposed the rest of this chapter, the data presented compare male and female *leaders*, not *cities* with male or female mayors.

Do female leaders have more general contact with community groups? In short, yes. Responding to the question "Have members of any of these groups contacted you in the last year regarding an issue in your city?" female leaders list more groups (more than eight different types of groups) than male leaders, who selected more than five types of groups. Female leaders listed more organizations and groups than male leaders did, even when controlling for other factors. Thus, a larger set of groups engages with female leaders, even when controlling for experience, position, and community factors.

Are women's issue groups more likely to contact female leaders? Identity theory, pluralism, and contextual-transactional leadership all suggest that women's issue groups would approach female leaders more frequently. More than half of female leaders (52 percent) were contacted by a women's issue group, compared to less than a third (31 percent) of male leaders, in accordance with the evidence from the survey of community members that the community views female mayors as more receptive to the interests of groups and individuals associated with women's interests. There are also differences in the contact rate for development groups: 97 percent of male leaders receive some contact from a development group, compared to 52 percent of female leaders. The data on group contact from the leader's perspective confirms that female leaders attract engagement from a more wide-ranging set of groups and individuals than male leaders do.

And You Put the Weight Right on Me: The Challenge of Constituent and Group Demands on Female City Leaders

> They tell you being mayor is a part-time job. What a joke.
> —Yvonne Johnson, former mayor of Greensboro, North Carolina, quoted in Kate Torgovnick, "The Cities Where Women Rule"

The increase in public contact in cities with female mayors can produce a more open and communal policy process, with a greater diversity in participation. However, the higher level of public participation has consequences. As revealed in interviews and by the data, each item the public participates in may require action on a variety of fronts, which results in a domino effect of policy making. Thus, a citizen who complains about garbage pickup on her street may set off a cascade of a reaction from the council, request for an investigation into the public works response to citizen complaints, meeting about ideal pickup days and times, response from the public works department, and reevaluation of whether the city needed to purchase the garbage truck last year that they cut from the budget. As one mayor said, "It isn't just them asking you about a crossing guard. You end up practically sending the National Guard half the time. And then, it really isn't enough."

Female mayors are associated with more business being conducted in city council meetings. The data from the city council minutes confirm the difficulty of leadership in a context of constant citizen involvement: even with controls for city demographics and form of government, the presence of a female mayor increases the number of items city councils address in their meetings by more than eighty over the course of a year. The same is true when the average number of items per meeting over time is evaluated in the case study cities in North Carolina and California: the total number of items under female mayors increases dramatically. The average number of comments per meeting increased by nearly five under female mayors. No similar increase occurred for male mayors who took office around the same time. In addition, the average number of comments per agenda item increased from 0.35 to 0.55 when the cities changed to female mayors but did not increase when the control cities changed to a male mayor.

The substantive change is very large in each of these cities; for example, in the California city with a white female mayor, the total number of items increased by twenty-three per month. The qualitative data demonstrate the significance of these findings for female mayors. In interviews, all the mayors indicated that handling citizen complaints was "central," "necessary," or "required." A representative male mayor said, "Sure, the time involved really surprised me at first, but then I got used to it and started using the city staff to handle things." The female mayors, however, focused on the problem of constituent demands. Comments from five of the six female mayors included statements that "keeping up with all the demands of the office," "staying on top of everything—particularly the service to the citizen requirements," and trying to handle "the ridiculous amount of crap people complain about" represented the *largest single challenge of being mayor.*

Female mayors find the job of leadership more challenging than their male counterparts do and with good reason. Citizens and groups exercise their voice more frequently with female mayors and other female leaders. The use of voice, as Albert Hirschman and others argue, limits exit of constituents and improves satisfaction only to the extent that it leads to change, which means that female mayors must not only interact more frequently with constituents but also *respond* effectively.[43] As one mayor put it, constituents "want you to police them all the time but leave them alone. They want trash pickup every day but no garbage trucks on the roads. They want the best schools but no taxes. They want lots of jobs but no development. Well, let me get out my magic wand." The increased demand by citizens (and the responses they require) restricts the ability of female mayors to engage in proactive policy making because the women are too busy reacting to these demands.

One of the principal reasons that fewer women than men run for political office is women's lack of interest in serving in public office.[44] Jennifer Lawless and Richard Fox's evaluations of women's lower levels of political ambition find that family members, friends, and those in influential political positions are more likely to ask men than women to run for political office.[45] Other research demonstrates that political elites often discount women's electoral viability. Women are less likely than men to believe in their qualifications for office or that they will ever be qualified to run. Once in office, women are also less likely to express progressive ambition.[46] The findings presented here suggest that women may be right to be cautious about assuming leadership roles, particularly given the increased pressure and time commitments they face, compared to their male colleagues. This may also depress progressive ambition; indeed, the findings by Sarah Fulton and her colleagues suggest that women wait for a combination of opportunity and ambition before serving, essentially producing women who are more qualified when they run for higher office than their male counterparts.[47] The experiences of women in my study reaffirm this inclination, with the added caveat that female mayors often express dismay with the amount of work associated with the job.

Intersecting identities may exacerbate the challenge of policy making in a demand-heavy environment. The female minority mayors expressed regret over not "having the time to get *my* things passed" or being kept so busy with "all the issues of the minority community and schools and child safety and everything else that I can't do anything new." Women's laments over a lack of time or resources to engage in innovative policy choices suggests that white male mayors implement more changes simply because they confront fewer citizen concerns; as a result, citizens may see white male mayors as more effective at responding to citizen concerns. Indeed, a male mayor said that he liked having the business community as an electoral base: "They don't want much. And what they do want I don't have a lot of control over. I can't change state taxes. I can't change the business climate. All I can do is make sure downtown has nice flowers."

5 /

Sex and the City

Policy Outcomes and Urban Leadership

> What does it matter what I think about these policies?
> What matters is what I *do* on each of these. And let me tell
> you, I get things done. I look for funding from the state
> and federal governments. I organize staff. And I find the
> money to pay for the programs that are important, even if
> I have to beg the Rotary to fund it. Kids get their summer
> programs, moms get their day care and their supplements
> [to WIC, the Special Supplemental Nutrition Program
> for Women, Infants, and Children], and I get to feel good
> about it.
> —FEMALE MAYOR, DISCUSSING ISSUES SHE THINKS ARE
> IMPORTANT BUT DO NOT RECEIVE ENOUGH ATTENTION

Local governments in the United States fund a wide variety of urban women's issue programs, spending more than $48 billion on
public welfare, health care and hospitals, and housing and community development in 2007, an increase over the $33.3 billion spent
in 1997 and the $37.2 billion in 2002.[1] Cities decide how to fund poli-
cies, which areas of city government will receive money for new programs, and whether to borrow money to fund these programs. Where
do urban women's issues fit in this? Can women in local office influence the allocation of scarce city budget dollars to these programs?
What kinds of constraints do these leaders face? Focusing on budgeting and the funding of women's issue programs, this chapter explores
whether female leaders change policy outcomes in cities.

Funding and budgeting represent key elements of urban public
policy making. Decisions about which programs to fund and how to

fund them (including whether to borrow money or seek grants for funds) represents concrete evidence of the preferences of political leaders and how institutions constrain those preferences.[2] All levels of government craft and implement budgets, but the fiscal constraints cities face make financial decisions that much more difficult and contentious.[3] State governments limit the ability of cities to make independent financial decisions, including on taxation and borrowing,[4] and local governments rely heavily on local taxes for funding. Because unhappy residents can move, taking their tax dollars with them, cities have a strong incentive to tailor policies to fit local demand, particularly from higher-income residents.[5]

From a variety of perspectives, cities should not fund women's urban issue programs. Paul Peterson and others argue that redistributive funding should be cut first and funded last.[6] The resources available to a city (in property value or tax base) thus should be an essential predictor of whether a city actively funds redistributional programs, an argument supported by scholarship on fiscal federalism.[7] Others point to local governments' lack of autonomy, because they operate under Dillon's Rule or Home Rule or under constraints put on them by their state and the federal government. These constraints lead to cities prioritizing the needs of businesses, and local governments bow to the interests of growth machines or form governing coalitions with private actors.[8] Although research suggests that local governments are unwilling or unable to engage in welfare programs, data show that cities routinely make large investments in social welfare, health, hospital, and community development programs.[9] In this chapter, I examine whether female leaders at the local level promote the funding of women's issues and discourage the funding of development issues. I investigate fund sources and ask whether cities with female leaders are more likely to receive intergovernmental or grant dollars and whether the gender of leaders influences the borrowing behavior of cities. The ultimate test of women's representation in local politics can be found in budgeting, especially given the fiscal constraints on cities and that these policy outcome measures represent a meaningful action of substantive representation. "The link between descriptive representation and substantive representation is most meaningful when descriptive representation affects not only a representative's attitudes and behavior *but also* the decisions made by the overall legislative body."[10] Evaluating budgeting as an outcome measure tests whether female leaders truly change urban politics.

Female Leaders and Policy Outcomes

Do women prioritize spending money on women's urban issues? The hundred-city survey asked leaders if they thought their city "spends too much, the correct amount, or not enough money" on a variety of areas.[11] Generally, leaders of both genders thought their city spent too much money on quality of life programs and not enough money on women's issues. Women were more likely to think that the city spent too much on development; men, too little. Next, leaders were asked, "If you controlled next year's budget in your city, would you decrease or increase spending on [general government, development, quality of life, and urban women's issues]?" Here, two gender differences emerged: men wanted to spend more on development (39 percent of male leaders would increase funding compared to 28 percent of female leaders), and women wanted to spend more on urban women's issues (81 percent of female leaders would increase spending compared to 65 percent of male leaders). The differences between male and female leaders persisted when the answers to questions on current and future spending were evaluated with additional controls for ideology and political position. Unlike the policy priorities explored in Chapter 2, gender has a significant relationship with attitudes about current and future spending on women's issues, even with additional controls.[12] The survey data indicate that female leaders want to fund women's issue programs, particularly if they control decision making on spending. These results suggest that women in positions of power—such as a mayor with independent power—may change policy outcomes.

Choosing to Fund Urban Women's Issues

By using multiple measures of policy outcomes, including spending, employment, attitudes, and overall budget information, this chapter presents a more comprehensive story of how female leaders at the local level are able to influence policy even in environments of fiscal restraint. Spending on women's urban issue programs (and the decisions whether to fund and how much to fund) represents a concrete action by leaders to prioritize these programs. Employment in these areas provides data on the long-term effects of women's representation in local politics on urban women's issues. Survey data provide gendered attitudes about spending in these programs, and budget data allow examining how women are able to pay for these programs.

To examine actual spending, data from coded city budgets from 2010 of the hundred-city sample are used. To ensure that the overrepresentation of cities with female mayors does not bias the results, I include data from the three-hundred-city sample described in Chapter 2.[13] The outcome variables come from coded city budgets: spending on women's issue programs, the percentage of city employees who work in women's issue programs, and revenue and bond data. See Appendix 5 for how I obtained and coded city budgets. I control for socioeconomic factors, all of which came from the 2000 U.S. census, and a city autonomy measure generated by previous scholars.[14] The key variables of interest are the presence of a female mayor, women's representation on the council, an interaction of female mayors and councilors, and a squared term representing the percentage of women on the council (to account for the possibility of critical mass).

Many cities simply do not fund urban women issue programs in any obvious way. In these cities, the majority of the budget funds public safety, public works, and general government, with some money going to recreation and development activities, which is consistent with theories of urban governance.[15] Thus, I evaluate the effect of female mayors and councilors in two ways: first, *whether* a city will fund programs related to women's issues, and second, *how much* a city allocates to urban women's issues.[16]

To Fund or Not: Female Leaders and the Decision to Fund a Program

Looking first at the general rate of participation in women's urban issue programs, more cities with female mayors fund some program relating to a women's urban issue (approximately 81 percent of cities) than cities with male mayors (61 percent) and spend more per resident on these programs ($31 per resident under female mayors compared to $23 under male mayors).

Female mayors continue to have a positive relationship with whether a city provides funding for women's issue programs when I control for city and political characteristics to evaluate whether female representatives influence city funding, with socioeconomic, institutional, and budgetary controls. Generally, the presence of a female mayor has a positive, significant relationship with the rate of participation in women's issue programs, as does the interaction between female mayors and a mayor-council form of government.[17] The percentage of women on the city council does not have a direct relationship with participation in women's issue programs but interacts with the presence of a female mayor for an accelerated effect: women on the council have a positive relationship with participation in these programs as their representation grows. As Figure 5.1 demonstrates, the relationship between women on the council and propensity to participate in women's issue programs increases as women's representation grows, no matter the mayoral gender. For example, 37 percent of cities with a city council that is less than 20 percent female fund urban women's issue programs, compared to 63 percent of cities with a city council over 40 percent female.

Examining the interaction of the percentage of women on each city's council and the presence of a female mayor finds that more female councilors increase the substantive effect of a female mayor on the likelihood of funding women's issue programs, but only if the percentage of women on the council exceeds 20 percent.[18] If a female mayor is present, the percentage of women on the council also substantively influences the propensity to fund. Figure 5.1 demonstrates the interactive effect of a female mayor and women on the council—women in both positions have a positive relationship with city participation in women's urban issue programs, producing a combined substantive effect of 89 percent of cities that have more than 40 percent female councilors and have a female mayor funding women's issue programs.

The interactive effect of a female mayor and women on the council suggests that women on city councils support funding women's

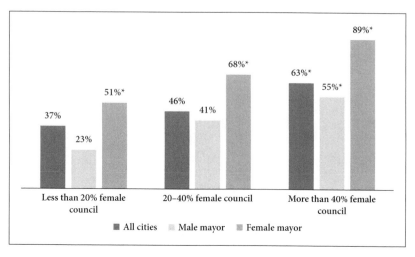

Figure 5.1   Critical mass effects of women on a city council and probability of providing women's urban issue services. Percentages indicate the likelihood of service provision, given the gender of the mayor and the percentage of women on the council. Predicted probabilities are estimated using the computer program Clarify and logistical analysis, with sociodemographic and political controls. Significance is calculated using linear combinations of estimators. * = Difference significant at the 0.05 level from the next-lowest level of women's representation on the council.

issue programs but that, to influence policy outcomes, they require a certain level of representation coupled with a female in the executive position. Female leaders said in interviews that they found it very hard to introduce new services, as it often required substantial discussions of whether the city should be providing the service at all. One particular stumbling block for many female leaders in convincing other leaders of the need for new policies was whether the policies would result in "authority creep" or whether the state was "just going to take all of it over as soon as [they got] it into place." All leaders—male and female—want to decrease state and federal governments' control in their cities and express particular concern about the usurping of authority. Leaders view new policies with suspicion because they may (and often do) involve developing new relationships with state or federal governments. Women's urban issue programs prompt more concern because leaders often seek alternative forms of funding, such as from the state and federal governments, for these programs. As a result, cities often rebuff female leaders' efforts to institute new policies, even when they are funded. As one female leader said, "[I had] all my ducks in a row and [was] preparing for everything. I wasn't prepared for them just to not want to [provide a job counselor for the food bank], even with the funding [being available]."

How Much to Give: Female Leaders and the Amount of Funding

Looking next at the effect of women in local office on spending on women's issue programs once the city decides to participate in them, I find that the presence of female mayors increases funding for women's urban issues, even when controlling for other factors. The percentage of female councilors does not have an independent effect on women's issue program spending, but it does as a squared term, demonstrating a critical mass effect.[19] As Figure 5.2 shows, the substantive effect

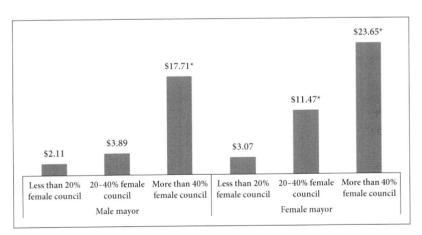

Figure 5.2 **Critical mass effects of women on city council and per-capita spending on women's urban issue services.** Significance calculated in left-truncated tobit model, with sociodemographic and political controls, using linear combinations of estimators. * = Difference significant at the 0.05 level from the next-lowest level of women's representation on the council.

of a female mayor grows as the female percentage of the city council increases. With a male mayor, the percentage of women on the city council does not have a statistically significant effect on spending on women's issue programs.

Examining the interaction of a female mayor with female council members reveals that the substantive effect of the percentage of women on the city council is large. Using some average data for an example may clarify the substantive effect: moving the 2010 mean percentage of women on the council (23 percent, as detailed in Chapter 1 and Table 1.2) up 10 percentage points, to 33 percent, would result in a $16.94 increase in per capita spending on women's issue programs, with a female mayor increasing spending by an additional $2.31.

The relationship between presence of a female mayor and provision of social welfare programs grows stronger as the percentage of female council members grows. The results presented here suggest several interesting patterns. First, women's representation on the council appears to have a critical mass effect that increases substantive relationships when women's representation on the council exceeds certain levels.[20] The number of women necessary varies with the presence or absence of a female mayor, suggesting that a specific critical mass level cannot be set and depends instead on each city's institutional characteristics and the number of female representatives in positions of power.[21] Specifically, the data show that the policy effects of women's representation on the council are *accelerated* by the presence of a female mayor; that is, substantive effects can occur with few women if they have a female mayor. For example, compare spending in Figure 5.2 for a council between 20 and 40 percent women under a male mayor ($3.89) and for one under a female mayor ($11.47).

The power of a political position continues to be important. Female mayors in mayor-council forms of government have an additionally positive relationship with funding women's urban issue programs, while female council members have an additional influence on spending when they serve in council-manager cities. Female mayors in mayor-council systems noted the power of the position. One mayor appreciated the amount of power she had, saying, "[I can make the council] talk about anything—I just put it on the agenda, and we have to talk about it. I've got the veto too. [*Pauses*] Not that I want to do that, but I can, you know, if it is important."

Where the Jobs Are: Female Leaders and Employment

Does the presence of female leaders have an effect on municipal employment in women's issue areas? City governments are large employers, provide a wide variety of jobs, and often compensate their employees well, including through pensions and benefits. In research conducted in the 1980s, female and minority mayors influenced hiring decisions by introducing affirmative action programs, changing the bureaucratic nature of employment, and directing funds for employment in particular programs.[22] Female representatives have two clear avenues for advocating for women's urban issues programs: creating lasting programs of interest and hiring in areas where women are often employed.

The effect of mayoral gender on municipal employment may be a more meaningful measure than spending in women's issue areas, because employment signifies that the city itself is running the program, as opposed to a subsidiary organization. In Table 5.1, the dependent variable is the percentage of employees in women's issue areas, which is derived from the number of employees in programs for affordable housing, health and hospitals, children's services, education, libraries, and public welfare divided by the number of employees in all categories of municipal employment.[23] The presence of a female mayor has a positive, significant relationship with the percentage of employees in women's issue areas, as do female councilors and the interaction of the two forms of representation. In addition, female mayors in mayor-council systems have an additional positive relationship with employment in women's urban issue areas. The percentage of the city that is nonwhite, city revenue, and dollar amount of grants awarded to the city also have significant relationships with the percentage of employees in these areas. Figure 5.3 presents the effect on municipal employment in women's issue areas by women's representation in council and mayoral positions. Here, male mayors and fewer women on the

TABLE 5.1   EMPLOYMENT IN WOMEN'S ISSUE AREAS (THREE-HUNDRED-CITY SAMPLE)

	Coefficient	Standard error
Female mayor	0.05**	0.01
Percentage female council	−0.02	0.13
Percentage female council, squared	1.88**	0.59
Female mayor × % female council	−0.13	0.27
Female mayor × % female council, squared	5.07**	1.80
Mayor-council	5.97	7.86
Female mayor × mayor-council	1.15**	0.23
Percentage female council × mayor-council	0.84	0.79
Median income	0.00	0.00
Percentage poverty	0.00	0.00
Percentage high school diploma	0.84	0.79
Percentage public assistance	1.16	1.54
Percentage nonwhite	0.29*	0.13
Revenue (per capita)	1.88†	1.16
Grants (per capita)	1.54*	0.79
Log of population	0.45	8.43
Autonomy	2.21	4.91
Constant	0.01	−0.02
N	258	
R^2	0.33	

Note: Ordinary least squares regression.

† $p < 0.10$, * $p < 0.05$, ** $p < 0.01$.

council are associated with lower employment in women's urban issue jobs, while more women on the council and female mayors are associated with higher employment in these areas.

The effect of a female mayor on the percentage of employees in women's issue areas demonstrates the long-term effect of electing women to local office. By increasing municipal employment in these areas, female mayors are institutionalizing their increased commitment to women's issues. In addition, because women often dominate employment in these fields, female mayors may be increasing jobs for women.

These findings suggest the importance of considering possible downstream effects of women's representation in cities, because women make up the significant majority of employees in these areas. Figure 5.4 presents nationwide employment data for traditionally

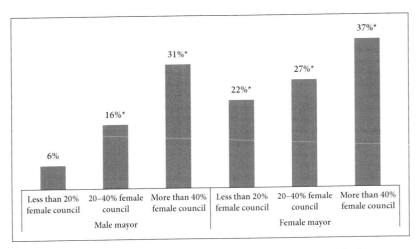

Figure 5.3   Substantive effects of female representation on municipal employment in women's issue areas. Significance calculated in left-truncated tobit model, with sociodemographic and political controls. * = Difference significant at the 0.05 level from the next-lowest level of women's representation on the council.

male and female occupations. Women make up the clear majority of employees in urban women's issue programs; thus, women's representation in urban government—and the subsequent positive relationship with municipal employment in women's urban issue areas—can produce substantial benefits for women living in American cities.

Female mayors acknowledged the differential effect of funding these programs on women's employment, noting on more than one occasion their awareness that women in their city would benefit from the creation and funding of programs in women's urban issue areas. In discussions of increasing funding for a job training program for low-income individuals and women reentering the workforce, a female mayor said that the program often hired its own more successful graduates and "lots of women. So when the moms go there, they can see all the success right there and have good role models." Another mayor, in discussing her city's new after-school and summer-care program, said that while "these might not be the best jobs in the world, a job is a job" and that these would make "great jobs" for moms transitioning back into the job market.

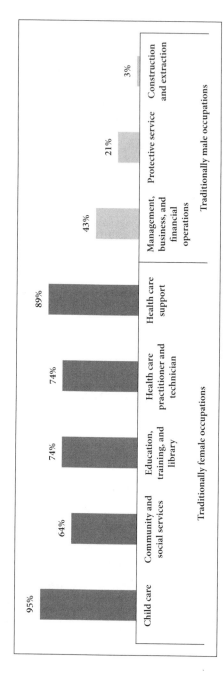

Figure 5.4 Female employees by occupation. Data come from U.S. Census Bureau, "Employed Civilians by Occupation, Sex, Race, and Hispanic Origin," 2010.

Paying for It: Female Leaders and Grants, Loans, and Intergovernmental Transfers

As previously discussed, cities operate within extreme finance constrictions. Subjected to mandates by state and federal governments, faced with the free movement of residents and businesses from city to city, and restricted in their ability to raise funds, city governments lack the extra resources to spend on women's urban issue programs.[24] Where does the funding come from?

I present four sets of data to examine how cities with female mayors and city council members pay for increased spending on women's issue programs: the total budget, the bond (debt) amount, the grant amount, and intergovernmental transfers. For all these measures, I use data from the three-hundred-city sample, because I am able to examine the measures while controlling for spending, loans,[25] grants, and transfers from the previous year. First, the gender of the mayor does not have a significant effect on the total spending in cities.[26] The lack of significance of gender of the mayor and city council (or any of the interactions) suggests that, perhaps, female leaders cut funding to other areas or find alternative revenue streams to pay for women's issue programs. The gender of the mayor also fails to influence debt payments per capita, as displayed in the "Spending of debt per capita" columns of Table 5.2.

The gender of the mayor does positively influence the per capita grant income and the per capita intergovernmental revenue (see Table 5.3). The presence of a female mayor increases per capita grant revenues significantly, and similar to spending on women's issues, interacts with the percentage of women on the city council to increase spending. That the rate of spending on social services connects to intergovernmental transfers and grants concurs with previous findings.[27] The substantively and statistically significant effect of women's representation on grant and intergovernmental amounts suggests that women find alternative sources for funding women's issue programs that do not threaten the economic future of the city or disenfranchise stakeholders. Indeed, female leaders often noted in interviews and surveys that they found alternative sources for their policy priorities.

TABLE 5.2   FEMALE MAYORS, TOTAL SPENDING, AND DEBT SPENDING (THREE-HUNDRED-CITY SAMPLE)

	Total spending per capita		Spending on debt per capita	
	Coefficient	Standard error	Coefficient	Standard error
Female mayor	3946.50	3877.50	122.20	198.09
Percentage female council	3648.03	2368.20	127.18	95.80
Percentage female council, squared	126.45	418.29	75.79	53.42
Female mayor × % female council	1887.06	4748.84	146.44	187.26
Female mayor × % female council, squared	933.96	876.16	149.52	116.04
Mayor-council	3905.61**	914.86	91.08	97.99
Female mayor × mayor-council	528.74	462.62	11.53	11.52
Percentage female council × mayor-council	325.75	488.02	25.42	20.52
Median income	0.00	0.01	0.00	0.00
Percentage poverty	0.00	0.00	0.00	0.00
Percentage high school diploma	0.42	0.53	0.54	0.89
Percentage public assistance	−0.99**	0.17	0.56**	0.00
Percentage nonwhite	0.73**	0.32	0.87**	0.15
2007 per capita spending	0.77*	0.36		
2007 debt spending			0.41**	0.18
Log of population	434.77	52.89	162.93	197.13
Autonomy	0.40	0.72	0.62	0.67
Constant	801.71	629.36	−141.31	174.05
N	253		253	
R^2	0.413		0.380	

Note: OLS regression.

* $p < 0.05$, ** $p < 0.01$.

These findings also suggest that female leaders may cause addition of mandates, accountability, and restrictions on local governments by the state and federal governments. Cities already face significantly eroded authority by increased power of state and federal governments, and many scholars point to this as a challenge for urban governance, a threat to local democracy, and a problem for citizen engagement with politics.[28] Others, however, suggest that oversight and engagement

TABLE 5.3   FEMALE MAYORS, GRANTS, AND INTERGOVERNMENTAL
SPENDING (THREE-HUNDRED-CITY SAMPLE)

	Grants per capita (2008)		Intergovernmental per capita revenue (2008)	
	Coefficient	Standard error	Coefficient	Standard error
Female mayor	40.62**	16.92	13.34**	5.76
Percentage female council	40.62	40.30	97.06	128.29
Percentage female council, squared	154.19	116.27	97.99**	25.42
Female mayor × % female council	118.64	170.15	163.05**	67.95
Female mayor × % female council, squared	197.13	163.48	159.28**	29.63
Mayor-council	−196.95**	40.71	−116.27**	20.52
Female mayor × mayor-council	175.57	142.48	61.75*	25.74
Percentage female council × mayor-council	38.27	78.15	68.24	58.63
Median income	0.0009**	0.00	0.0007**	0.00
Percentage poverty	105.45	132.28	97.06	128.29
Percentage high school diploma	83.14	156.35	143.29	100.10
Percentage public assistance	−5.06**	1.17	4.73	1.89
Percentage nonwhite	7.78**	2.67	7.003**	2.59
2007 grants per capita	0.00	0.02		
2007 intergovernmental per capita			4.73**	1.89
Log of population	185.11**	52.38	125.13**	47.65
Autonomy	−0.73*	0.31	0.712†	0.34
Constant	137.03	193.01	117.07**	72.90
N	232		232	
R^2	0.106		0.145	

Note: OLS regression.

† $p < 0.10$, * $p < 0.05$, ** $p < 0.01$.

in local politics by higher levels of government lead to better policy making, more accountability, and improved services.[29] The positive relationship between women's representation and intergovernmental transfers suggests that women might be more willing than men to trade urban autonomy for their policy priorities.

Bringing All Together: Female Leaders and Policy Outcomes

The presence of a female mayor has a positive and substantively significant relationship on a variety of policy outcomes. The percentage of female city council members has no direct effect on participation in or spending on women's issue programs but does have a positive effect when a female mayor is present and their representation reaches certain levels. In addition, female leaders are associated with not only more employees in women's issue programs but more female employees. Thus, female leaders are associated with the policy outcome of more jobs for women in their cities. Finally, female leaders do not increase budgets or loan amounts to pay for these programs but do increase intergovernmental revenues and grant funding.

One important finding from the research presented in this chapter is that to identify the traditional relationship between women in office and policy outcomes at the urban level, it may be necessary to have a female leader in a position of power. Female mayors have a positive effect on spending for women's issue areas, and while female city council members do not appear to have a significant straightforward effect on spending, they do positively influence spending in the presence of a female mayor. The presence of a female mayor also increases municipal employment in women's issue areas, suggesting long-term consequences from the election of women to municipal office. My findings here dovetail with extant research on the importance of representative bureaucracy; in particular, the number of women in bureaucracies leads to the representation of women's interests across a variety of measures.[30] Thus, electing a woman to office increases city employment in areas where women work, thus employing more women in the community and providing the opportunity for representation in local bureaucracies as well.

The research presented here demonstrates the importance of including local political factors in explanations of municipal policy making and spending patterns. The gender of the mayor influences both participation in and funding of women's issue programs. Examinations of the realities of municipal funding—particularly the realities of women's issue funding—must include evaluations of the effect of political leaders on these decisions.

6 /

For the Good and the Bad of the City

Female Leaders and Urban Interests

Ann[1] has been the mayor of her city for four years and has seen "a lot of change" over that time. She spends a significant amount of time on the job—up to sixty hours a week for this supposedly part-time job—which pays $5,000 a year. She said, "I'm happiest when I get to actually talk to people. You know, get out there and chat with people in neighborhoods, see what the kids are up to. . . . I got to check out the revamped playground last week, and there were all these kids there with smiles on their faces. I felt like I was maybe a little responsible for that by funding [the new playground equipment]. That's what I like about this job." Ann is not resentful of the amount of time the job takes—she is semiretired and understood the "demands of the job" before running for office. She expressed great satisfaction with passing a balanced budget, saving money on the city bus system by figuring out more efficient routes "that got to everyone, not just those that live on the main drags," and authorizing a census of city parks and programs that revealed significant disparities in programs offered in rich versus poor neighborhoods. Elected to office with the support of the PTA and members from a variety of organizations (including the Junior League and the local American Association of University Women), Ann often refers to these community connections

when discussing the policies that matter to her and how she conceptualizes women's issues in her city. In speaking about women's activism in the city, Ann's pride in "how involved [women are] and how
much they clearly care about the community—about what is good for
the community"—was clear. Although reluctant to identify herself as
an advocate for women's issues—"I am a mayor who happens to be a
woman, not a female mayor"—Ann's actions in office demonstrate her
interest in representing urban women's issues.

Robert, like Ann, has been mayor for four years and "loves the job."
Also like Ann, he particularly likes interacting with members of the
community, "going to chamber events, working with local small businesses, and just chatting, you know, with the people that really understand what I have gotten accomplished. He [the previous mayor] was
perceived as sort of antibusiness—not that he didn't like them; he just
didn't spend time with them. Didn't care about them. I do, and they
notice." Robert noted that his connection with the business community also related to his background—as a small-business owner in the
community, he knew many of these people before he was elected and
relied on their support when running for office. His biggest achieve-
ment was getting a large mixed-use development project passed by the
council that will bring "jobs and money—the important things" to
the city. When asked about urban women's issues, Robert shrugged,
smiled, and suggested that I ask one of his female city council members. Later, when discussing how women are active in his community,
he said, "[Education] would probably be in that category, right? Of
women's issues? The PTA here, they are bulldogs if they think you are
taking something away from them. Those women, they are impressive. I wish that businesses would get together like that." Thus, while
able to identify areas of city politics that he views as related to women's
issues, Robert was reluctant to speak for women in his community and
circled back to a discussion of jobs and economic development.

The sentiments these two mayors expressed illustrate many of the
components of why women's representation at the local level matters.
The office of mayor or city council entails making difficult decisions
about how to protect and advance the interests of the city. Beyond
facing the normal demands on any public figure, local public officials
lead in an environment in which citizens and businesses can relocate

to another city and extensive mandates from state and federal governments restrict action. These constraints limit a city's ability to raise
revenue from taxes. Within this context, is it reasonable or even right
to expect gender to influence the actions of municipal leaders? I argue
that the extensive restrictions on the actions of leaders make urban
governance the most resistant to substantive representation of
women's interests. Yet dispute this resistance, I find that *gender does
matter at the local level.* Female leaders influence the policy process,
the participation of groups in urban politics, and policy outcomes so
that the presence of female mayors (and to some extent, council members) has a positive effect on the discussion and funding of policies
relating to urban women's issues.

Women's Urban Issues

In this book, I conceptualize and operationalize urban women's issues
as those under the purview of urban governance that have a history
of women's political activism and disproportionality influence the
lives of contemporary women in urban America. In this definition, I
include policies that address children, education, affordable housing,
social welfare, and violence against women. To make this definition,
I explore women's activism in urban politics throughout American
history, demonstrating deep connections between women's nascent
political activism in the nineteenth century and today's urban wom-
en's issues. I use this definition to demonstrate how women in local
politics privilege policy making within this set of issues. In concep-
tualizing urban women's issues as I do, I demonstrate that a subset of
issues that women care about does exist at the urban level, contrary to
scholars who suggest otherwise.[2]

   Men and women in local office value development and women's urban issues in very similar ways: development is important and women's
urban issues are not. When I conceptualize representation in urban
politics as crossing the formal-informal divide and look at the large
segment of female leaders who establish relationships with women and
women's organizations in their city, differences emerge. Specifically,
by focusing on those women who indicate feeling a responsibility to
represent women's issue groups, I find that these preferable descriptive

representatives consider education, health, domestic violence, and welfare policies to be important and work more often on education, health, affordable housing, and welfare. At the same time, gender alone is an insignificant predictor in most circumstances. Comparing a descriptive representative and a preferable descriptive representative reveals distinctive differences between the two in policy preferences and goals, ideas about the power of women, attitudes toward other women, and whom they feel a responsibility to represent. The results in Chapter 2 demonstrate the importance of connections between informal and formal politics for the advancement of urban women's issues.

Does the presence of a female mayor and female council members change the substance of policy making in cities? As I show in Chapter 3, cities with female mayors discuss women's issues much more often than those with male leaders, even when I account for city characteristics and the varying nature of city council meetings. In a confirmatory analysis that looks at several cities over time, cities that change from a male to a female mayor increase the number of discussions related to women's issues and time spent on them. A detailed discussion of one of the women's equality policies that local governments control—domestic violence and rape prevention—reveals similar patterns. Specifically, under female mayors, cities pass more policies and increase discussion of issues relating to domestic and sexual violence. In interviews, female mayors noted feeling protective of women in their cities who are threatened by intimate partner violence. An analysis of the discussion of domestic violence issues over time reveals that many female mayors promote and pass policies right after getting into office and after having essentially exhausted the extent of existing policies regulating the issue. Discussion of these issues then declines after a female mayor's first year in office.

What effect do women have on the process of urban governance and citizen participation in policy making? Scholars have argued that women develop a unique sense of morality, which influences their approach to policy making.[3] Specifically, women's morality centers on an ethos of "responsibility and care."[4] As a result, policy production under women should be more open, involve more participants, and be less focused on the identification of a single right answer. Chapter 4 demonstrates that the presence of a female mayor leads to an increase in public participation in urban policy making, and this increase lengthens the general policy-making process. Examining the causes of the increase in public comments reveals that, under female mayors, the public comments on agenda items relating to women's issues much more frequently than they do under male mayors.

What are the community's perceptions of female and male mayors? I identify individuals active in ten cities through city council minutes and lists from leaders discussed in Chapter 4 and find that in cities with female mayors, a larger diversity of organizations and individuals are involved in the public elements of policy making. In addition, community members with concerns relating to women's issues are much more likely to be active in cities with female mayors. In turn, community members consider female mayors more responsive to their interests, a result driven almost entirely by the group of community members with women's issue concerns. In cities with male mayors, the active community members contacted the government more for issues relating to development.

Although many scholars have found significant connections between women and policy changes in the state, federal, and international arenas, previous research on local representatives rarely identifies these gender differences.[5] My research presents alternative evidence that female mayors increase spending on welfare programs, an effect that intensifies as the percentage of women on the city council grows. Additionally, cities with female mayors have a larger percentage of their employees working in women's issue occupations than cities with male mayors, suggesting female mayors have long-lasting effects on policy changes in urban governance.

Female Leaders and Theories of Urban Politics

The findings presented here suggest several important implications for the general urban politics scholarship. As previously discussed, urban politics scholars often argue that cities operate in a constrained environment of limited financial resources and control. Here I present three theories of urban politics and examine how women's representation—and the effect of women's representation—fits into each of these dominant views of local politics. In doing so, I ask: Are the effects that female leaders have on urban policy a good thing? Do we want women who matter in local politics?

Fiscal federalism argues that urban politics is transactional and good policy advances the interests of the city through development. Paul Peterson and others focus on the easy movement of people from city to city, as families and businesses shop for the city that offers the services they want at the price they can afford.[6] In this context, in which residents can move easily from city to city, urban governments should provide allocative and developmental policies to rein in the exodus of high-income residents. Because female local leaders are associated with preferring, discussing, and funding a variety of redistributional policies, perhaps the effect of female mayors on the city is a net negative. By focusing on urban women's issues and downplaying the significance of developmental policies, female leaders work against what scholars would consider the interests of the city.[7]

Regime theory challenges fiscal federalism by arguing that governing coalitions guide urban politics. The scarce resources available to local governments means that leaders do not have the ability to meet the demands made on cities. To satisfy citizen interests, local leaders must collaborate with private business interests.[8] These regimes consist of informal, long-term coalitions of political leaders and private actors who make important policy decisions for the city.[9] Women are much less likely than men to belong to the groups that make up the traditional regime, and urban women's issues may run perpendicular to the interests of businesses.[10] What are the consequences of a city leader being resistant to a regime? First, the regime may cease to exist.[11] Although city governments can exist without these partnerships, the absence of a regime presents a long-term, constant threat to the city; New Orleans' lack of response to Hurricane Katrina typifies the problems associated with a lack of a regime.[12] Second, the regime may react by restricting the actions of a female leader. Regimes, and business elites in general, can immobilize any person or group that challenges the current system.[13] Women in local government may be successful in creating issue-based regimes for urban women's issues, but these coalitions "do not possess the resources that allow them to serve as permanent leaders of the city."[14]

Another perspective on power in urban governance posits that small groups of elites make policy decisions and promote their interests at the expense of the public.[15] The concentrated view of urban power argues that property owners and developers use a combination of public and private resources to perpetuate a culture of development to advance their fortunes. When the desires and demands of a small group of elites determine policy, a female leader who bucks this trend and seeks alternative policy courses promotes urban democracy and is good for urban politics. Indeed, as detailed in Chapter 4, city policy making under a female mayor seems to represent a much larger group of citizen interests than that in cities with male mayors. Thus, the introduction of women into urban political leadership may challenge Floyd Hunter's finding that urban government is "just a smokescreen for dominant economic interests."[16]

Organizations active in urban women's issues see female leaders as more responsive to their interests and engage in the policy-making process more often with them. Communities with a female mayor also respond by participating more in urban politics. This reinforces previous findings that gender influences leadership styles and relationships: "Constituents are more important to women, not because they need votes, but because they have strong commitments to community service and representing community needs."[17] Many female leaders in my survey were dedicated to opening up government to those previously excluded: these women have found success in this goal, particularly for community members associated with women's urban issues. In welcoming new participants to the policy process, female leaders promote strong democracy, loyalty to the city, and the use of voice.[18]

Results presented throughout this book reaffirm the general centrality of business and development in urban politics. According to survey data, close to 100 percent of the leaders worked with someone in the community on development issues, and both male and female leaders considered development issues very important. A large group of leaders (mostly male) felt a responsibility to represent the interests of developers, business leaders, and property owners. Leaders generally also believed that businesses have the correct amount of power in their cities. As Figure 6.1 shows, the vast majority of leaders

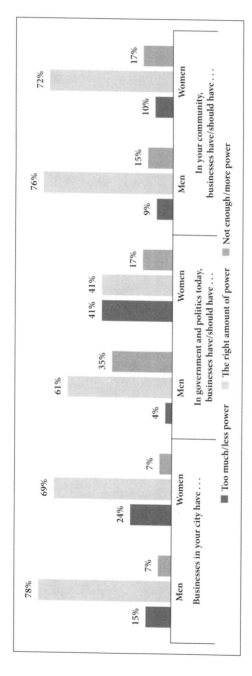

Figure 6.1   Leaders' perceptions of the power of businesses, by gender. Data come from the hundred-city survey of mayors and city council members. Because of rounding, total percentages may not equal 100.

were satisfied with the amount of power that businesses have in their communities. Figure 6.1 also shows the belief of some female leaders that businesses in their community and government *currently have too much power* but their power *should not change*. To the question of whether "businesses in your city have too much power, the right amount of power, or not enough power," nearly a quarter of women answered that businesses have too much power. However, when asked, "In your community, do you think that businesses should have more power, have the right amount of power, or should have less power?" only 10 percent of female leaders believe businesses should have less power.

Development discussions compose just under one-third of all city council discussions. Development is also the subject of many public comments on city council items; more than one-fifth of development items involved a public comment. These results indicate that issues relating to development are important to both leaders and community members. Groups interested in development issues make up just under half the organizations I identified as active in the cities by viewing city council meeting minutes and asking for names from leaders; individuals interested in development make up 40 percent of those identified as active in the community. Development projects occupy a much larger portion of city budgets than women's issue programs, regardless of the gender of the mayor or the gender composition of the city council. Overall, development is certain to be at the center of urban politics and policy making, regardless of the gender of the leaders in a city.

Exit, Voice, and Female Leaders

Cities struggle with attracting and keeping residents and businesses in their communities. Because businesses and wealthy residents value development, a female leader's pursuit of women's urban issue policies may lead to their exit and resulting fiscal consequences for cities. However, looking at tax revenue for cities (see Table 6.1), the gender of the mayor and the city council's gender composition are both significant and positive. These results demonstrate the absence of a negative effect for female leaders, suggesting that the promotion of urban

TABLE 6.1   PER CAPITA TAX REVENUE IN 2008 (THREE-HUNDRED-CITY SAMPLE)

	Coefficient	Standard error
Female mayor	223.578**	88.709
Percentage female council	652.7	333.305
Percentage female council, squared	83.035	52.905
Female mayor × % female council	67.359**	23.133
Female mayor × % female council, squared	275.722	159.538
Mayor-council	90.957	99.439
Female mayor × Mayor-council	66.865**	26.995
Percentage female council × Mayor-council	34.834	34.264
Median income	47.998**	17.708
Percentage poverty	−72.092**	14.404
Percentage high school diploma	99.439	65.350
Percentage public assistance	−63.292*	23.545
Percentage nonwhite	18.135	90.957
Log of population)	190.527†	84.973
Autonomy	19.113	17.240
Constant	191.681	283.939
N	232	
R^2	0.414	

† $p < 0.10$, * $p < 0.05$, ** $p < 0.01$.

women's interests does not lead to an immediate reduction of tax revenues. The gender composition of the council seems to have no effect on the per capita revenue of the city, while traditional indicators like the median income and percentage in poverty do have the expected effect. It may be that the price a city pays for a mayor who does not value development over all other policies is further down the road.

It also may be that, as discussed in Chapter 5, female leaders find alternative funding for women's issue policies, and therefore do not endanger the city by reducing money for development or by raising taxes. Still, Peterson and others argue that by providing these services—regardless of the funding source—the city risks attracting low-income residents who do not pay taxes and alienating residents who choose not to support women's issue programs.[19] I find little evidence of this, with the exception that community members associated with and active in development are less likely to support female mayors, but this takes the form of an electoral consequence for the mayor, not a fiscal consequence for the city.

Do the differences in community perceptions of leaders and contacts with them in male- and female-governed cities influence support and votes for the mayors? Both genders of mayors enjoy relatively high overall approval from their communities (3.2 for female mayors, 3.4 for male mayors, on a 1–5 scale, with 5 being strong approval) and indications of overall support in the next election (4.1 for female mayors, 4.0 for male mayors, on a 1–5 scale, with 5 being definite support). As Figure 6.2 shows, differences emerge when the interests of community members are compared to support for the mayors. Comparing community members who said they contacted an elected official or attended a meeting about a development issue or a women's issue shows clear differences. Among the group with development concerns, the male mayors get extremely high marks of approval and support, while the female mayors do not.[20] Conversely, the female mayors enjoy much higher levels of support from those concerned with women's issues but much lower levels from those with development concerns.[21]

What are the other consequences of electing female mayors to positions of power in local politics? One primary consequence of interest is

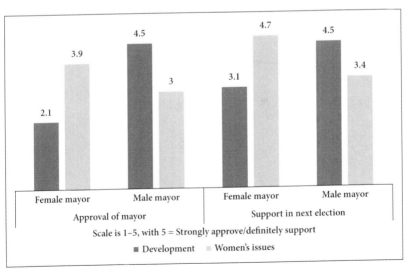

Figure 6.2   Approval and support of mayor by community members. Data come from a survey of community members in ten cities. See Chapter 4 for a discussion of the selection and contact of these community members.

that public participation in city council meetings increased markedly in cities with female mayors, particularly compared to the prior male mayors or similar cities with male mayors. In addition, the increase in public participation accompanied an increase in the overall length of city council meetings, measured by the number of items discussed in each council meeting. In general, meetings under female mayors were 60 percent longer than meetings under male mayors and involved a much greater diversity of participants. By participating in policy making, city residents may feel they can exert control over the political process, and this may increase satisfaction with government.[22]

Female leaders are thus promoting what Albert Hirschman calls voice, or "any attempt at all to change, rather than escape from, an objectionable state of affairs."[23] However, Hirschman and others argue that what matters is not simply the use of voice but the effectiveness of that use.[24] By encouraging public participation, female leaders may be encouraging public engagement in the political system through voice. Community members find female mayors more responsive, and the large number and types of groups that contact female leaders reflect the increased use of voice under female leaders.

Conclusion

I begin the book by asking whether it mattered if only 17 percent of large cities had female mayors. Is the lack of gender parity in local office okay? What kinds of implications does this have for urban politics? For women's representation? After six chapters, hundreds of city council minutes, responses to surveys, interviews with leaders, feedback from community members, and evaluation of budget and employment data, I can conclude that *women in local office make a difference* across a multitude of measures and outcomes.

My findings demonstrate that, although cities do not have control over many policies that address the equality and rights of women in society, female leaders still are able to promote policies of importance to their constituents, particularly their female constituents. However, these leaders also face two significant challenges: First, the universe of policies available to municipal leaders that directly address the position of women in society is limited. Thus, using survey questions designed for evaluating policy making of state or federal legislative bodies in the urban context is inappropriate. Second, the strong institutional, fiscal, and service constraints of municipal office severely limit the ability of leaders to accomplish widespread policy changes. The problem of resources (whether money, time, or energy) seems to expand for female mayors. If women have a more difficult experience as leaders than men, this suggests consequences for a political pipeline consisting of women in local government, because "women's ranks in national and state offices will grow only when they make substantial gains at the local level."[25] My findings also dovetail with research on women's general and progressive political ambition, in which women, before initially seeking office and then running for higher office, feel like they need to be better qualified than their male counterparts believe themselves to be.[26]

The findings presented here have significant implications for the general study of women in politics. I both confirm and deny the extant scholarship on women's representation in that I find significant gender differences across a wide variety of measures, which is consistent with a broad body of scholarship that generally finds that "women in office do make a difference."[27] While all leaders—male and female—may "cite taxes and development as the most important issues in the community," women in local office use a variety of mechanisms to *also* represent women's urban issues.[28] The findings presented here also demonstrate the power of informal connections for improving the lives of women and the need to have women at all levels of office. My results suggest that women's reluctance to run for political office may be rooted in the (correct) perception that the job is harder for women than it is for men.

Women's representation in urban politics has a variety of policy and democratic consequences. Among the primary consequences are an increased focus on providing programs relating to women's issues, the representation of women's interests in public deliberation, increase in participation of the public and urban women's interest groups in urban policy making, and increases in both the rate and level of funding of women's issue programs. Women leaders, particularly mayors, reflect the gender differences that exist in the general population, in which women are more supportive of women's urban issues and more hesitant to support the power of business. That women are nowhere near half of local representatives poses a serious and long-lasting challenge to the fundamental idea of representative democracy. Women in local government clearly think, speak, act, and lead in a different manner, and until women are fully represented in electoral institutions, the perspectives of women are underrepresented and democracy is incomplete.

Appendixes

Chapter 2

A: Hundred-City Survey

The hundred-city survey solicited information about policies and practices that mayors and city council members deal with on a day-to-day basis. I based survey questions on other surveys of women in state legislatures and Congress, adjusted for an urban focus, and scholarship on group membership.[1] Generally, the survey evaluated whether the gender of mayors and city council members influences attitudes toward the importance of policies. It asked about their experience in office, their views of the job of a representative, and groups in their community and city they interact with regularly and solicited background information. The questions are as follows:

1. What is the name of the city you represent?
2. What state is your city in?
3. What position do you hold?
4. For council members: Are you elected at large, by a district, or by a ward?
5. How long (in years) have you held your current position?
6. What has been your biggest success since assuming this office?
7. What has been your biggest challenge since assuming this office?
8. What are your goals, in terms of city policy, in the next year?
9. There are many policy areas that demand attention from you as a leader. How important is each of the following interests to you? Please rank the following areas by level of importance, with 1 being the most important and 5 being the least important. Feel free to indicate N/A if

your city does not handle the issue. (Policy areas: affordable housing, children, development, domestic violence, education, general government, library, public works, parks and recreation, race and ethnicity, public safety, transportation and infrastructure, environment, welfare and health, and women.)

10. How about in your community? Please rank these areas by level of importance to your community. (Policy areas are same as above.)
11. Have you ever worked with other council members on any of these issues? (Policy areas are same as above.)
12. How often does your city council discuss these issues? (Policy areas are same as above.) (Once a meeting, once every few months or more, once a year or more, rarely, never)
13. Do you think your city spends too much, the correct amount, or not enough time discussing each of these areas? (Policy areas are same as above.)
14. What about in budgeting? Do you think your city spends too much, the correct amount, or not enough money on each of these areas? (Policy areas are same as above.)
15. If you controlled next year's budget in your city, would you decrease or increase spending on these areas? (Policy areas are same as above.)
16. Do you feel a specific responsibility to represent the interests of any of the following groups? (Whites, blacks, Hispanics, Asians, women, men, liberals, conservatives, independents, business owners, developers, property owners, feminists, middle class, poor, rich, people at your place of worship, people in your neighborhood, people at your place of work, Americans in general)
17. Which of these groups do you feel the strongest responsibility to represent? (Groups same as above.)
18. Have members of any of these groups contacted you regarding an issue in your city? (Groups same as above.)
    a. Please indicate which groups (if any) have contacted you. (Groups same as above.)
19. Which groups do you feel particularly close to—people who are most like you in their ideas and interests and feelings? (Groups same as above.)
20. Of the groups mentioned, which one do you feel the *most* close to? (Groups same as above.)

I would like to get your feelings about the power of some groups. I am interested in whether you think that certain groups have too much, the right amount, or too little power and whether they should have more or less power.

21. Do you think businesses have too much power, the right amount of power, or not enough power in your city?

22. Thinking about how you would like things to be in government and politics today, do you think that businesses should have more power and influence, have the right amount of power and influence, or should have less power and influence?

23. How about in your community? Thinking about how you would like things to be in your community, do you think that businesses should have more power and influence, have the right amount of power and influence, or should have less power and influence?

24. Do you think the poor have too much power, the right amount of power, or not enough power in your city?

25. Thinking about how you would like things to be in government and politics today, do you think that the poor should have more power and influence, have the right amount of power and influence, or should have less power and influence?

26. How about in your community? Thinking about how you would like things to be in your community, do you think that the poor should have more power and influence, have the right amount of power and influence, or should have less power and influence?

27. Do you think women have too much power, the right amount of power, or not enough power in your city?

28. Thinking about how you would like things to be in government and politics today, do you think that women should have more power and influence, have the right amount of power and influence, or should have less power and influence?

29. How about in your community? Thinking about how you would like things to be in your community, do you think that women should have more power and influence, have the right amount of power and influence, should have less power and influence?

30. What is your gender? (Male, female) For women:
    a. How often do you find yourself feeling a sense of pride as a woman in the accomplishments of other women in public office? (Almost never; occasionally; some of the time; most of the time; all the time)
    b. When reading or listening to the news, how much attention do you pay to issues that especially affect women as a group? (No attention at all; a little attention; some attention; a lot of attention)
    c. If all the elected leaders in your city were female, do you think policies would change? (No, yes) If yes, how?

31. Generally speaking, do you usually think of yourself as a Republican, a Democrat, an independent, or what? (Strong Democrat; Democrat; weak Democrat; independent—leaning Democrat; independent; independent—leaning Republican; weak Republican; Republican; strong Republican)

32. We hear a lot of talk these days about liberals and conservatives. Here is a scale on which the political views that people might hold are arranged

from extremely liberal to extremely conservative. Where would you place yourself on this scale? (Extremely liberal; liberal; slightly liberal; moderate or middle of the road; slightly conservative; conservative; extremely conservative; don't know)

33. Where would you generally place your constituents on this scale? (Extremely liberal; liberal; slightly liberal; moderate or middle of the road; slightly conservative; conservative; extremely conservative; don't know)

34. Thinking of the other elected officials in your city, where would you place them on this scale? (Extremely liberal; liberal; slightly liberal; moderate or middle of the road; slightly conservative; conservative; extremely conservative; don't know)

35. What is your present or prior occupation?

36. What is your race or ethnicity?

Thank you for taking the time to complete this study. If you are interested in receiving notice of results from this study, please place your contact information below.

B: Three-Hundred-City Survey

The three-hundred-city survey was similar to the hundred-city survey but solicited less information on gender and more on general characteristics. The questions are as follows:

1. What is the name of the city you represent?

2. What state is your city in?

3. What position do you hold?

4. For council members: Are you elected at large, by a district, or by a ward?

5. How long (in years) have you held your current position?

6. Is this your first position in city government? (Yes, no) If no, what other positions have you held?

7. What has been your biggest success since assuming this office?

8. What has been your biggest challenge since assuming this office?

9. Please indicate which response most accurately reflects your experiences. (Strongly agree; agree; slightly agree; neither agree nor disagree; slightly disagree; disagree; strongly disagree)

   a. I have the same policy goals as other members of the city council.

   b. I have a combative relationship with other members of city government.

   c. I work well with other leaders in my city.

   d. I feel respected by other members of the city council.

10. Please indicate how often you feel the following statement accurately describes your experiences as a municipal leader. (Never; rarely; sometimes; often; always) How often do
    a. you feel your opinion matters on the city council?
    b. you have conflicts with other members of the city council or the mayor?
    c. you put items on the agenda at city council meetings?
    d. other members of the city council seek out your opinion or expertise on an issue?
        i. Which issues are you asked about the most?
11. There are many interests demanding attention from you as a leader. How important is each of the following interests to you? Please rank the following issues by level of importance, with 1 being the most important and 11 being the least important. (Domestic violence, infrastructure and transportation, welfare services, economic development, affordable housing, parks and recreation, public works, public safety, education, culture and arts, health and human services)
12. Have you ever worked with other council members on any of these issues? (Same issues as above.)
13. How often do you propose legislation relating to the same issues as above? (Once a meeting; once every few months or more; once a year or more; rarely; never)
14. Are there any groups whose interests you feel are underrepresented in your city? (No, yes) If yes, which groups?
15. Many public officials feel they represent specific groups in office, beyond their electoral constituencies. Do you feel any responsibility toward representing any specific group or groups?
    a. Which groups do you feel a responsibility to represent?
    b. Why do you feel a responsibility to represent these groups?
16. Generally speaking, do you usually think of yourself as a Republican, a Democrat, an independent, or what? (Strong Democrat; Democrat; weak Democrat; independent—leaning Democrat; independent; independent—leaning Republican; weak Republican; Republican; strong Republican)
17. We hear a lot of talk these days about liberals and conservatives. Here is a scale on which the political views that people might hold are arranged from extremely liberal to extremely conservative. Where would you place yourself on this scale? (Extremely liberal; liberal; slightly liberal; moderate or middle of the road; slightly conservative; conservative; extremely conservative; don't know)
18. When it comes to politics, where would you generally place your constituents on this scale? (Extremely liberal; liberal; slightly liberal;

        moderate or middle of the road; slightly conservative; conservative; extremely conservative; don't know)

19. Thinking of the other elected officials in your city, where would you place them on this scale? (Extremely liberal; liberal; slightly liberal; moderate or middle of the road; slightly conservative; conservative; extremely conservative; don't know)
20. What is your present or prior occupation?
21. What is your race or ethnicity?
22. What is your gender? (Male, female)

Thank you for taking the time to complete this study. If you are interested in receiving notice of results from this study, please place your contact information below.

Chapter 3

A: Coding of City Council Minutes' Subject Matter

Affordable housing: Affordable housing, housing costs, housing developments that include set-asides for low-income residents, rent subsidies for low-income residents, public housing, unsafe housing.

Children: Child safety, activities for children, children presenting to the council, drug free programs, fairs for kids, fingerprinting, Amber alerts, missing children, pedophilia, sex offenders databases, crimes against children.

Development: Economic development, attracting businesses, retaining businesses, location of businesses, large-scale developments.

Domestic and sexual violence: Domestic violence, rape, sexual assault, rape crisis response.

Education: Scholarships, achievements, presentations by schoolchildren, recognition of achievements by children in schools, reports by schools.

Environment: Environmental degradation, global warming, clean air, clean water, open space.

General: Hiring employees, firing employees, raises, promotions, general council business, authorizing purchases, office equipment, office supplies, legal issues.

Library: Library buildings, fines, exhibits, books, fund-raising, hiring, firing, promoting library employees.

Race and ethnicity: Race, ethnicity, diversity, Martin Luther King Jr., Cesar Chavez, discrimination, harassment, day laborers, racism.

Parks and recreation: Parks, park rentals, sports, hiring and firing park employees, pools, baseball fields, golf courses, parks equipment.

Public safety: Police, fire, EMT, appropriate responses to crimes, equipment, canine units, drug task forces, police training, liquor licenses and enforcement, underage drinking, crime prevention, flooding, forest fires.

Public works: Roads, electricity, water, gas, utilities, trash, recycling.

Transportation: Public transportation, transportation issues, traffic, buses, trains.

Urban women's issues: Composite of affordable housing, children, education, domestic and sexual violence, welfare and health, and women.

Welfare and health: Redistribution of resources, public assistance programs, food stamps, scholarships, public health, free clinics, health fairs, health epidemics, health preparedness, responses to health issues.

Women: Gender, women's health, discrimination, harassment, female leaders, sexism.

Zoning: Zoning changes, building permits, small development projects, historic homes, fences, zoning violations.

B: Interview Questions for Mayors and City Council Members

1. What is the best part of being a [mayor/city council member]?
2. What is the most frustrating part of being a [mayor/city council member]?
3. Why did you run for office?
4. What are the most important issues in [city]?
5. Are there issues in [city] that you think are important but don't receive enough attention?
   a. What are these issues?
   b. Why do you think that they don't receive enough attention?
6. What policies are you most proud of? Why?
7. Are there any groups that you feel are underrepresented in [city]?
   a. Which groups?
   b. Why do you think that they are underrepresented?
8. Are there any groups that you feel a special responsibility to represent?
   a. Which groups?
   b. Why do you feel responsible to represent them?
9. Are women active in your city? How?
10. What would you consider women's issues or women's policies in your city?
11. What groups are you involved with?
    a. Did any of these groups help you in your campaign? How?
12. Which are the most powerful groups in [city]? (Prompt to list organizations.)

13. Which are the least powerful? (Prompt to list organizations.)
14. If you could give a new [mayor/city council member] some advice about being a leader, what would it be?

For women only:
15. Do you think that your gender affected your actions in office?
    a. How? Why?

For minorities only:
16. Do you think that your race affected your actions in office?
    a. How? Why?

For city council members in office with both mayors:
17. Do you think that changing mayors matters?
    a. Why?
18. What was the biggest change you saw with the change in mayors?
19. What did you expect when the mayor changed?
20. Did [name of second mayor] surprise you in any way?

For mayors only:
1. What are the most important changes you accomplished in office?
2. What were your goals when you ran for mayor?
    a. Do you feel you accomplished these goals?
    b. Why or why not?
    c. What was the biggest challenge to accomplishing these goals?
3. What is the best thing about [city]?
4. What one thing would you change about [city]?
5. What distinguishes you from your predecessor?
6. In what ways are you the same as your predecessor?
7. Is there anything else you would like to tell me about being mayor of [city]?

C: Mayoral Gender and Community Discussions

TABLE 3C.1   THE EFFECT OF MAYORAL CHANGE ON DISCUSSIONS OF ITEMS
ON DOMESTIC AND SEXUAL VIOLENCE

	City 1	City 2	City 3	City 4 (control)	City 5	City 6 (control)	City 7	City 8
Mayoral change	0.164*	0.172*	0.137*	0.016	0.030*	0.012	0.129*	0.072*
OPG standard error	0.028	0.029	0.016	0.008	0.009	0.033	0.010	0.020
Constant	0.138*	0.297	0.249*	0.135†	0.040*	0.034	0.145†	0.095*
OPG standard error	0.027	0.127	0.083	0.079	0.003	0.078	0.089	0.038

Note: OPG = outer product of gradients.

† $p < 0.10$; * $p < 0.05$.

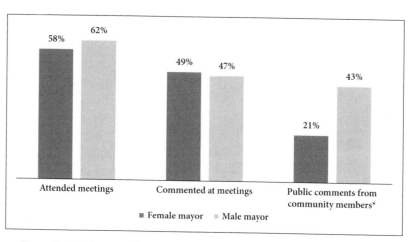

Figure 3C.1   Community members attending and commenting at meetings (community survey). * = Difference significant at the 0.05 level.

Chapter 4

A: Organizations and Individuals Active in Cities

TABLE 4A.1 ORGANIZATIONS AND INDIVIDUALS IN CITIES WITH
FEMALE OR MALE MAYORS FOUND IN CITY COUNCIL MINUTES AND
NAMED BY LEADERS

	Female mayors	Male mayors
Number of organizations or individuals		
Number of organizations in minutes	23	17
Number of organizations named by leaders	32	30
Number of organizations both in minutes and named by leaders	18	12
Number of individuals in minutes	12 women, 14 men	7 women, 14 men
Number of individuals named by leaders	26 women, 12 men	12 women, 13 men
Number of individuals both in minutes and named by leaders	8 women, 6 men	3 women, 8 men
Type of organization (in minutes or named by leaders)		
Economic development or business	7 (in minutes) 12 (named)	11 (in minutes) 21 (named)
Quality of life	1 (in minutes) 3 (named)	0 (in minutes) 5 (named)
Women's issues	16 (in minutes) 15 (named)	5 (in minutes) 2 (named)
Miscellaneous	0 (in minutes) 2 (named)	0 (in minutes) 3 (named)

B: Questions for Citizens Active in the Community (Paper and E-mail Questionnaire)

1. What do you think the biggest issue facing [city] is today?
2. Have you, in the past year, tried to influence public policy in [city]?
   a. If yes, how?
3. In the past year, have you contacted a public official in your city?
   a. If yes, how many times?
   b. If yes, why did you contact an elected official?
4. Do you think that local elected officials are responsive to you?
   a. Why or why not?
5. Have you attended a city council meeting in the past year?
   a. If yes, how many city council meetings have you attended?
   b. If yes, why did you attend a city council meeting?
   c. If no, why haven't you attended a city council meeting?
   d. If yes, did you make a public comment at any of these meetings?
      i. If yes, what was your comment about?
6. If you contacted an official but had not attended a meeting, why did you contact an elected official instead of attending a city council meeting?
7. Do you think that local officials are responsive to your interests?
   a. Yes
   b. No
8. Do you think that the mayor is responsive to your interests?
   a. Yes
   b. No
9. Do you think that the city council is responsive to your interests?
   a. Yes
   b. No
10. Do you approve of the job the mayor is doing in your city? Why?
    a. Strongly approve
    b. Approve
    c. Neither approve or disapprove
    d. Disapprove
    e. Strongly disapprove
11. Do you approve of the job the city council is doing in your city? Why?
    a. Strongly approve
    b. Approve
    c. Neither approve or disapprove
    d. Disapprove
    e. Strongly disapprove
12. What is one area in which you would like to see the city change its policy?

13. Will you be supporting the mayor in the next election?
    a. Definitely support
    b. Support
    c. Don't know/undecided
    d. Oppose
    e. Definitely oppose
    f. N/A/mayor isn't running/don't vote
14. For those contacted as a member of an organization:
    a. What are [your organization's] goals in the city?
    b. Does your organization have a particular member of the city government that it approaches with problems?
    c. Do you think that local officials are responsive to your organization's interests?
    d. Do you think that the mayor is responsive to your organization's interests?
    e. Do you think that the city council is responsive to your organization's interests?

Chapter 5

Budget Coding Information

I obtained and coded each city's 2010 budget, looking at the level for funding for social welfare programs, including funding for health and human services, hospitals, welfare programs, community development, affordable housing, and child care and child welfare services. I obtained and coded budgets in the following ways. First, if the city was located in a state that requires reporting of budgets to a central clearinghouse, like Michigan, Massachusetts, or Utah, I obtained the budgets from that state clearinghouse and used their coding for "health and human services" or "social welfare services" and "community development." In these circumstances, all the budgets were obtained from this central clearinghouse, and I did not need to obtain individual budgets. For those states where these clearinghouses were unavailable, I obtained budgets from city websites. If I could not get the budgets from the state or the city's website, I contacted the city clerk or city finance director and asked for an electronic or paper copy of the budget. I then coded the budgets by hand, summing all expenditures in the health and human services, hospitals, welfare programs, community development, affordable housing, and child care and child welfare services categories. I coded only funds spent from the city's general budget. I used budgets rather than expenditures for several reasons. First, budgets are more widely available than exact expenditures, because cities are required to provide their budgets to the public. Second, leaders have more control over budgets (the planning) than expenditures (the output), because expenditures are controlled by city employees implementing the budget. Finally, the scholarship on government budgeting conflates the two, given the high level of correspondence, particularly at the subcategory level, between budgets and expenditures.

As with the model presented in Table 5.1, analysis of budgets in the hundred-city sample shows that the presence of a female mayor has a positive effect on both the provision of urban women's issues and the amount of funding dedicated to these services (see Table 5A.1). In addition, there is a significant interaction between the presence of the female mayor and the percentage of the council who are female, as well as an interaction between the form of government and a female leader.

TABLE 5A.1   WOMEN'S URBAN REPRESENTATION AND THE PROVISION OF WOMEN'S ISSUE PROGRAMS (ONE-HUNDRED-CITY SAMPLE)

	Provision of service		Amount of funding	
	Coefficient	Standard error	Coefficient	Standard error
Female mayor	0.82**	−0.23	32.62**	10.12
Percentage female council	0.33	−1.26	5.33	10.20
Percentage female council, squared	1.122†	−0.57	2.12	1.30
Female mayor × % female council	0.91**	−0.41	11.12*	4.98
Female mayor × % of council female, squared	3.00**	−1.00	1.02†	5.12
Mayor-council	0.09	−0.52	9.12**	3.54
Female mayor × mayor-council	0.713**	−0.22	4.66*	2.92
Percentage female council × mayor-council	2.19	−3.23	−1.11†	0.55
Median income	0.00	0.00	0.00	0.00
Percentage poverty	2.12	−9.12	23.17**	10.12
Percentage high school diploma	−0.32	−4.21	2.13	4.97
Percentage public assistance	3.91*	−1.88	30.82*	10.99
Percentage nonwhite	0.21*	−0.09	2.134*	1.00
Revenue (per capita)	0.00	0.00	0.003**	0.00
Grants (per capita)	0.00	0.00	0.41**	0.00
Log of population	0.25**	−0.01	12.01**	0.02
Autonomy	−0.901†	−0.46	0.13	0.46
Constant	−1.12	−1.89	178.34	101.98
Sigma			109.9**	10.14
N	85		56 (23 left-truncated)	
Pseudo R^2	0.2413		0.512	

Note: I used logistical regression for analysis of provision of service, because the dependent variable takes a dichotomous form (yes or no for funding). I used tobit regression to analyze the amount of provision, with left truncation to drop those cities without funding for women's issue programs.

† $p < 0.10$; * $p < 0.05$; ** $p < 0.01$.

Notes

Chapter 1

1. The letter was sent to Mayor Salter with a pair of pants drawn on the card.

2. While in office, Mayor Salter "discharge[d] the duties of her office in the most acceptable manner," taking up only those policies traditionally addressed by the council. *Rushville (Indiana) Republican*, August 18, 1887, quoted in Monroe Billington, "Susanna Madora Salter—First Woman Mayor," *Kansas Historical Quarterlies* 21, no. 3 (1954): 178.

3. Throughout the book, I use "leaders" to mean mayors and city council members; where a mayor or city council member is specifically meant, I use "mayor," "councilor," or "council member."

4. Center for American Women and Politics, *Women Mayors in U.S. Cities, 2011* (New Brunswick, NJ: CAWP Eagleton Institute of Politics, 2011), 625.

5. Janet Boles, "Local Elected Women and Policy-Making: Movement Delegates or Feminist Trustees?" in *The Impact of Women in Public Office*, ed. Susan Carroll (Bloomington: Indiana University Press, 2001), 69; Lynne A. Weikart, Greg Chen, Daniel W. Williams, and Haris Hromic, "The Democratic Sex: Gender Differences and the Exercise of Power," *Journal of Women, Politics and Policy* 28, no. 1 (2007): 119–140; Susan Abrams Beck, "Gender and the Politics of Affordable Housing," in *Gender in Urban Research*, ed. Judith Garber and Robyne Turner (New York: Sage, 1995), 119–135.

6. Feminist urban scholars have often called for a stronger evaluation of women's issues in urban politics and the incorporation of gender as a politically relevant term in urban studies, because "urban scholars are greatly unaccustomed to thinking about gender"; while urbanists have answered with extensive research, these calls have largely gone unheeded in political science. Judith Garber and Robyne Turner, *Gender and Urban Research*, Urban Affairs Annual Review 42 (Thousand Oaks, CA: Sage, 1995), xv; see also Ruth Fincher and Jacinta McQuillen, "Women in Urban Social Movements," *Urban Geography* 10, no. 6 (1989): 604–613; Ruth Fincher, "Class and Gender Relations in the Local Labor Market and the Local State," in *The Power of Geography: How Territory Shapes Social Life*, ed. Jennifer Wolch and Michael Dear (Boston: Unwin Hyman, 1989), 93–117; Ruth Fincher, "Women in the City: Feminist Analyses of Urban Geography," *Australian Geographical Studies* 28, no. 1 (1990): 29–37; Liz Bondi, "Gender, Class, and Urban Space: Public and Private Space in Contemporary Urban Landscapes," *Urban Geography* 19, no. 2 (1998): 160–185; Judith N. DeSena, *Gender in an Urban World*, Research in Urban Sociology 9 (Bingley, UK: Emerald Group, 2008); Judith N. DeSena, "Local Gatekeeping Practices and Residential Segregation," *Sociological Inquiry* 64, no. 3 (1994): 307–321; Judith N. DeSena, "Women: The Gatekeepers of Urban Neighborhoods," *Journal of Urban Affairs* 16, no. 3 (1994): 271–283.

7. Throughout the text, I refer to these interchangeably as "urban women's issues," "women's urban issues," and occasionally, "women's issues."

8. Thus, these areas are those that female leaders define for themselves as women's issues, meeting the call of Beth Reingold and Michele Swers to endogenously define women's issues. See "An Endogenous Approach to Women's Interests: When Interests Are Interesting in and of Themselves," *Politics and Gender* 7, no. 3 (2011): 429–435.

9. Virginia Sapiro, "Research Frontier Essay: When Are Interests Interesting? The Problem of Political Representation of Women," *American Political Science Review* 75, no. 3 (1981): 703.

10. By creating a subset of urban women's issues that meet these criteria, I rely on previous work that addresses those traditionally associated with women, identifies where a gendered difference in public opinion emerges, or discusses issues disproportionately affecting women while still allowing female leaders to address what they consider women's urban issues: Susan J. Carroll, ed., *The Impact of Women in Public Office* (Bloomington: University of Indiana Press, 2001); Debra L. Dodson and Susan J. Carroll, *Reshaping the Agenda: Women in State Legislatures* (New Brunswick, NJ: Center for American Women and Politics, 1991); Barbara Burrell, *A Woman's Place in the House: Campaigning for Congress in the Feminist Era* (Ann Arbor: University of Michigan Press, 1994); Beth Reingold, *Representing Women: Sex, Gender, and Legislative Behavior in Arizona and California* (Chapel Hill: University of North Carolina Press, 2000); Susan Welch, "Are Women More Liberal Than Men in the U.S. Congress?"

Legislative Studies Quarterly 10, no. 1 (1985): 125–135; Michele Swers, "Understanding the Policy Impact of Electing Women: Evidence from Research on Congress and State Legislatures," *PS: Political Science and Politics* 34, no. 2 (2001): 217–220; Michele Swers, *The Difference Women Make: The Policy Impact of Women in Congress* (Chicago: University of Chicago Press, 2002); Beth Reingold and Adrienne R. Smith, "Welfare Policymaking and Intersections of Race, Ethnicity, and Gender in U.S. State Legislatures," *American Journal of Political Science* 56, no. 1 (2012): 131–147; Reingold and Swers, "An Endogenous Approach to Women's Interests."

11. Stefania Abrar, Joni Lovenduski, and Helen Margetts, "Sexing London: The Gender Mix of Urban Policy Actors," *International Political Science Review* 19, no. 2 (1998): 147–171.

12. Virginia Sapiro, *The Political Integration of Women: Roles, Socialization, and Politics* (Urbana: University of Illinois Press, 1983); Eleanor Flexner, *Century of Struggle: The Women's Rights Movement in the United States* (Cambridge, MA: Harvard University Press, 1975); Linda Kerber, "The Republican Mother: Women and the Enlightenment—an American Perspective," *American Quarterly* 28, no. 2 (1976): 187–205; Paula Baker, "The Domestication of Politics: Women and American Political Society, 1780–1920," *American Historical Review* 89, no. 3 (1984): 620–647.

13. Holly J. McCammon, Karen E. Campbell, Ellen M. Granberg, and Christine Mowery, "How Movements Win: Gendered Opportunity Structures and U.S. Women's Suffrage Movements, 1866 to 1919," *American Sociological Review* 66, no. 1 (2001): 49–70; Holly McCammon, "'Out of the Parlors and into the Streets': The Changing Tactical Repertoire of the U.S. Women's Suffrage Movements," *Social Forces* 81, no. 3 (2003): 787–818.

14. Baker, "Domestication of Politics," 635.

15. Ibid., 625; Kerber, "The Republican Mother."

16. Christine Stansell, *City of Women: Sex and Class in New York, 1789–1860* (Urbana: University of Illinois Press, 1987); Lori D. Ginzberg, *Women and the Work of Benevolence: Morality, Politics, and Class in the Nineteenth-Century United States* (New Haven, CT: Yale University Press, 1992); Daniel Scott Smith, "Family Limitation, Sexual Control, and Domestic Feminism in Victorian America," in *Clio's Consciousness Raised*, ed. Mary Hartman and Lois Banner (New York: Harper and Row, 1974), 23–27.

17. African American, poor, and non-Protestant women often formed alternative benevolence societies to "challenge the hegemony of wealthy white Protestant women's associations," with varying success. Anne M. Boylan, *The Origins of Women's Activism: New York and Boston, 1797–1840* (Chapel Hill: University of North Carolina Press, 2002), 13.

18. Michael McGerr, "Political Style and Women's Power, 1830–1930," *Journal of American History* 77, no. 3 (1990): 864–885; Baker, "Domestication of Politics."

19. Barbara J. Berg, *The Remembered Gate: Origins of American Feminism; The Woman and the City, 1800–1860* (New York: Oxford University Press, 1978); Seth Koven and Sonya Michel, eds., *Mothers of a New World: Maternalist Politics and the Origins of Welfare States* (New York: Routledge, 1993); Kathryn Kish Sklar, *Florence Kelley and the Nation's Work: The Rise of Women's Political Culture, 1830–1900* (New Haven, CT: Yale University Press, 1997); Joanne L. Goodwin, *Gender and the Politics of Welfare Reform: Mothers' Pensions in Chicago, 1911–1929* (University of Chicago Press, 1997).

20. Karen J. Blair, *The Clubwoman as Feminist: True Womanhood Redefined, 1868–1914* (New York: Holmes and Meier, 1980), 99.

21. Blair, *Clubwoman as Feminist.*

22. Mary P. Ryan, *Womanhood in America: From Colonial Times to the Present* (New York: New Viewpoints, 1975); Agnes Hooper, *Women Journalists and the Municipal Housekeeping Movement, 1868–1914* (Lewiston, NY: Edwin Mellen, 2001).

23. Blair, *Clubwoman as Feminist*, 106. See also Tiffany Lewis, "Municipal Housekeeping in the American West: Bertha Knight Landes's Entrance into Politics," *Rhetoric and Public Affairs* 14, no. 3 (2011): 465–491; Georgia Pulsifer Porter, *Maine Federation of Women's Clubs: Historical Sketches, 1892–1924* (Lewiston, ME: Lewiston Journal Printshop, 1925), 72.

24. Rheta Childe Dorr, *What Eight Million Women Want* (Boston: Small, Maynard, 1910), 327.

25. Maud Nathan, *The Story of an Epoch-Making Movement* (New York: Doubleday, 1926), 19.

26. Early benevolence work, women's clubs, the municipal housekeeping movement, and settlement houses all promoted to some extent the primary female bond. Blair, *Clubwoman as Feminist*; Ryan, *Womanhood in America*; Helen Winslow, *The President of Quex: A Women's Club Story* (Boston: Lothrop, Lee, and Shepard, 1906), 185–186.

27. Contemporary work on the topic is in France Willard, *Women and Temperance; Or, the Work and Workers of the Women's Christian Temperance Union* (Hartford, CT: Park, 1883). Mothers Against Drunk Driving represents modern women's efforts regarding alcohol.

28. The regulation of restaurants by local health inspectors is a clear exception to the movement of health issues to the state and national levels.

29. Blair, *Clubwoman as Feminist*; Baker, "Domestication of Politics"; Gerda Lerner, *The Creation of Patriarchy* (New York: Oxford University Press, 1986). Others (contentiously) suggest that the city itself is partially responsible for changes in women's status. Margaret Gibbons Wilson, *The American Woman in Transition: The Urban Influence, 1870–1920* (Westport, CT: Greenwood, 1979).

30. James L. Leloudis II, "School Reform in the New South: The Woman's Association for the Betterment of Public School Houses in North Carolina, 1902–1919," *Journal of American History* 69, no. 4 (1983): 886–909; Koven and Michel, *Mothers of a New World*; Seth Koven and Sonya Michel, "Womanly

Duties: Maternalist Politics and the Origins of Welfare States in France, Germany, Great Britain, and the United States, 1880–1920," *American Historical Review* 95, no. 4 (1990): 1076–1108.

31. In many ways, early women's education activism ran parallel to rural women's activism through the grange movement, but rural women soon focused their attention on pushing state colleges to admit women, while urban women's activism focused on basic public education and the provision of trade schools and training opportunities for younger children. Koven and Michel, *Mothers of a New World*; Koven and Michel, "Womanly Duties."

32. Robert H. Whitten, "Political and Municipal Legislation in 1903," *Annals of the American Academy of Political and Social Science* 23 (March 1904): 128; Anne C. Rose, *Transcendentalism as a Social Movement, 1830–1850* (New Haven, CT: Yale University Press, 1981).

33. Florence Kelly, "Forbid Home Work and End Child Labor," *New York Globe*, December 7, 1912, quoted in Eileen Boris, "Reconstructing the 'Family': Women, Progressive Reform, and the Problem of Social Control," in *Gender, Class, Race, and Reform in the Progressive Era*, ed. Noralee Frankel and Nancy Dye (Lexington: University Press of Kentucky, 1991), 79. See also Blair, *Clubwoman as Feminist*.

34. Jane Bernard Powers, *The "Girl Question" in Education: Vocational Education for Young Women in the Progressive Era*, Studies in Curriculum History Series (New York: Routledge, 2012), 73; Blair, *Clubwoman as Feminist*; Marlene Stein Wortman, "Domesticating the Nineteenth-Century American City," *Prospects* 3 (1977): 531–572; Lori D. Ginzberg, *Women and the Work of Benevolence: Morality, Politics, and Class in the Nineteenth-Century United States* (New Haven, CT: Yale University Press, 1992); Jennie Croly, *The History of the Woman's Club Movement in America* (New York: Henry G. Allen, 1898); Nancy Hewitt, "Politicizing Domesticity: Anglo, Black, and Latin Women in Tampa's Progressive Movements," in Frankel and Dye, *Gender, Class, Race, and Reform in the Progressive Era*, 24–42.

35. Boylan, *Origins of Women's Activism*, 18; Berg, *Remembered Gate*; Ginzberg, *Women and the Work of Benevolence*.

36. Mrs. T. J. Bowlker, "Women's Home-Making Function Applied to the Municipality," *American City* 6 (1912): 863.

37. This is the mission statement of the Junior Leagues in 1910, quoted in Stephen Birmingham, *The Grandes Dames* (New York: Simon and Schuster, 1982), 2.

38. Virginia Sapiro, "The Gender Basis of American Social Policy," *Women, the State, and Welfare* (Madison: University of Wisconsin Press, 1990). For example, in 1921, women's efforts toward the provision of welfare services triumphed at the federal level with the passage of the Sheppard-Towner Act, which provided support for the health of mothers and children. Although urban women's progressive activism saw a decline in the 1920s, the substance of future welfare services at the urban, state, and national levels emerged from women's prior efforts.

39. Paula Baker, "The Domestication of Politics," in *Women, the State, and Welfare*, ed. Linda Gordon (Madison: University of Wisconsin Press, 1990), 70.

40. Mary Ritter Beard, *Woman's Work in Municipalities* (New York: D. Appleton, 1915), 221.

41. Stansell, *City of Women*, 207.

42. Sklar, *Florence Kelley and the Nation's Work*; Bowlker, "Women's Home-Making Function Applied to the Municipality"; Joanna Mathews, *A Short History of the Orphan Asylum Society in the City of New York* (New York: Anson D. F. Randolph, 1893); Elizabeth Mason North, *Consecrated Talents, or, the Life of Mrs. Mary W. Mason* (New York: Carlton and Lanahan, 1870).

43. Jacob August Riis, *How the Other Half Lives: Studies among the Tenements of New York* (New York: Penguin, 1901); Dorothy Schneider and Carl J. Schneider, *American Women in the Progressive Era, 1900–1920* (New York: Facts on File, 1993); Ruth Crocker, *Social Work and Social Order: The Settlement Movement in Two Industrial Cities, 1889–1930* (Champaign: University of Illinois Press, 1992).

44. Gail Radford, *Modern Housing for America: Policy Struggles in the New Deal Era* (Chicago: University of Chicago Press, 2008).

45. William Thomas Stead, *If Christ Came to Chicago!* (New York: Larid and Lee, 1894); Jane Addams, *A New Conscience and an Ancient Evil* (New York: Macmillan, 1912); Charlotte Perkins Gilman, *Women and Economics: A Study of the Economic Relation between Men and Women as a Factor in Social Evolution* (Courier Dover, 1898); Blair, *Clubwoman as Feminist*.

46. Addams, *New Conscience and an Ancient Evil*. World War I—and a greater availability of birth control and (thus) sex within marriage—diminished demand for and concern about prostitution in cities. Janet Beer and Katherine Joslin, "Diseases of the Body Politic: White Slavery in Jane Addams' *A New Conscience and an Ancient Evil* and Selected Short Stories by Charlotte Perkins Gilman," *Journal of American Studies* 33, no. 1 (1999): 1–18.

47. Mazie Hough, "Are You or Are You Not Your Sister's Keeper? A Radical Response to the Treatment of Unwed Mothers in Tennessee," in *Before the New Deal: Social Welfare in the South, 1830–1930*, ed. Elna C. Green (Athens: University of Georgia Press, 1999), 100–119; Boylan, *Origins of Women's Activism*; Nancy Cott, *The Bonds of Womanhood: "Women's Sphere" in New England, 1785–1835* (New Haven, CT: Yale University Press, 1978); Ruth H. Bloch, "The Gendered Meanings of Virtue in Revolutionary America," *Signs* 13, no. 1 (1987): 37–58.

48. For a larger discussion of the history of legal responses to domestic violence, see Lynette Feder, "Domestic Violence and Police Response in a Pro-arrest Jurisdiction," *Women and Criminal Justice* 8, no. 4 (1997): 79–98.

49. Fulgham v. State, 46 Ala. 146 (1871).

50. Elizabeth Pleck, *Domestic Tyranny: The Making of American Social Policy against Family Violence from Colonial Times to the Present* (New York: Oxford University Press, 2004); Thomas L. Hafemeister, "If All You Have Is a

Hammer: Society's Ineffective Response to Intimate Partner Violence," *Catholic University Law Review* 60, no. 1 (2010): 919–1002.

51. See *Bruno v. Codd*, 396 N.Y.S.2d 974 (N.Y. Sup. Ct. 1977); *Scott v. Hurt*, no. C-76-2395 (N.D. Cal. 1976); *Thomas v. Los Angeles Police Department*, no. 572 (L.A. Superior Ct. 1979); and *Thurman v. City of Torrington*, 595 F. Supp. 1521 (1985).

52. Patricia Mutpfay, "Domestic Violence Legislation and the Police," *Women and Politics* 18, no. 2 (1997): 27–53; Caroline Andrew, "Getting Women's Issues on the Municipal Agenda: Violence against Women," in *Gender in Urban Research*, ed. Judith Garber and Robyne Turner (New York: Sage, 1995), 99–118; Sue Brownill and Susan Halford, "Understanding Women's Involvement in Local Politics: How Useful Is a Formal/Informal Dichotomy?" *Political Geography Quarterly* 9, no. 4 (1990): 396–414.

53. Beard, *Woman's Work in Municipalities*, x.

54. Wortman, "Domesticating the Nineteenth-Century American City"; Beard, *Woman's Work in Municipalities*; Wilson, *American Woman in Transition*; Leloudis, "School Reform in the New South"; Dorr, *What Eight Million Women Want*.

55. Blair, *Clubwoman as Feminist*; Daphne Spain, *How Women Saved the City* (Minneapolis: University of Minnesota Press, 2001).

56. Kristi Andersen, "The Gender Gap and Experiences with the Welfare State," *PS: Political Science and Politics* 32, no. 1 (1999): 17–19; Robert Shapiro and Harpreet Mahajan, "Gender Differences in Policy Preferences: A Summary of Trends from the 1960s to the 1980s," *Public Opinion Quarterly* 50, no. 1 (1986): 42–61; Karen M. Kaufmann and John R. Petrocik, "The Changing Politics of American Men: Understanding the Sources of the Gender Gap," *American Journal of Political Science* 43, no. 3 (1999): 864–887.

57. Mark Schlesing and Caroline Heldman, "Gender Gap or Gender Gaps? New Perspectives on Support for Government Action and Policies," *Journal of Politics* 63, no. 1 (2001): 59–92.

58. Shapiro and Mahajan, "Gender Differences in Policy Preferences"; Erin O'Brien, "The Double-Edged Sword of Women's Organizing," *Women and Politics* 26, nos. 3–4 (2004): 25–56.

59. Data are from the American National Election Studies (ANES) Longitudinal data set, *The ANES Guide to Public Opinion and Electoral Behavior* (Ann Arbor: University of Michigan, Center for Political Studies, 1982–2008), available at http://www.electionstudies.org.

60. See, for example, Meg Bostrom, "Education, Gender and Race: A Review of Current Public Opinion," 2000, available at http://www.buildinitiative.org/portals/0/uploads/documents/resource-center/educationgenderandrace.pdf; Alice H. Eagly, Amanda B. Diekman, Mary C. Johannesen-Schmidt, and Anne M. Koenig, "Gender Gaps in Sociopolitical Attitudes: A Social Psychological Analysis," *Personality and Social Psychology* 87, no. 6 (2004): 796–816.

61. Alissa Pollitz Worden and Bonnie E. Carlson, "Attitudes and Beliefs about Domestic Violence: Results of a Public Opinion Survey; II. Beliefs about Causes," *Journal of Interpersonal Violence* 20, no. 10 (2005): 1219–1243.

62. Hart Research Associates and HousingWorksRI, "Affordable Housing in Rhode Island," 2010, p. 7, available at http://www.housingworksri.org/sites/default/files/SurveyResultsPresentation.pdf; Neighborhood Partnership Fund, "Talking about Housing: Developing Effective Messages," 2004, available at http://housingtrustfundproject.org/campaigns/making-your-case/messages-that-work/public-opinion-research.

63. Sapiro, *Political Integration of Women*; Paul Schumaker and Nancy Elizabeth Burns, "Gender Cleavages and the Resolution of Local Policy Issues," *American Journal of Political Science* 32, no. 4 (1988): 1070–1095; Nancy Elizabeth Burns and Paul Schumaker, "Gender Differences in Attitudes about the Role of Local Government," *Social Science Quarterly* 68, no. 1 (1987): 138–148.

64. Schumaker and Burns, "Gender Cleavages and the Resolution of Local Policy Issues."

65. Nicholas O. Alozie and Catherine McNamara, "Gender Differences in Willingness to Pay for Urban Public Services," *Urban Affairs Review* 45, no. 3 (2010): 377–390.

66. Stephen L. Klineberg, *Kinder Houston Area Survey, 1982–2010: Successive Samples of Harris County Residents* (Ann Arbor, MI: Inter-university Consortium for Political and Social Research, 2011). I include in Table 1.1 control questions about the environment to demonstrate that, while women do support social welfare and school funding at the local level, they are less interested in other forms of municipal policies and that the difference between men and women in social welfare funding is not simply an artifact of women's willingness to pay more taxes at the local level. Indeed, although women are more likely to support taxes to pay for local health care, they are not more willing spend more to protect the environment.

67. Gertrude Schaffner Goldberg and Eleanor Kremen, *The Feminization of Poverty: Only in America?* (New York: Praeger, 1990); Sara McLanahan and Erin Kelly, "The Feminization of Poverty: Past and Future," in *Handbook of the Sociology of Gender*, ed. J. Chafetz (New York: Plenum, 2001), 127–145; Diane Pearce, "The Feminization of Poverty: Women, Work, and Welfare," *Urban and Social Change Review* 11, nos. 1–2 (1978): 28–36.

68. Lynne M. Casper, Sara S. McLanahan, and Irwin Garfinkel, "The Gender-Poverty Gap: What We Can Learn from Other Countries," *American Sociological Review* 59, no. 4 (1994): 594–605; Eugenie Hildebrandt and Patricia Stevens, "Impoverished Women with Children and No Welfare Benefits: The Urgency of Researching Failures of the Temporary Assistance for Needy Families Program," *American Journal of Public Health* 99, no. 5 (2009): 793–801; Mark Harvey, "Welfare Reform and Household Survival: The Interaction of Structure and Network Strength in the Rio Grande Valley, Texas," *Journal of Poverty* 15, no. 1 (2011): 43–64.

69. Swers, *Difference Women Make*, 4.

70. Mary Ellen Guy and Meredith A. Newman, "Women's Jobs, Men's Jobs: Sex Segregation and Emotional Labor," *Public Administration Review* 64, no. 3 (2004): 289–298; Markus Gangl and Andrea Ziefle, "Motherhood, Labor Force Behavior, and Women's Careers: An Empirical Assessment of the Wage Penalty for Motherhood in Britain, Germany, and the United States," *Demography* 46, no. 2 (2009): 341–369.

71. Lynn Appleton, "The Gender Regimes of American Cities," in *Gender in Urban Research*, ed. Judith Garber and Robyne Turner (Thousand Oaks, CA: Sage, 1995), 44–59.

72. Hanna Fenichel Pitkin, *The Concept of Representation* (Berkeley: University of California Press, 1967).

73. Beth Reingold, "Women as Officeholders: Linking Descriptive and Substantive Representation," in *Political Women and American Democracy*, ed. Christina Wolbrecht, Karen Beckwith, and Lisa Baldez (New York: Cambridge University Press, 2008), 129; see also Carroll, *Impact of Women in Public Office*; Noelle Norton, "Uncovering the Dimensionality of Gender Voting in Congress," *Legislative Studies Quarterly* 24, no. 1 (1999): 65–86; Swers, *Difference Women Make*.

74. Sue Thomas, "The Impact of Women on State Legislative Policies," *Journal of Politics* 53, no. 4 (1991): 958–976; Sarah Poggione, "Exploring Gender Differences in State Legislators' Policy Preferences," *Political Research Quarterly* 57, no. 2 (2004): 305–314; Reingold and Smith, "Welfare Policymaking and Intersections of Race, Ethnicity, and Gender in U.S. State Legislatures"; Brianne Heidbreder and Katherine Felix Scheurer, "Gender and the Gubernatorial Agenda," *State and Local Government Review* 45, no. 1 (2013): 3–13; Jason A. MacDonald and Erin E. O'Brien, "Quasi-Experimental Design, Constituency, and Advancing Women's Interests: Reexamining the Influence of Gender on Substantive Representation," *Political Research Quarterly* 64, no. 2 (2011): 472–486; Judith R. Saidel and Karyn Loscocco, "Agency Leaders, Gendered Institutions, and Representative Bureaucracy," *Public Administration Review* 65, no. 2 (2005): 158–170; Jane Mansbridge, "Should Blacks Represent Blacks and Women Represent Women? A Contingent 'Yes,'" *Journal of Politics* 61, no. 3 (1999): 628–657. However, some scholars fail to find such differences; see Arturo Vega and Juanita M. Firestone, "The Effects of Gender on Congressional Behavior and the Substantive Representation of Women," *Legislative Studies Quarterly* 20, no. 2 (1995): 213–222; Kim L. Fridkin and Patrick J. Kenney, "The Role of Gender Stereotypes in U.S. Senate Campaigns," *Politics and Gender* 5, no. 3 (2009): 301–324; Leonie Huddy, "The Political Significance of Voters' Gender Stereotypes," *Research in Micropolitics* 4 (1994): 169–193; Jeffery Koch, "Do Citizens Apply Gender Stereotypes to Infer Candidates' Ideological Orientations?" *Journal of Politics* 62, no. 2 (2008): 414–429; Jan E. Leighley, *Strength in Numbers? The Political Mobilization of Racial and Ethnic Minorities* (Princeton, NJ: Princeton University Press, 2001); and Kira Sanbonmatsu, "Gender

Stereotypes and Vote Choice," *American Journal of Political Science* 46, no. 1 (2002): 20–34.

75. Burns and Schumaker, "Gender Differences in Attitudes about the Role of Local Government"; Lynne A. Weikart, Greg Chen, Daniel W. Williams, and Haris Hromic, "The Democratic Sex: Gender Differences and the Exercise of Power," *Journal of Women, Politics, and Policy* 28, no. 1 (2007): 119–140; Janet Flammang, "Female Officials in the Feminist Capital: The Case of Santa Clara County," *Western Political Science Quarterly* 38, no. 1 (1985): 94–118; Susan Gluck Mezey, "Perceptions of Women's Role on Local Councils in Connecticut," in *Women in Local Office*, ed. Debra Stewart (London: Scarecrow, 1980), 177–197; Melissa Marie Deckman, "School Board Candidates and Gender: Ideology, Party, and Policy Concerns," *Journal of Women, Politics and Policy* 28, no. 1 (2007): 541–563; Adrienne J. Smith, "'Cities Where Women Rule': Female Political Incorporation and the Allocation of Community Development Block Grant Funding" (paper presented at the American Political Science Association annual meeting, Washington, DC, September 2010); Grace Hall Saltzstein, "Female Mayors and Women in Municipal Jobs," *American Journal of Political Science* 30, no. 1 (1986): 140–164; Brinck Kerr, Will Miller, and Margaret Reid, "Determinants of Female Employment Patterns in U.S. Cities," *Urban Affairs Review* 33, no. 4 (1998): 559–578; Jesse Donahue, "The Non Representation of Gender," *Women and Politics* 20, no. 3 (1999); Jesse Donahue, "It Doesn't Matter: Some Cautionary Findings about Sex and Representation from School Committee Conversations," *Policy Studies Journal* 25, no. 4 (1997): 630–647; Susan Abrams Beck, "Rethinking Municipal Governance: Gender Distinctions on Local Councils," in *Gender and Policymaking*, ed. Debra Dodson (Rutgers, NJ: Center for American Women and Politics, Eagleton Institute of Politics, 1991), 103–113; Fernando V. Ferreira and Joseph Gyourko, "Does Gender Matter for Political Leadership? The Case of U.S. Mayors" (working paper, Wharton School, University of Pennsylvania, 2011); James M. Vanderleeuw, Maria E. Sandovici, and Christopher A. Jarmon, "Women City Leaders and Postmaterialist Values: Gender Differences in Economic Development Priorities," *Journal of Women, Politics and Policy* 32, no. 3 (2011): 211–236.

76. Beck, "Gender and the Politics of Affordable Housing," 123. See also Smith, "Cities Where Women Rule"; Saltzstein, "Female Mayors and Women in Municipal Jobs"; Kerr, Miller, and Reid, "Determinants of Female Employment Patterns in U.S. Cities"; Donahue, "The Non Representation of Gender"; Donahue, "It Doesn't Matter"; Beck, "Rethinking Municipal Governance." Many of these studies argue that the lack of traditional women's issues at the local level could be the primary driver behind the lack of gender differences.

77. Although for a few differences, see Ferreira and Gyourko, "Does Gender Matter for Political Leadership?"; Donahue, "The Non Representation of Gender"; Donahue, "It Doesn't Matter"; Beck, "Rethinking Municipal Governance"; and Sue Tolleson-Rinehart, "Do Women Leaders Make a Difference: Substance,

Style and Perception," in *The Impact of Women in Public Office*, ed. Susan Carroll (Bloomington: University of Indiana Press, 2001), 149–165.

78. Smith, "Cities Where Women Rule"; Saltzstein, "Female Mayors and Women in Municipal Jobs"; Kerr, Miller, and Reid, "Determinants of Female Employment Patterns in U.S. Cities"; Ferreira and Gyourko, "Does Gender Matter for Political Leadership?"

79. Kathleen Bratton and Leonard Ray, "Descriptive Representation, Policy Outcomes, and Municipal Day-Care Coverage in Norway," *American Journal of Political Science* 46, no. 2 (2002): 428–437; Maud Eduards, *Women's Representation and Women's Power* (Stockholm: Forskningsrapport, Stockholms Universitet, Statsvetenskapliga Institutionen, 1980); Raghabendra Chattopadhyay and Esther Duflo, "Women as Policy Makers: Evidence from a Randomized Policy Experiment in India," *Econometrica* 72, no. 5 (2004): 1409–1443.

80. Beck, "Gender and the Politics of Affordable Housing," 133; Lynne A. Staeheli, "Gender Relations in Urban Growth Politics," in *Marginalized Places and Populations: A Structurationist Agenda*, ed. D. Wilson and J. O. Huff (Westport, CT: Praeger, 1994), 129–148; Schumaker and Burns, "Gender Cleavages and the Resolution of Local Policy Issues."

81. Dillon's Rule and Home Rule govern the relationship between state and local governments. Dillon's rule is named after Judge John Dillon, who made the 1868 ruling in *City of Clinton v. Cedar Rapids & Missouri River R.R.*, 24 Iowa 455 (1868), that states have ultimate power over cities, because "municipal corporations owe their origin to, and derive their powers and rights wholly from, the legislature. It breathes into them the breath of life, without which they cannot exist. As it creates, so may it destroy. If it may destroy, it may abridge and control." Alternatively, the city-state relationship may be governed by a Home Rule charter that sets forth certain rights and responsibilities for the city and state but allows a degree of independence for the city. For summary information on Home Rule and Dillon's Rule by state, see Dale Krane, Planton Rigos, and Melvin Hill, *Home Rule in America: A Fifty-State Handbook* (Washington, DC: CQ Press, 2001).

82. Krane, Rigos, and Hill, *Home Rule in America*; G. Ross Stephens, "State Centralization and the Erosion of Local Autonomy," *Journal of Politics* 36, no. 1 (1974): 44–76; David R. Berman and Lawrence L. Martin, "State-Local Relations: An Examination of Local Discretion," *Public Administration Review* 48, no. 2 (1988): 637–641.

83. Paul Peterson, *City Limits* (Chicago: University of Chicago Press, 1981); Charles Tiebout, "A Pure Theory of Local Expenditures," *Journal of Political Economy* 64 (1956): 416–424; Albert O. Hirschman, *Exit, Voice, and Loyalty: Responses to Decline in Firms, Organizations, and States* (Cambridge, MA: Harvard University Press, 1970); Berman and Martin, "State-Local Relations."

84. Tiebout, "Pure Theory of Local Expenditures"; James M. Buchanan, "Principles of Urban Fiscal Strategy," *Public Choice* 11 (1971): 1–16.

85. Wallace Oates, *Fiscal Federalism* (New York: Harcourt Brace Jovanovich, 1972); Wallace E. Oates, "An Essay on Fiscal Federalism," *Journal of Economic Literature* 37, no. 3 (1999): 1120–1149.

86. Clarence N. Stone, *Regime Politics: Governing Atlanta, 1946–1988,* Studies in Government and Public Policy (Lawrence: University Press of Kansas, 1989); Hirschman, *Exit, Voice, and Loyalty.*

87. Karen Kaufmann, *The Urban Voter* (Ann Arbor: University of Michigan Press, 2004); Peterson, *City Limits*; John Logan and Harvey Molotch, *Urban Fortunes: The Political Economy of Place* (Los Angeles: University of California Press, 1987); Stone, *Regime Politics.*

88. Peterson, *City Limits.*

89. Richard E. DeLeon, "The Urban Antiregime," *Urban Affairs Review* 27, no. 4 (1992): 555–579; Martin Shefter, *Political Crisis/Fiscal Crisis: The Collapse and Revival of New York City* (New York: Columbia University Press, 1992); Joel Rast, "Governing the Regimeless City," *Urban Affairs Review* 42, no. 1 (2006): 81–112.

90. Clarence N. Stone, "Urban Regimes and the Capacity to Govern: A Political Economy Approach," *Journal of Urban Affairs* 15, no. 1 (1993): 1–28.

91. Karen Mossberger and Gary Stoker, "The Evolution of Urban Regime Theory: The Challenges of Conceptualization," *Urban Affairs Review* 36 (2001): 813; see also Stone, *Regime Politics*; Stephen L. Elkin, *City and Regime in the American Republic* (Chicago: University of Chicago Press, 1987); Peter Burns and Matthew O. Thomas, "The Failure of the Nonregime," *Urban Affairs Review* 41, no. 4 (2006): 517–527.

92. Stone, *Regime Politics*, 7. Even in a progressive or opportunity expansion regime, the participation of business is a key component of the formation and maintenance of the regime. Rast, "Governing the Regimeless City," 85.

93. Rufus Browning, Dale Marshall, and David Tabb, *Protest Is Not Enough* (Berkeley: University of California Press, 1984); Peter Burns, *Electoral Politics Is Not Enough: Racial and Ethnic Minorities and Urban Politics* (New York: State University of New York Press, 2006).

94. Susan Welch, "The Impact of Black Elected Officials on Urban Social Expenditures," *Policy Studies Journal* 7, no. 4 (1979): 707–714; Albert K. Karnig and Susan Welch, *Black Representation and Urban Policy* (Chicago: University of Chicago Press, 1980); Harold Wolman, John Strate, and Alan Melchior, "Does Changing Mayors Matter?" *Journal of Politics* 58, no. 1 (1996): 201–223; Leonard Cole, *Blacks in Power: A Comparative Study of Black and White Elected Officials* (Princeton, NJ: Princeton University Press, 1976); Edmond Keller, "The Impact of Black Mayors on Urban Policy," *Annals of the American Academy of Political and Social Science* 439 (1978): 40–52; William E. Nelson, *Black Politics in Gary: Problems and Prospects* (Washington, DC: Joint Center for Political Studies, 1972); John Pelissero, David Holian, and Laura Tomaka, "Does Political Incorporation Matter? The Impact of Minority Mayors over Time," *Urban Affairs*

Review 36 (2000): 84–92; James Button, *Blacks and Social Change: Impact of the Civil Rights Movement in Southern Communities* (Princeton, NJ: Princeton University Press, 1989); Michael Preston, "Limitations on Black Urban Power: The Case of Black Mayors," in *The New Urban Politics*, ed. L. Masotti and R. Lineberry (Cambridge, MA: Ballinger, 1976), 111–132; Charles Bullock, "The Election of Blacks in the South: Preconditions and Consequences," *American Journal of Political Science* 19, no. 4 (1975): 727–739; J. Phillip Thompson, *Double Trouble: Black Mayors, Black Communities, and the Call for a Deep Democracy*, Transgressing Boundaries (Oxford: Oxford University Press, 2006).

95. Clarence N. Stone, "Systemic Power in Community Decision Making: A Restatement of Stratification Theory," *American Political Science Review* 74, no. 4 (1980): 978–990; Jessica Trounstine, "Dominant Regimes and the Demise of Urban Democracy," *Journal of Politics* 68, no. 4 (2006): 879–893.

96. Peterson, *City Limits*, 116; Bryan D. Jones and Lynn Bachelor, *The Sustaining Hand: Community Leadership and Corporate Power* (Lawrence: University of Kansas Press, 1993).

97. Andrew, "Getting Women's Issues on the Municipal Agenda"; Elizabeth L. Sweet and Sara Ortiz Escalante, "Planning Responds to Gender Violence: Evidence from Spain, Mexico and the United States," *Urban Studies* 47, no. 10 (2010): 2129–2147.

98. Browning, Marshall, and Tabb, *Protest Is Not Enough*; Burns, *Electoral Politics Is Not Enough*; Thomas R. Dye and James Renick, "Political Power and City Jobs: Determinants of Minority Employment," *Social Science Quarterly* 62, no. 4 (1981): 475–486; Barbara Ferman, *Challenging the Growth Machine: Neighborhood Politics in Chicago and Pittsburg* (Lawrence: University of Kansas Press, 1996).

99. Browning, Marshall, and Tabb, *Protest Is Not Enough*.

100. Reingold, *Representing Women*.

101. Trounstine, "Dominant Regimes and the Demise of Urban Democracy"; Stone, "Systemic Power in Community Decision Making"; Peterson, *City Limits*; Logan and Molotch, *Urban Fortunes*; Abrar, Lovenduski, and Margetts, "Sexing London"; Stefania Abrar, Joni Lovenduski, and Helen Margetts, "Feminist Ideas and Domestic Violence Policy Change," *Political Studies* 48, no. 2 (2000): 239–262.

102. Burns and Schumaker, "Gender Differences in Attitudes about the Role of Local Government"; Schumaker and Burns, "Gender Cleavages and the Resolution of Local Policy Issues"; Sapiro, *Political Integration of Women*; Andersen, "The Gender Gap and Experiences with the Welfare State"; Ronald Inglehart and Pippa Norris, "The Developmental Theory of the Gender Gap: Women's and Men's Voting Behavior in Global Perspective," *International Political Science Review* 21, no. 4 (2000): 441–463; Kaufmann and Petrocik, "Changing Politics of American Men"; Schlesing and Heldman, "Gender Gap or Gender Gaps?"

103. Studying urban politics offers a variety of challenges, such as the lack of a central database of information about cities' politics and number of women in office. While an ideal study of urban government would include smaller as well as larger cities, the tyranny of available data forces an overreliance on larger cities. I used data from the U.S. Conference of Mayors, which tracks data from cities with population over thirty thousand, and from the Center for American Women and Politics (CAWP), whose data originate with the Conference of Mayors. Advantages of using larger cities include having more information about the city from the Internet and a greater likelihood that I could access city council minutes, demographic information about leaders, and contact information for them.

104. When I discuss the hundred-city sample, I am referring to this group of cities and their leaders. Using MatchIt, a nonparametric matching program, I matched cities with female mayors to the entirety of cities with a population over thirty thousand, excluding cities listed by CAWP as having female mayors and a population over thirty thousand, and identified fifty cities with female mayors and the best-matched group of fifty cities with male mayors. Center for American Women and Politics, *Women Mayors in U.S. Cities, 2007* (New Brunswick, NJ: CAWP, Eagleton Institute of Politics, 2007). I matched cities by population, poverty rate, and median income. All demographic data come from the 2000 U.S. census.

105. Women are more likely to be elected in cities with council-manager systems or, more generally, into positions with less power. Adrienne J. Smith, Beth Reingold, and Miles Owens, "The Political Determinants of Women's Descriptive Representation in Cities," *Political Research Quarterly* 64, no. 2 (2011): 315–329; Farida Jalalzai, "Women Rule: Shattering the Executive Glass Ceiling," *Politics and Gender* 4, no. 2 (2008): 205–231.

106. Suzanne Dovi, "Preferable Descriptive Representatives: Will Just Any Woman, Black, or Latino Do?" *American Political Science Review* 96, no. 4 (2002): 729–744.

Chapter 2

1. Susan Abrams Beck, "Acting as Women: The Effects and Limitations of Gender in Local Governance," in *The Impact of Women in Public Office*, ed. Susan Carroll (Bloomington: Indiana University Press, 2001), 49–67; Beth Reingold, *Representing Women: Sex, Gender, and Legislative Behavior in Arizona and California* (Chapel Hill: University of North Carolina Press, 2000); Susan Gluck Mezey, "Women and Representation: The Case of Hawaii," *Journal of Politics* 40, no. 2 (1978): 369–385; Mezey, "Perceptions of Women's Role on Local Councils in Connecticut," in *Women in Local Office*, ed. Debra Stewart (London: Scarecrow, 1980), 61–85; Lynne A. Weikart, Greg Chen, Daniel W. Williams, and Haris Hromic, "The Democratic Sex: Gender Differences and the Exercise of

Power," *Journal of Women, Politics and Policy* 28, no. 1 (2007): 119–140; Janet Boles, "A Policy of Our Own: Local Feminist Networks and Social Services for Women and Children," *Review of Policy Research* 8, no. 3 (1989): 638–647.

2. R. Darcy, S. Welch, and J. Clark, *Women, Elections, and Representation* (Lincoln: University of Nebraska Press, 1994).

3. Kira Sanbonmatsu, Susan Carroll, and Darcy Walsh, "Poised to Run: Women's Pathways to the State Legislatures" (New Brunswick: Center for American Women and Politics, Eagleton Institute of Politics, State University of New Jersey, 2009); Melissa Marie Deckman, "School Board Candidates and Gender: Ideology, Party, and Policy Concerns," *Journal of Women, Politics and Policy* 28, no. 1 (2007): 87–117; Kathleen Dolan and Lynne Ford, "Change and Continuity among Women State Legislators: Evidence from Three Decades," *Political Research Quarterly* 50, no. 1 (1997): 137–151.

4. Caroline Andrew, "Getting Women's Issues on the Municipal Agenda: Violence against Women," in *Gender in Urban Research*, ed. Judith Garber, Judith and Robyne Turner (New York: Sage, 1995), 99–118; Elizabeth L. Sweet and Sara Ortiz Escalante, "Planning Responds to Gender Violence: Evidence from Spain, Mexico and the United States," *Urban Studies* 47, no. 10 (2010): 2129–2147; Sue Brownill and Susan Halford, "Understanding Women's Involvement in Local Politics: How Useful Is a Formal/Informal Dichotomy?" *Political Geography Quarterly* 9, no. 4 (1990): 396–414; Stefania Abrar, "Feminist Intervention and Local Domestic Violence Policy," *Parliamentary Affairs* 49, no. 1 (1996): 191–205; Stefania Abrar, Joni Lovenduski, and Helen Margetts, "Sexing London: The Gender Mix of Urban Policy Actors," *International Political Science Review* 19, no. 2 (1998): 147–171; Stefania Abrar, Joni Lovenduski, and Helen Margetts, "Feminist Ideas and Domestic Violence Policy Change," *Political Studies* 48, no. 2 (2000): 239–262.

5. Jane Mansbridge, "Should Blacks Represent Blacks and Women Represent Women? A Contingent 'Yes,'" *Journal of Politics* 61, no. 3 (1999): 628–657.

6. Suzanne Dovi, "Preferable Descriptive Representatives: Will Just Any Woman, Black, or Latino Do?" *American Political Science Review* 96, no. 4 (2002): 729–744; Lani Guinier, *The Tyranny of the Majority: Fundamental Fairness in Representative Democracy* (New York: Free Press, 1994).

7. Anne Phillips, *Feminism and Politics* (London: Oxford University Press, 1998); Guinier, *Tyranny of the Majority*; Rufus Browning, Dale Marshall, and David Tabb, *Racial Politics in American Cities* (New York: Longman, 2003); Dovi, "Preferable Descriptive Representatives."

8. Dovi, "Preferable Descriptive Representatives," 737.

9. Ibid.

10. The cities in the three-hundred-city survey were from forty-two of the fifty states, with cities in California (twenty-eight), Texas (nineteen), and Illinois (eighteen) representing a large portion. The cities ranged in population from 6,599 to 1,953,631, with an average of just under 43,000. I was able to locate

contact information for 216 mayors and 1,101 city council members of the three hundred cities. An incorrect or invalid e-mail address rendered 233 surveys undeliverable, resulting in a bounce-back rate of 18 percent. Of the remainder, 149 chose to opt out, for a nonparticipation rate of 11 percent. Taking the bounce-back and opt-out numbers into account, the overall response rate was 38 percent: 40 percent for city council members and 35 percent for mayors. Of the 357 responses received, 97 (27 percent) were from female leaders and 260 were from male leaders. Of the mayoral respondents, 25 percent were female and 75 percent were male, while among the city council members, 41 percent were female and 59 percent were male.

11. An additional twenty-nine surveys were undeliverable because of an incorrect or invalid e-mail address or because the respondent opted out, for a bounce-back rate of 5 percent. Taking the bounce-back and opt-out rates into account, the overall response rate is 48 percent: 49 percent for city council members and 47 percent for mayors.

12. Weikart, Chen, Williams, and Hromic, "Democratic Sex."

13. Don A. Dillman et al., "Response Rate and Measurement Differences in Mixed-Mode Surveys Using Mail, Telephone, Interactive Voice Response (IVR) and the Internet," *Social Science Research* 38, no. 1 (2009): 1–18; Daniel Underwood, Heather Kim, and Michael Matier, "To Mail or to Web: Comparisons of Survey Response Rates and Respondent Characteristics" (paper presented at the Fortieth Annual Meeting of the Association for Institutional Research, Cincinnati, Ohio, May 2000).

14. These subject areas were chosen carefully from an examination of the duties of municipal government and by a review of each city's budget, which provided insight into spending on resources and what was reasonable to consider as being within the jurisdiction of municipal government.

15. The possible answers to how frequently the city council discussed a particular issue were "once a meeting," "once every few months or more," "once a year or more," "rarely," or "never."

16. This is significant to the 0.10 level.

17. The mayors and their responses are included in these data.

18. Survey respondents could be mayors or city council members as long as the leaders were from the same city. In nine of these cities, either more than one woman or more than one man responded to the survey. For these nine cities, I evaluated all possible combinations of the respondents and as the average of the multiple respondents.

19. I used one-way repeated measures ANOVA to evaluate whether female leaders differ from their male colleagues. The differences are not significant whether using the regular, Huynh-Feldt, Greenhouse-Geisser, or Box's conservative measure.

20. A higher number for a variable indicates a more frequent action. Specifically, "never" = 0; "rarely" = 1; "once a year or more" = 2; "once every few months or more" = 3; "once a meeting" = 4.

21. Leaders' responses in cities with male and female mayors are very similar: almost every leader reported working on general government and development more than on quality of life or women's issues. There were no differences between leaders who serve with male or female mayors; the results also do not vary when the paired representative responses are evaluated.

22. Andrew, "Getting Women's Issues on the Municipal Agenda"; Susan Abrams Beck, "Gender and the Politics of Affordable Housing," in *Gender in Urban Research*, ed. Judith Garber and Robyne Turner (New York: Sage, 1995), 119–135; Abrar, Lovenduski, and Margetts, "Sexing London."

23. The coding scheme allows for a clean presentation of the overall impression of the issue.

24. Both of these differences are significant to the 0.05 level.

25. The list of groups is derived from the American National Election Studies Pilot study 1991, with other groups central to urban politics (developers, property owners, and people in a neighborhood) added. The full list is whites, blacks, Hispanics, Asians, women, men, liberals, conservatives, independents, business owners, developers, property owners, feminists, middle class, poor, rich, people at one's place of worship, people in one's neighborhood, people at one's place of work, and Americans in general.

26. Dovi, "Preferable Descriptive Representatives."

27. Issue priorities are measured on a 1 to 5 scale, with higher values indicating a higher priority; community priorities are measured on a 1 to 5 scale, with higher values indicating a higher priority; and frequency of working on issues is measured on a 0 to 5 scale, with higher numbers indicating a higher frequency of working on issues. Because all the measures are continuous or ordered ordinal data, I used traditional ordinary least squares regression. Ideology and partisanship are included as controls to measure the relationship between gender, gender consciousness, and policy preferences without concern that the more liberal nature of women in the sample could produce the differences. Controls for the leader's position and number of years in office are included to account for any effect of experiences from a longer tenure in office or whether a specific office's responsibilities influenced priorities.

28. Ideally, I would be able to interact gender with the preferable descriptive representation measure, but the data do not allow this.

29. Gender, preferable descriptive representation, party, and ideology are all insignificant in the models of importance of general government, development, or quality of life.

30. Party affiliation and ideology are significant indicators of attitudes about women's issues and how the council should spend its time. Mayors are more likely to think that the council does not spend enough time on women's issues.

31. The leaders were chosen through matching, after controlling for the type of city and the position of the leader.

32. Data are discussed in the abstract to protect the confidentiality of respondents. Verbatim speech of leaders is set off with quotation marks.

Chapter 3

1. John Parkinson, "Legitimacy Problems in Deliberative Democracy," *Political Studies* 51, no. 1 (2003): 180.

2. Lani Guinier, *The Tyranny of the Majority: Fundamental Fairness in Representative Democracy* (New York: Free Press, 1994); Jürgen Habermas, *Between Facts and Norms: Contributions to a Discourse Theory of Law and Democracy* (Cambridge, MA: MIT Press, 1996); Anne Phillips, *The Politics of Presence* (London: Oxford University Press, 1995); Melissa Williams, *Voice, Trust and Memory: Marginalized Groups and the Failings of Liberal Representation* (Princeton, NJ: Princeton University Press, 1998); Melissa Williams, "The Uneasy Alliance of Group Representation and Deliberative Democracy," in *Citizenship in Diverse Societies*, ed. Will Kymlicka and Wayne Norman (New York: Oxford University Press, 2000), 124–152.

3. Christina Wolbrecht, *The Politics of Women's Rights: Parties, Positions, and Change* (Princeton, NJ: Princeton University Press, 2000).

4. Jane Mansbridge, "Should Blacks Represent Blacks and Women Represent Women? A Contingent 'Yes,'" *Journal of Politics* 61, no. 3 (1999): 628–657.

5. Joel Lieske, "The Political Dynamics of Urban Voting Behavior," *American Journal of Political Science* 33, no. 1 (1989): 150–174.

6. Martin Saiz and Hans Geser, *Local Parties in Political and Organizational Perspective* (Boulder, CO: Westview, 1999).

7. Approximately two-thirds of all cities with population over five thousand have nonpartisan elections. Saiz and Geser, *Local Parties in Political and Organizational Perspective*. See also Phillips Cutright, "Measuring the Impact of Local Party Activity on the General Election Vote," *Public Opinion Quarterly* 27 (Fall 1963): 327–386; Susan Welch and Timothy Bledsoe, "The Partisan Consequences of Nonpartisan Elections and the Changing Nature of Urban Politics," *American Journal of Political Science* 30, no. 1 (1986): 128–139; Timothy Bledsoe and Susan Welch, "Patterns of Political Party Activity among U.S. Cities," *Urban Affairs Review* 23, no. 2 (1987): 249–269; Charles R. Adrian, "A Typology for Nonpartisan Elections," *Western Political Science Quarterly* 12, no. 2 (1959): 449–458; and Willis D. Hawley, *Nonpartisan Elections and the Case for Party Politics* (New York: Wiley Interscience, 1973).

8. Issues related to public works, transportation, and development are not "owned" by either party, so leaders are not bound to a party platform when working on them.

9. For details on the substance of each subject, see Appendix 3A. These categories were developed through coding a random sample of council minutes from all the cities in my data set and condensing that coding into these sixteen categories. For example, coding the original random sample of city council minutes revealed that the library was a frequent subject of discussion; in most states, public libraries are under the funding umbrella of local cities (as opposed to counties or states). Thus, the category of library emerged as an obvi-

ous choice, because many topics relating to libraries were evident in the initial coding, including a capital works project, honoring a retiring librarian, summer reading series, and lengthy discussions of funding for library services.

10. The remaining eight cities did not publish their minutes, did not respond to my requests for their minutes, or provided only a portion of the minutes from 2010.

11. Using the percentage rather than the average number controls for the variation in the scope of policies covered by each city's council, the number of agenda items city councils consider during any given meeting, and the number of meetings the city council has in a year.

12. As previously discussed, these areas align with traditional expectations of what kinds of policies cities *should* discuss.

13. The difference between male and female mayors in discussions on general government, development, and urban women's issues are significant to the 0.05 level in difference of means tests.

14. Manon Tremblay, "The Substantive Representation of Women and PR: Some Reflections on the Role of Surrogate Representation and Critical Mass," *Politics and Gender* 2, no. 4 (2006): 502–511; Rosabeth Moss Kanter, "Some Effects of Proportions on Group Life: Skewed Sex Ratios and Responses to Token Women," *American Journal of Sociology* 82, no. 5 (1977): 965–990; Rosabeth Moss Kanter, *Men and Women of the Corporation* (New York: Basic Books, 1977); Beth Reingold, "Women as Office Holders: Linking Descriptive and Substantive Representation," in *Political Women and American Democracy*, ed. Christina Wolbrecht, Karen Beckwith, and Lisa Baldez (New York, NY: Cambridge University Press, 2008), 128–147; Drude Dahlerup, "From a Small to a Large Minority: Women in Scandinavian Politics," *Scandinavian Political Studies* 11, no. 4 (1988): 275–298; Drude Dahlerup, "The Story of the Theory of Critical Mass," *Politics and Gender* 2, no. 4 (2006): 511–522; Kathleen Bratton and Leonard Ray, "Descriptive Representation, Policy Outcomes, and Municipal Day-Care Coverage in Norway," *American Journal of Political Science* 46, no. 2 (2002): 428–437.

15. Dahlerup, "The Story of the Theory of Critical Mass," 512 (italics in original).

16. Sandra Grey, "Numbers and Beyond: The Relevance of Critical Mass in Gender Research," *Gender and Politics* 2, no. 4 (2006): 492–502; Thomas L. Hafemeister, "If All You Have Is a Hammer: Society's Ineffective Response to Intimate Partner Violence," *Catholic University Law Review* 60, no. 1 (2010): 919–1002; Jocelyn Elise Crowley, "When Tokens Matter," *Legislative Studies Quarterly* 29 (February 2004): 109–136; Beth Reingold, *Representing Women: Sex, Gender, and Legislative Behavior in Arizona and California* (Chapel Hill: University of North Carolina Press, 2000).

17. Adrienne J. Smith, Beth Reingold, and Miles Owens, "The Political Determinants of Women's Descriptive Representation in Cities," *Political Research Quarterly* 64, no. 2 (2011): 315–329; Bratton and Ray, "Descriptive Representation, Policy Outcomes, and Municipal Day-Care Coverage in Norway."

18. Smith, Reingold, and Owens, "Political Determinants of Women's Descriptive Representation in Cities"; Robert Darcy, Susan Welch, and Janet Clark, *Women, Elections, and Representation* (Lincoln: University of Nebraska Press, 1994); Rebekah Herrick and Susan Welch, "The Impact of At-Large Elections on the Representation of Black and White Women," in *Ethnic Politics and Civil Liberties*, ed. Lucius Barker (New Brunswick, NJ: Transaction, 1992), 62–77; Jessica Trounstine and Melody E. Valdini, "The Context Matters: The Effects of Single-Member versus At-Large Districts on City Council Diversity," *American Journal of Political Science* 52 (2008): 554–569.

19. Kathy Hayes and Chang Semoon, "The Relative Efficiency of City Manager and Mayor-Council Forms of Government," *Southern Economic Journal* 57, no. 1 (1990): 167–177. I estimate the models with both the direct and squared percentages of women on the council to test the possibility of a nonlinear effect. Bratton and Ray, "Descriptive Representation, Policy Outcomes, and Municipal Day-Care Coverage in Norway."

20. Richard C. Feiock and Jae-Hoon Kim, "Form of Government, Administrative Organization, and Local Economic Development Policy," *Journal of Public Administration Research and Theory* 11, no. 1 (2001): 29–50. But for a finding of no clear gender differences in type of city, see Sue Tolleson-Rinehart, "Do Women Leaders Make a Difference: Substance, Style and Perception," in *The Impact of Women in Public Office*, ed. Susan Carroll (Bloomington: University of Indiana Press, 2001), 149–165.

21. Keep in mind that the unit of observation is the percentage of the council's discussion that relates to women's issues, or a city-level observation; thus, there are ninety-six observations.

22. The presence of a ward system has a positive relationship with discussions of women's interests. Other scholarship has found that ward systems lead to a more localized representation of interests. Trounstine and Valdini, "Context Matters," Susan Welch and Albert K. Karnig, "Correlates of Female Office Holding in City Politics," *Journal of Politics* 41, no. 2 (1979): 478–491. The significance of the ward system variable possibly reflects the localized representation of interests. The percentage of the population with a high school diploma has a positive relationship.

23. I promised confidentiality to the leaders in each city and so do not refer to the cities by their name. In addition, I have rounded some of the descriptive characteristics to prevent identification of cities and their leaders.

24. Hayes and Semoon, "The Relative Efficiency of City Manager and Mayor-Council Forms of Government"; Elaine Sharp and Steven Maynard-Moody, "Theories of the Local Welfare Role," *American Journal of Political Science* 35, no. 4 (1991): 934–950.

25. Raymond E. Wolfinger and John Osgood Field, "Political Ethos and the Structure of City Government," *American Political Science Review* 60, no. 2 (1966): 306–326; Pamela S. Tolbert and Lynne G. Zucker, "Institutional Sources

of Change in the Formal Structure of Organizations: The Diffusion of Civil Service Reform, 1880–1935," *Administrative Science Quarterly* 28, no. 1 (1983): 22–39; Rodney E. Hero, "Latinos and Politics in Denver and Pueblo, Colorado: Differences, Explanations, and the 'Steady-State' of the Struggle for Equality," in *Racial Politics in American Cities*, ed. Rufus Browning, Dale Marshall, and David Tabb (New York: Longman, 1997), 247–258.

26. Smith, Reingold, and Owens, "The Political Determinants of Women's Descriptive Representation in Cities."

27. Mayors were asked about their organizational background. In addition, I looked at campaign materials and biographies to supplement the list in Table 3.3.

28. I use a per month measurement, because the councils met at varying frequencies; one council met every week, another met once a month, five councils met every two weeks, and one council met once a month and had an additional, special meeting once a month.

29. Each change is significant in an autoregressive integrated moving average (ARIMA) model; full details are available in Appendix 3C. The exponential decay function is evident as an autocorrelation function (ACF):

$$R = \frac{\sum \left(Y_{t-1} - \overline{Y} \right) \cdot \left(Y_{t-k} - \overline{Y} \right)}{\sum \left(Y_t - \overline{Y} \right)^2}.$$

30. The lack of change in the control city allows me to rule out that a state or regional event prompted the increase in discussion of domestic and sexual violence. The discussions relating to domestic violence over time show a clear decay function (see Appendix 3C), suggesting that being the first female mayor in a city may have an effect. Each change is significant in an ARIMA model; the exponential decay function is evident as an ACF.

31. Patricia Collins, "Learning from the Outsider Within: The Sociological Significance of Black Feminist Thought," *Social Problems* 33, no. 1 (1986): 14–32; Patricia Collins, *Black Feminist Thought: Knowledge, Consciousness, and the Politics of Empowerment* (New York: Routledge, 1990); George T. Felkenes and Jean Reith Schroedel, "A Case Study of Minority Women in Policing," *Women and Criminal Justice* 4, no. 2 (1993): 65–89.

32. The method used was a time-series model with fixed effects.

Chapter 4

1. Benjamin R. Barber, *Strong Democracy: Participatory Politics for a New Age* (Berkeley: University of California Press, 2003); Jane Mansbridge, *Beyond Adversary Democracy* (Chicago: University of Chicago Press, 1983); James A. Morone, *The Democratic Wish: Popular Participation and the Limits of American Government* (New Haven, CT: Yale University Press, 1998); John Stuart

Mill, *Considerations on Representative Government* (Boston: Harper and Brothers, 1862); Jean Jacques Rousseau, *The Social Contract* (New York: Penguin, 1968).

2. Albert O. Hirschman, *Exit, Voice, and Loyalty: Responses to Decline in Firms, Organizations, and States* (Cambridge, MA: Harvard University Press, 1970).

3. Stacy G. Ulbig, "Voice Is Not Enough: The Importance of Influence in Political Trust and Policy Assessments," *Public Opinion Quarterly* 72, no. 3 (2008): 523–539.

4. Groups and group membership are important in promoting participation, because group identity suppresses self-interested behavior. Linnda R. Caporael, Robyn M. Dawes, John M. Orbell, and Alphons J. C. van de Kragt, "Selfishness Examined: Cooperation in the Absence of Egoistic Incentives," *Behavioral and Brain Sciences* 12, no. 4 (1989): 683–699; Katherine McComas, "Theory and Practice of Public Meetings," *Communication Theory* 11, no. 1 (2001): 36–55; William T. Gormley, "The Representation Revolution: Reforming State Regulation through Public Representation," *Administration and Society* 18, no. 2 (1986): 179–196; Kathleen G. Gundry and Thomas A. Heberlein, "Research Report: Do Public Meetings Represent the Public?" *Journal of the American Planning Association* 50, no. 2 (1984): 175–182; Caron Chess and Kristen Purcell, "Public Participation and the Environment: Do We Know What Works?" *Environmental Science and Technology* 33, no. 16 (1999): 2685–2692.

5. Matthew A. Crenson, *Neighborhood Politics* (Cambridge, MA: Harvard University Press, 1983); Brian Adams, "Public Meetings and the Democratic Process," *Public Administration Review* 64, no. 1 (2004): 43–54; Gordana Rabrenovic, *Community Builders: A Tale of Neighborhood Mobilization in Two Cities* (Philadelphia: Temple University Press, 1996).

6. John Logan and Harvey Molotch, *Urban Fortunes: The Political Economy of Place* (Los Angeles: University of California Press, 1987); Jeffrey M. Berry, Kent E. Portney, and Ken Thomson, *The Rebirth of Urban Democracy* (Washington, DC: Brookings Institution, 1993).

7. Stefania Abrar, "Feminist Intervention and Local Domestic Violence Policy," *Parliamentary Affairs* 49, no. 1 (1996): 191–205; Christina Batistich, "Breaking the Silence: A Critical Analysis of Integrating a Community Level Intervention Model within a Domestic Violence Public Awareness Campaign in New Zealand" (master's thesis, Auckland University Technology, 2004); Caroline Andrew, "Getting Women's Issues on the Municipal Agenda: Violence against Women," in *Gender in Urban Research*, ed. Judith Garber and Robyne Turner (New York: Sage, 1995), 99–118; Sue Brownill and Susan Halford, "Understanding Women's Involvement in Local Politics: How Useful Is a Formal/Informal Dichotomy?" *Political Geography Quarterly* 9, no. 4 (1990): 396–414.

8. Carol Gilligan, "In a Different Voice: Women's Conception of the Self and of Morality," *Harvard Educational Review* 47, no. 4 (1977): 481; Lyn Kathlene,

"Uncovering the Political Impacts of Gender: An Exploratory Study," *Political Research Quarterly* 42, no. 3 (1989): 397–421; Lyn Kathlene, "Power and Influence in State Legislative Policymaking: The Interaction of Gender and Position in Committee Hearing Debates," *American Political Science Review* 88 (September 1994): 560–576; Lyn Kathlene, "Alternative Views of Crime: Legislative Policymaking in Gendered Terms," *Journal of Politics* 57, no. 3 (1995): 696–723; Georgia Duerst-Lahti and Cathy Johnson, "Gender and Style in Bureaucracy," *Women and Politics* 10, no. 1 (1990): 67–120; Louise Tilly and Patricia Gurin, *Women, Politics, and Change* (New York: Russell Sage Foundation, 1990); Judy Rosener, "How Women Lead," *Harvard Business Review*, November–December 1990, pp. 119–125; Esther Lang-Takac and Zahava Osterweil, "Separateness and Connectedness: Differences between the Genders," *Sex Roles* 27, no. 1 (1992): 277–289.

9. Denise Antolini, "Women in Local Government: An Overview," in *Political Women: Current Roles in State and Local Government*, ed. Janet Flammang (Beverly Hills, CA: Sage, 1984), 23–40; Susan Abrams Beck, "Rethinking Municipal Governance: Gender Distinctions on Local Councils," in *Gender and Policymaking*, ed. Debra Dodson (Rutgers, NJ: Center for the American Woman and Politics, Eagleton Institute of Politics, 1991), 103–113; Sharyne Merritt, "Sex Differences in Role Behavior and Policy Orientations of Suburban Officeholders: The Effect of Women's Employment," in *Women in Local Politics*, ed. Debra Stewart (London: Scarecrow, 1980), 115–129; Janet Flammang, *Women's Political Voice: How Women Are Transforming the Practice and Study of Politics* (Philadelphia: Temple University Press, 1997); Melissa Marie Deckman, "School Board Candidates and Gender: Ideology, Party, and Policy Concerns," *Journal of Women, Politics and Policy* 28, no. 1 (2007): 87–117.

10. Alice H. Eagly, Mary C. Johannesen-Schmidt, and Marloes L. van Engen, "Transformational, Transactional, and Laissez-Faire Leadership Styles: A Meta-Analysis Comparing Women and Men," *Psychological Bulletin* 129, no. 4 (2003): 569–591; Flammang, *Women's Political Voice*.

11. Alice Eagly and Blair Johnson, "Gender and Leadership Style: A Meta-Analysis," *Psychology Bulletin* 108, no. 2 (1990): 233–256; Janet Flammang, "Female Officials in the Feminist Capital: The Case of Santa Clara County," *Western Political Science Quarterly* 38, no. 1 (1985): 94–118; Kathlene, "Uncovering the Political Impacts of Gender"; Kathlene, "Power and Influence in State Legislative Policymaking"; Kathlene, "Alternative Views of Crime"; Rosener, "How Women Lead"; Tilly and Gurin, *Women, Politics, and Change*.

12. David R. Morgan and Sheilah S. Watson, "The Effects of Mayoral Power on Urban Fiscal Policy," *Policy Studies Journal* 23, no. 2 (1995): 232.

13. Ibid.; James H. Svara, "The Mayor in Council-Manager Cities: Recognizing Leadership Potential," *National Civic Review* 75 (1986): 271–305; James H. Svara, "Mayoral Leadership in Council-Manager Cities: Preconditions versus Preconceptions," *Journal of Politics* 49 (1987): 207–227.

14. Thomas Webler, Seth Tuler, and R.O.B. Krueger, "What Is a Good Public Participation Process? Five Perspectives from the Public," *Environmental Management* 27, no. 3 (2001): 435–450. In the same way, a deliberative process that includes minority groups lends legitimacy to policies produced by the body. John S. Dryzek, "Legitimacy and Economy in Deliberative Democracy," *Political Theory* 29, no. 5 (2001): 651–669. Similarly, Jane Mansbridge argues that deliberative bodies "should ideally include at least one representative who can speak for every group that might provide new information, perspectives, or ongoing insights relevant to the understanding that leads to a decision." "Should Blacks Represent Blacks and Women Represent Women? A Contingent 'Yes,'" *Journal of Politics* 61, no. 3 (1999): 634. Thus, if policies affect women and women are unrepresented in the process, the policies are illegitimate.

15. Paul Peterson, *City Limits* (Chicago: University of Chicago Press, 1981); Jones and Bachelor, *Sustaining Hand*; Berry, Portney, and Thomson, *Rebirth of Urban Democracy*.

16. Barry Checkoway, "The Politics of Public Meetings," *Journal of Applied Behavioral Science* 17, no. 4 (1981): 566–582; Ray Kemp, "Planning, Public Meetings and the Politics of Discourse," in *Critical Theory and Public Life*, ed. John Forester (Cambridge, MA: MIT Press, 1985), 177–201; Gene Rowe and Lynn J. Frewer, "Public Participation Methods: A Framework for Evaluation," *Science, Technology and Human Values* 25, no. 1 (2000): 3–29; Richard L. Cole and David A. Caputo, "The Public Hearing as an Effective Citizen Participation Mechanism: A Case Study of the General Revenue Sharing Program," *American Political Science Review* 78, no. 2 (1984): 404–416.

17. Katherine McComas, "Public Meetings about Local Waste Management Problems: Comparing Participants to Nonparticipants," *Environmental Management* 27, no. 1 (2001): 135–147.

18. Logan and Molotch, *Urban Fortunes*; G. William Domhoff, *Who Rules America? Power and Politics, and Social Change* (Boston: McGraw-Hill, 2006); Floyd Hunter, *Community Power Structure* (Chapel Hill: University of North Carolina Press, 1953); Xinsheng Liu, Eric Lindquist, Arnold Vedlitz, and Kenneth Vincent, "Understanding Local Policymaking: Policy Elites' Perceptions of Local Agenda Setting and Alternative Policy Selection," *Policy Studies Journal* 38, no. 1 (2010): 69–91.

19. Again, I use a per agenda item count to control for the wide-ranging nature of city council meetings.

20. Additional costs may be associated with participation in local politics; many scholars have noted that "participation through normal institutional channels has little impact on the substance of government politics." Ned Crosby, Janet M. Kelly, and Paul Schaefer, "Citizens Panels: A New Approach to Citizen Participation," *Public Administration Review* 46, no. 2 (1986): 172.

21. The average number of public comments is calculated on a per month basis. The difference in the average number of comments per agenda item is significant to the 0.05 level.

22. Iris Marion Young, "Gender as Seriality: Thinking about Women as a Social Collective," *Signs* 19, no. 3 (1994): 713–738; Williams, "The Uneasy Alliance of Group Representation and Deliberative Democracy"; Joan Acker, "From Sex Roles to Gendered Institutions," *Contemporary Sociology* 21, no. 5 (1992): 565–569.

23. Alice Eagly and Mary Johannesen-Schmidt, "The Leadership Styles of Men and Women," *Journal of Social Issues* 57, no. 4 (2001): 781–797; Eagly and Johnson, "Gender and Leadership Style."

24. Malcolm E. Jewell and Marcia Lynn Whicker, *Legislative Leadership in the American States* (Ann Arbor: University of Michigan Press, 1994); Paul Mussen, Stephen Harris, Eldred Rutherford, and Charles B. Keasey, "Honesty and Altruism among Preadolescents," *Developmental Psychology* 3 (1970): 169–194.

25. Tilly and Gurin, *Women, Politics, and Change*, 556; also see Kathlene, "Uncovering the Political Impacts of Gender."

26. Adams, "Public Meetings and the Democratic Process," 52.

27. Tilly and Gurin, *Women, Politics, and Change*, 556; Karen Korabik, Galen L. Baril, and Carol Watson, "Managers' Conflict Management Style and Leadership Effectiveness: The Moderating Effects of Gender," *Sex Roles* 29, nos. 5–6 (1993): 405–420.

28. As before, discussions fall into four general categories: development, general government, quality of life, and women's issues. However, public comments on items of general government were so few that I do not include them in the analysis. Essentially, no one comments when the city council authorizes someone to replace the carpet in the police station or the city clerk to buy a copier.

29. I made transcriptions of video or audio tapes of council meetings and did supplementary newspaper research for background. I counted a comment's number of lines in the typed text of the transcription. A person had multiple comments if they were separated by another person's comments. Speakers were identified by how they described themselves in their comments to the city clerk or by searching the Internet for the speaker's name in conjunction with the event.

30. The actions are different enough to merit some skepticism about their equivalency, but because the two policies serve as examples only, I am comfortable comparing them.

31. James M. Burns, *Leadership* (New York: Harper and Row, 1978); James MacGregor Burns, *Transforming Leadership* (New York: Grove Press, 2004); Kathlene, "Uncovering the Political Impacts of Gender"; Lyn Kathlene, "In a Different Voice: Women and the Policy Process," in *Women and Elective Office: Past, Present and Future*, ed. Sue Thomas and Clyde Wilcox (New York: Oxford University Press, 1998), 188–202; Eagly and Johannesen-Schmidt, "Leadership Styles of Men and Women"; Eagly and Johnson, "Gender and Leadership Style."

32. Eagly and Johnson, "Gender and Leadership Style"; Kathlene, "Alternative Views of Crime."

33. I used websites and city resources to obtain the contact information for the member of each organization and individuals whose names I gleaned from city council minutes. In many circumstances, I had a phone number, and I called the person, explained the purpose of the survey, and e-mailed a survey. See Peter Burns, *Electoral Politics Is Not Enough: Racial and Ethnic Minorities and Urban Politics* (New York: State University of New York Press, 2006); Adams, "Public Meetings and the Democratic Process."

34. This is 73 percent of the total list of names compiled for cities with a female mayor; 68 percent for those with a male mayor. The difference is not statistically different.

35. Stefania Abrar, Joni Lovenduski, and Helen Margetts, "Sexing London: The Gender Mix of Urban Policy Actors," *International Political Science Review* 19, no. 2 (1998): 147–171.

36. Community members were asked the same question about local officials and the city council; significant differences between male- and female-governed cities do not emerge in their answers.

37. To calculate the rate of public comments from organization members, I compared my list of individuals' names to a list of those who commented at the meetings; each comment was coded as either from an organization member (1) or not (0).

38. Logan and Molotch, *Urban Fortunes*; Domhoff, *Who Rules America?*; Hunter, *Community Power Structure*.

39. Abrar, "Feminist Intervention and Local Domestic Violence Policy"; Suzanne Dovi, "Preferable Descriptive Representatives: Will Just Any Woman, Black, or Latino Do?" *American Political Science Review* 96, no. 4 (2002): 729–744; Brownill and Halford, "Understanding Women's Involvement in Local Politics."

40. Clarence N. Stone, "Urban Regimes and the Capacity to Govern: A Political Economy Approach," *Journal of Urban Affairs* 15, no. 1 (1993): 1–28; Logan and Molotch, *Urban Fortunes*.

41. Coding of tone is similar to methods used to code newspaper articles, public comments, or political debates. Joseph Phelps, William Gonzenbach, and Edward Johnson, "Press Coverage and Public Perception of Direct Marketing and Consumer Privacy," *Journal of Direct Marketing* 8, no. 2 (1994): 9–22.

42. The full list of possible groups is whites, blacks, Hispanics, Asians, women, men, liberals, conservatives, independents, business owners, developers, property owners, feminists, middle class, poor, rich, people at one's place of worship, people in one's neighborhood, people at one's place of work, and Americans in general.

43. Hirschman, *Exit, Voice, and Loyalty*.

44. Miki Caul Kittilson, *Challenging Parties, Changing Parliaments: Women and Elected Office in Contemporary Western Europe* (Columbus: Ohio State University Press, 2006); Richard L. Fox and Jennifer L. Lawless, "If Only They'd Ask: Gender, Recruitment, and Political Ambition," *Journal of Politics* 72, no. 2 (2010): 310–326; Jennifer L. Lawless and Richard L. Fox, *It Takes a*

Candidate: Why Women Don't Run for Office (New York: Cambridge University Press, 2005); Jennifer L. Lawless and Richard L. Fox, *It Still Takes a Candidate: Why Women Don't Run for Office* (New York: Cambridge University Press, 2010); Pippa Norris and Joni Lovenduski, *Political Recruitment: Gender, Race and Class in the British Parliament* (New York: Cambridge University Press, 1995); Leslie Schwindt-Bayer, "Women Who Win: Social Backgrounds, Paths to Power, and Political Ambition in Latin American Legislatures," *Politics and Gender* 7, no. 1 (2011): 1–33.

45. Fox and Lawless, "If Only They'd Ask"; Lawless and Fox, *It Takes a Candidate*.

46. Jeffrey Koch, "Candidate Gender and Women's Psychological Engagement in Politics," *American Politics Quarterly* 25, no. 1 (1997): 118–133; Sidney Verba, Nancy Burns, and Kay Lehman Schlozman, "Knowing and Caring about Politics: Gender and Political Engagement," *Journal of Politics* 59, no. 4 (1997): 1051–1072; Sarah A. Fulton, Cherie D. Maestas, L. Sandy Maisel, and Walter J. Stone, "The Sense of a Woman: Gender, Ambition, and the Decision to Run for Congress," *Political Research Quarterly* 59, no. 2 (2006): 235–248; Timothy Bledsoe and Susan Welch, "Patterns of Political Party Activity among U.S. Cities," *Urban Affairs Review* 23, no. 2 (1987): 249–269; Kira Sanbonmatsu, "Political Parties and the Recruitment of Women to State Legislatures," *Journal of Politics* 64, no. 3 (2002): 791–809.

47. Fulton, Maestas, Maisel, and Stone, "Sense of a Woman"; Sarah F. Anzia and Christopher R. Berry, "The Jackie (and Jill) Robinson Effect: Why Do Congresswomen Outperform Congressmen?" *American Journal of Political Science* 55, no. 3 (2011): 478–493.

Chapter 5

1. U.S. Census Bureau, "Local Government Finances by Type of Government and State: 2006–07," in *2007 Census of Governments: Finance* (Washington, DC: U.S. Census Bureau, 2007).

2. Frank R. Baumgartner and Bryan D. Jones, *Agendas and Instability in American Politics*, American Politics and Political Economy Series (Chicago: University of Chicago Press, 1993).

3. Ibid.

4. Dale Krane, Planton Rigos, and Melvin Hill, *Home Rule in America: A Fifty-State Handbook* (Washington, DC: CQ Press, 2001); G. Ross Stephens, "State Centralization and the Erosion of Local Autonomy," *Journal of Politics* 36, no. 1 (1974): 44–76; Wallace Oates, *Fiscal Federalism* (New York: Harcourt Brace Jovanovich, 1972); Wallace Oates, "An Essay on Fiscal Federalism," *Journal of Economic Literature* 37, no. 3 (1999): 1120–1149.

5. James M. Buchanan, "Principles of Urban Fiscal Strategy," *Public Choice* 11 (1971): 1–16; Charles Tiebout, "A Pure Theory of Local Expenditures," *Journal of Political Economy* 64 (1956): 416–424.

6. Paul Peterson, *City Limits* (Chicago: University of Chicago Press, 1981); Paul Kantor, *The Dependent City Revisited: The Political Economy of Urban Development and Social Policy* (Boulder, CO: Westview Press, 1995).

7. Larry Isaac and William R. Kelly, "Racial Insurgency, the State, and Welfare Expansion: Local and National Level Evidence from the Postwar United States," *American Journal of Sociology* 86, no. 6 (1981): 1348–1386; Elaine Sharp and Steven Maynard-Moody, "Theories of the Local Welfare Role," *American Journal of Political Science* 35, no. 4 (1991): 934–950.

8. Clarence N. Stone, *Regime Politics: Governing Atlanta, 1946–1988*, Studies in Government and Public Policy (Lawrence: University Press of Kansas, 1989).

9. See, for example, U.S. Census Bureau, "Local Government Finances by Type of Government and State: 2006–07."

10. Kathleen Bratton and Leonard Ray, "Descriptive Representation, Policy Outcomes, and Municipal Day-Care Coverage in Norway," *American Journal of Political Science* 46, no. 2 (2002): 428 (italics in original).

11. As in earlier chapters, I have aggregated the policy areas into general government, development, quality of life, and urban women's issues.

12. The dependent variable is the preferences averaged across the subtopic area, which makes the variable continuous and OLS regression appropriate. Including the preferable descriptive representation variable in the model improves the model on current spending on women's issues but is not significant in the other models.

13. The data on the gendered composition of municipal leadership were collected through a combination of consulting a city's website (when available) and calling city clerks.

14. As previously discussed, the fiscal condition of the city influences funding of redistributive programs, so the revenues raised per capita and the per capita grant revenue are controlled for in many models. Per capita grant revenue is the per capita dollars that the city receives from grants. Peterson, *City Limits*. The economic state of residents can influence demand for urban women's issue programs and the city's ability to provide them. Similarly, racial diversity influences local provision of social services. Michael Craw, "Deciding to Provide: Local Decisions on Providing Social Welfare," *American Journal of Political Science* 54, no. 4 (2010): 906–920; Michael Craw, "Overcoming City Limits: Vertical and Horizontal Models of Local Redistributive Policy Making," *Social Science Quarterly* 87, no. 2 (2006): 361–379; Mitchell Chamlin, "General Assistance among Cities: An Examination of the Need, Economic Threat, and Benign Neglect Hypotheses," *Social Science Quarterly* 68 (1987): 834–846. The type of government (council-manager or mayor-council) is also accounted for and interacted with the presence of a female mayor and women on the council.

15. Peterson, *City Limits*; Karen Kaufmann, *The Urban Voter* (Ann Arbor: University of Michigan Press, 2004).

16. In the first, a logit model predicts whether a city will fund programs related to women's issues, and in the second, a left-truncated tobit model looks at only those with funding.

17. The percentage of the city that is nonwhite also has a significant, positive relationship with participation in women's issue programs, as does reliance on public assistance funding and the log of the population, meaning that as a city becomes more diverse, more reliant on social services, and larger, this has a positive relationship with the decision to provide women's urban issue programs. Analysis of the three-hundred-city sample finds similar results.

18. The substantive effects for the interactive terms were calculated using the linear combinations of estimators (lincom) command in the computer program Stata, which computes point estimates and significance for interactive terms.

19. Funding for welfare programs is estimated *only* for those cities that have them, which reduces the number of observations but avoids problems with modeling data with excessive zeros.

20. Drude Dahlerup, "The Story of the Theory of Critical Mass," *Politics and Gender* 2, no. 4 (2006): 511–522; Bratton and Ray, "Descriptive Representation, Policy Outcomes, and Municipal Day-Care Coverage in Norway"; Manon Tremblay, "The Substantive Representation of Women and PR: Some Reflections on the Role of Surrogate Representation and Critical Mass," *Politics and Gender* 2, no. 4 (2006): 502–511.

21. Karen Beckwith and Kimberly Cowell-Meyers, "Sheer Numbers: Critical Representation Thresholds and Women's Political Representation," *PS: Political Science and Politics* 5, no. 3 (2007): 553–565.

22. Grace Hall Saltzstein, "Female Mayors and Women in Municipal Jobs," *American Journal of Political Science* 30, no. 1 (1986): 140–164. See also Joshua Behr, "Black and Female Municipal Employment: A Substantive Benefit of Minority Political Incorporation?" *Journal of Urban Affairs* 22, no. 3 (2000): 243–264; Paula D. McClain, "The Changing Dynamics of Urban Politics: Black and Hispanic Municipal Employment—Is There Competition?" *Journal of Politics* 55, no. 2 (1993): 399–414; Peter K. Eisinger, "Black Employment in Municipal Jobs: The Impact of Black Political Power," *American Political Science Review* 76, no. 2 (1982): 380–392; Bratton and Ray, "Descriptive Representation, Policy Outcomes, and Municipal Day-Care Coverage in Norway."

23. Replicating the model with data from the hundred-city sample finds very similar results. See Table 5A.1.

24. Roger Friedland, Frances Fox Piven, and Robert R. Alford, "Political Conflict, Urban Structure, and the Fiscal Crisis," *International Journal of Urban and Regional Research* 1, nos. 1–4 (1977): 447–471; William A. Fischel, "Property Taxation and the Tiebout Model: Evidence for the Benefit View from Zoning and Voting," *Journal of Economic Literature* 30, no. 1 (1992): 171–177; Tiebout, "A Pure Theory of Local Expenditures"; Oates, *Fiscal Federalism*,

Oates, "An Essay on Fiscal Federalism"; Clarence N. Stone, "Urban Regimes and the Capacity to Govern: A Political Economy Approach", *Journal of Urban Affairs* 15, no. 1 (1993): 1–28; Stone, *Regime Politics*.

25. Measuring loans and borrowing is difficult, because I coded only data from the general expenditures budget, and often bonds are separated into a different budget, particularly if they are used for a capital project. Thus, the dependent variable here is the per capita amount from the general budget spent on debt payments.

26. A mayor-council system, population, median income, public assistance use in the population, percentage of nonwhite population (see Table 5.2, columns 2 and 4), and 2007 rate of spending all have a positive relationship with spending.

27. Michael Craw, "Overcoming City Limits: Vertical and Horizontal Models of Local Redistributive Policy Making," *Social Science Quarterly* 87, no. 2 (2006): 361–379; Craw, "Deciding to Provide"; Kantor, *Dependent City Revisited*. Many scholars have argued that using intergovernmental and grant funds for city expenditures on social service programs is a faulty strategy, because intergovernmental dollars come with strings and high administrative costs or are not a fixed amount of money. Robert M. Stein, "Federal Categorical Aid: Equalization and the Application Process," *Western Political Science Quarterly* 32 (1979): 396–408. Also see Robert M. Stein, "Municipal Public Employment: An Examination of Intergovernmental Influences," *American Journal of Political Science* 28, no. 4 (1984): 636–653.

28. Michael P. Brown, "The Possibility of Local Autonomy," *Urban Geography* 13, no. 3 (1992): 257–279; Stephens, "State Centralization and the Erosion of Local Autonomy"; Stein, "Municipal Public Employment."

29. Robert E. Deyle and Richard A. Smith, "Local Government Compliance with State Planning Mandates: The Effects of State Implementation in Florida," *Journal of the American Planning Association* 64, no. 4 (1998): 457–469; Richard K. Norton, "More and Better Local Planning: State-Mandated Local Planning in Coastal North Carolina," *Journal of the American Planning Association* 71, no. 1 (2005): 55–71; David R. Berman, *Local Government and the States: Autonomy, Politics, and Policy* (Armonk, NY: M. E. Sharpe, 2003).

30. Lael R. Keiser, Vicky M. Wilkins, Kenneth J. Meier, and Catherine A. Holland, "Lipstick and Logarithms: Gender, Institutional Context, and Representative Bureaucracy," *American Political Science Review* 96, no. 3 (2002): 553–564; Julie Dolan, "The Senior Executive Service: Gender, Attitudes, and Representative Bureaucracy," *Journal of Public Administration Research and Theory* 10, no. 3 (2000): 513–530; Kenneth J. Meier and Jill Nicholson-Crotty, "Gender, Representative Bureaucracy, and Law Enforcement: The Case of Sexual Assault," *Public Administration Review* 66, no. 6 (2006): 850–860; Richard Fox and Robert Schuhmann, "Gender of Local Government: A Comparison of Women and Men City Managers," *Public Administration Review* 59, no. 3 (1999): 231–242.

Chapter 6

1. The mayors' names are changed.

2. Lynne A. Weikart, Greg Chen, Daniel W. Williams, and Haris Hromic, "The Democratic Sex: Gender Differences and the Exercise of Power," *Journal of Women, Politics and Policy* 28, no. 1 (2007): 119–140.

3. Carol Gilligan, *In a Different Voice: Psychological Theory and Women's Development* (Cambridge, MA: Harvard University Press, 1982); Lyn Kathlene, "Power and Influence in State Legislative Policymaking: The Interaction of Gender and Position in Committee Hearing Debates," *American Political Science Review* 88, no. 3 (1994): 560–576; Lyn Kathlene, "Alternative Views of Crime: Legislative Policymaking in Gendered Terms," *Journal of Politics* 57, no. 3 (1995): 696–723; Lyn Kathlene, "Position Power versus Gender Power: Who Holds the Floor?" in *Gender Power, Leadership, and Governance*, ed. Georgia Duerst-Lahti and Rita Mae Kelly (Ann Arbor: University of Michigan Press, 1995), 167–194; Lyn Kathlene, "In a Different Voice: Women and the Policy Process," in *Women and Elective Office: Past, Present and Future*, ed. Sue Thomas and Clyde Wilcox (New York: Oxford University Press, 1998), 188–202.

4. Gilligan, *In a Different Voice*, 105.

5. Michele Swers, "Are Congresswomen More Likely to Vote for Women's Issue Bills than Their Male Colleagues?" *Legislative Studies Quarterly* 23, no. 4 (1998): 435–448; Michele Swers, "Understanding the Policy Impact of Electing Women: Evidence from Research on Congress and State Legislatures," *PS: Political Science and Politics* 34, no. 2 (2001): 217–220; Michele Swers and Carin Larson, "Women in Congress: Do They Act as Advocates for Women's Issues?" in *Women and Elective Office*, ed. Sue Thomas and Clyde Wilcox (New York: Oxford University Press, 2005), 110–128; Barbara Burrell, *A Woman's Place in the House: Campaigning for Congress in the Feminist Era* (Ann Arbor: University of Michigan Press, 1994); Susan J. Carroll, "Woman Candidates and Support for Feminist Concerns: The Closet Feminist Syndrome," *Western Political Science Quarterly* 37, no. 2 (1984): 307–323; Susan Welch, "Are Women More Liberal than Men in the U.S. Congress?" *Legislative Studies Quarterly* 10, no. 1 (1985): 125–134; Michele Swers, *The Difference Women Make: The Policy Impact of Women in Congress* (Chicago: University of Chicago Press, 2002); Arturo Vega and Juanita M. Firestone, "The Effects of Gender on Congressional Behavior and the Substantive Representation of Women," *Legislative Studies Quarterly* 20, no. 2 (1995): 213–222; Julie Dolan, "Support for Women's Interests in the 103rd Congress: The Distinct Impact of Congressional Women," *Women and Politics* 18, no. 1 (1997): 81–94.

6. Paul Peterson, *City Limits* (Chicago: University of Chicago Press, 1981); Wallace Oates, *Fiscal Federalism* (New York: Harcourt Brace Jovanovich, 1972); Wallace E. Oates, "An Essay on Fiscal Federalism," *Journal of Economic Literature* 37, no. 3 (1999): 1120–1149; Avinash Dixit and John Londregan, "Fiscal Federalism and Redistributive Politics," *Journal of Public Economics* 68, no. 2

(1998): 153–180; Charles Tiebout, "A Pure Theory of Local Expenditures," *Journal of Political Economy* 64 (1956): 416–424.

7. Peterson, *City Limits*; Oates, *Fiscal Federalism*.

8. Peter Burns, *Electoral Politics Is Not Enough: Racial and Ethnic Minorities and Urban Politics* (New York: State University of New York Press, 2006); Clarence N. Stone, *Regime Politics: Governing Atlanta, 1946–1988*, Studies in Government and Public Policy (Lawrence: University Press of Kansas, 1989); Karen Mossberger and Gary Stoker, "The Evolution of Urban Regime Theory: The Challenges of Conceptualization," *Urban Affairs Review* 36 (2001): 810–835.

9. Stone, *Regime Politics*; Clarence N. Stone, "Urban Regimes and the Capacity to Govern: A Political Economy Approach," *Journal of Urban Affairs* 15, no. 1 (1993): 1–28.

10. Nancy Elizabeth Burns and Paul Schumaker, "Gender Differences in Attitudes about the Role of Local Government," *Social Science Quarterly* 68, no. 1 (1987): 138–148.

11. Richard E. DeLeon, "The Urban Antiregime," *Urban Affairs Review* 27, no. 4 (1992): 555–579; Joel Rast, "Governing the Regimeless City," *Urban Affairs Review* 42, no. 1 (2006): 81–112.

12. Peter Burns and Matthew O. Thomas, "The Failure of the Nonregime," *Urban Affairs Review* 41, no. 4 (2006): 517–527.

13. Clarence N. Stone, "Systemic Power in Community Decision Making: A Restatement of Stratification Theory," *American Political Science Review* 74, no. 4 (1980): 987; Louise Jezierski, "Class and Inequality in the City," in *Handbook of Research on Urban Politics and Policy in the United States*, ed. Ronald K. Vogel (Westport, CT: Greenwood, 1997), 90–106.

14. Burns and Thomas, "Failure of the Nonregime," 519.

15. John Logan and Harvey Molotch, *Urban Fortunes: The Political Economy of Place* (Los Angeles: University of California Press, 1987); Allan Cochrane, "Redefining Urban Politics for the Twenty-First Century," in *The Urban Growth Machine: Critical Perspectives Two Decades Later*, ed. Andrew E. G. Jonas and David Wilson (Albany: State University of New York Press, 1999), 109–124; Floyd Hunter, *Community Power Structure* (Chapel Hill: University of North Carolina Press, 1953).

16. Hunter, *Community Power Structure*, 82.

17. Sue Thomas, "Effects of Race and Gender on Constituency Service," *Western Political Quarterly* 45, no. 1 (1992): 170; Richard Fox and Robert Schuhmann, "Gender of Local Government: A Comparison of Women and Men City Managers," *Public Administration Review* 59, no. 3 (1999): 231–242; Janet Flammang, *Women's Political Voice: How Women Are Transforming the Practice and Study of Politics* (Philadelphia: Temple University Press, 1997); Irene Diamond, *Sex Roles in the State House* (New Haven, CT: Yale University Press, 1977); Thomas, "Effects of Race and Gender on Constituency Service"; Susan Abrams Beck, "Rethinking Municipal Governance: Gender Distinctions on Local Councils," in *Gender and Policymaking*, ed. Debra Dodson (Rutgers,

NJ: Center for the American Woman and Politics, Eagleton Institute of Politics, 1991), 103–113.

18. Albert O. Hirschman, *Exit, Voice, and Loyalty: Responses to Decline in Firms, Organizations, and States* (Cambridge, MA: Harvard University Press, 1970); Benjamin R. Barber, *Strong Democracy: Participatory Politics for a New Age* (Berkeley: University of California Press, 2003); Arend Lijphart, "Unequal Participation: Democracy's Unresolved Dilemma," *American Political Science Review* 91, no. 1 (1997): 1–14.

19. Peterson, *City Limits*; Oates, *Fiscal Federalism*; Oates, "An Essay on Fiscal Federalism"; Dixit and Londregan, "Fiscal Federalism and Redistributive Politics"; Tiebout, "A Pure Theory of Local Expenditures."

20. Difference in support of male and female mayors is significant to the 0.05 level on both approval and support among the development group.

21. Difference in support of male and female mayors is significant to the 0.05 level on both approval and support among the women's issues group.

22. Tom R. Tyler and Andrew Caine, "The Influence of Outcomes and Procedures on Satisfaction with Formal Leaders," *Journal of Personality and Social Psychology* 41, no. 4 (1981): 642–655; Tom R. Tyler, Kenneth A. Rasinski, and Kathleen M. McGraw, "The Influence of Perceived Injustice on the Endorsement of Political Leaders," *Journal of Applied Social Psychology* 15, no. 8 (1985): 700–725.

23. Hirschman, *Exit, Voice, and Loyalty*, 30.

24. Ibid.; Stacy G. Ulbig, "Voice Is Not Enough: The Importance of Influence in Political Trust and Policy Assessments," *Public Opinion Quarterly* 72, no. 3 (2008): 523–539; John R. Hibbing and Elizabeth Theiss-Morse, *Stealth Democracy: Americans' Beliefs about How Government Should Work* (New York: Cambridge University Press, 2002); Elizabeth Theiss-Morse and John R. Hibbing, "Citizenship and Civic Engagement," *Annual Review of Political Science* 8 (2005): 227–249.

25. Melissa Marie Deckman, "Gender Differences in the Decision to Run for School Board," *American Politics Research* 35, no. 4 (2007): 541.

26. Sarah A. Fulton, Cherie D. Maestas, L. Sandy Maisel, and Walter J. Stone, "The Sense of a Woman: Gender, Ambition, and the Decision to Run for Congress," *Political Research Quarterly* 59, no. 2 (2006): 235–248; Richard L. Fox and Jennifer L. Lawless, "To Run or Not to Run for Office: Explaining Nascent Political Ambition," *American Journal of Political Science* 49, no. 3 (2005): 642–659; Jennifer L. Lawless and Richard L. Fox, *It Still Takes a Candidate: Why Women Don't Run for Office* (New York: Cambridge University Press, 2010).

27. Beth Reingold, "Women as Officeholders: Linking Descriptive and Substantive Representation," in *Political Women and American Democracy*, ed. Christina Wolbrecht, Karen Beckwith, and Lisa Baldez (New York: Cambridge University Press, 2008), 129.

28. Adrienne J. Smith, "'Cities Where Women Rule': Female Political Incorporation and the Allocation of Community Development Block Grant Funding" (paper presented at the American Political Science Association annual meeting,

September 2010); Grace Hall Saltzstein, "Female Mayors and Women in Municipal Jobs," *American Journal of Political Science* 30, no. 1 (1986): 140–164; Brinck Kerr, Will Miller, and Margaret Reid, "Determinants of Female Employment Patterns in U.S. Cities," *Urban Affairs Review* 33, no. 4 (1998): 559–578; Jesse Donahue, "The Non Representation of Gender," *Women and Politics* 20, no. 3 (1999): 65–81; Jesse Donahue, "It Doesn't Matter: Some Cautionary Findings about Sex and Representation from School Committee Conversations," *Policy Studies Journal* 25, no. 4 (1997): 630–647; Beck, "Rethinking Municipal Governance"; Beck, "Gender and the Politics of Affordable Housing," in *Gender in Urban Research*, ed. Judith Garber and Robyne Turner (New York: Sage, 1995), 123.

Appendix 2

1. Irene Diamond, *Sex Roles in the State House* (New Haven, CT: Yale University Press, 1977); Sue Thomas, *How Women Legislate* (London: Oxford University Press, 1994); Sue Thomas and Susan Welch, "The Impact of Gender on Activities and Priorities of State Legislators," *Western Political Quarterly* 44, no. 2 (1991): 445–456; Carol Hardy-Fanta, Christine Marie Sierra, Pei-te Lien, Dianne M. Pinderhughes, and Wartyna L. Davis, "Race, Gender, and Descriptive Representation: An Exploratory View of Multicultural Elected Leadership in the United States" (paper presented at the American Political Science Association annual meeting, Washington, DC, September 2005); Cara Wong, *Group Closeness—1997 National Election Study Pilot Report*, no. nes008587 (Ann Arbor, MI: American National Election Studies, 1998); Patricia Johnston Conover, "The Role of Social Groups in Political Thinking," *British Journal of Political Science* 18, no. 1 (1988): 51–76; Patricia Johnston Conover, "Feminists and the Gender Gap," *Journal of Politics* 50, no. 4 (1988): 985–1010.

Bibliography

Abrar, Stefania. "Feminist Intervention and Local Domestic Violence Policy." *Parliamentary Affairs* 49, no. 1 (1996): 191–205.

Abrar, Stefania, Joni Lovenduski, and Helen Margetts. "Feminist Ideas and Domestic Violence Policy Change." *Political Studies* 48, no. 2 (2000): 239–262.

———. "Sexing London: The Gender Mix of Urban Policy Actors." *International Political Science Review* 19, no. 2 (1998): 147–171.

Acker, Joan. "From Sex Roles to Gendered Institutions." *Contemporary Sociology* 21, no. 5 (1992): 565–569.

Adams, Brian. "Public Meetings and the Democratic Process." *Public Administration Review* 64, no. 1 (2004): 43–54.

Addams, Jane. *A New Conscience and an Ancient Evil.* New York: Macmillan, 1912. Available at http://www.gutenberg.org/files/15221/15221-h/15221-h.htm.

Adrian, Charles R. "A Typology for Nonpartisan Elections." *Western Political Science Quarterly* 12, no. 2 (1959): 449–458.

Alozie, Nicholas O., and Catherine McNamara. "Gender Differences in Willingness to Pay for Urban Public Services." *Urban Affairs Review* 45, no. 3 (2010): 377–390.

American National Election Studies. *The ANES Guide to Public Opinion and Electoral Behavior.* Ann Arbor: University of Michigan Center for Political Studies, 1982–2008.

Andersen, Kristi. "The Gender Gap and Experiences with the Welfare State." *PS: Political Science and Politics* 32, no. 1 (1999): 17–19.

Andrew, Caroline. "Getting Women's Issues on the Municipal Agenda: Violence against Women." In *Gender in Urban Research*, edited by Judith Garber and Robyne Turner, 99–118. New York: Sage, 1995.

Antolini, Denise. "Women in Local Government: An Overview." In *Political Women: Current Roles in State and Local Government*, edited by Janet Flammang, 23–40. Beverly Hills, CA: Sage, 1984.

Anzia, Sarah F., and Christopher R. Berry. "The Jackie (and Jill) Robinson Effect: Why Do Congresswomen Outperform Congressmen?" *American Journal of Political Science* 55, no. 3 (2011): 478–493.

Appleton, Lynn. "The Gender Regimes of American Cities." In *Gender in Urban Research*, edited by Judith Garber and Robyne Turner, 44–59. Thousand Oaks, CA: Sage, 1995.

Baker, Paula. "The Domestication of Politics: Women and American Political Society, 1780–1920." *American Historical Review* 89, no. 3 (1984): 620–647.

Barber, Benjamin R. *Strong Democracy: Participatory Politics for a New Age.* Berkeley: University of California Press, 2003.

Batistich, Christina. "Breaking the Silence: A Critical Analysis of Integrating a Community Level Intervention Model within a Domestic Violence Public Awareness Campaign in New Zealand." Master's thesis, Auckland University Technology, 2004.

Baumgartner, Frank R., and Bryan D. Jones. *Agendas and Instability in American Politics.* American Politics and Political Economy Series. Chicago: University of Chicago Press, 1993.

Beard, Mary Ritter. *Woman's Work in Municipalities.* New York: D. Appleton, 1915.

Beck, Susan Abrams. "Acting as Women: The Effects and Limitations of Gender in Local Governance." In *The Impact of Women in Public Office*, edited by Susan Carroll, 49–67. Bloomington: Indiana University Press, 2001.

———. "Gender and the Politics of Affordable Housing." In *Gender in Urban Research*, edited by Judith Garber and Robyne Turner, 119–135. New York: Sage, 1995.

———. "Rethinking Municipal Governance: Gender Distinctions on Local Councils." In *Gender and Policymaking*, edited by Debra Dodson, 103–113. Rutgers, NJ: Center for American Women and Politics, Eagleton Institute of Politics, 1991.

Beckwith, Karen, and Kimberly Cowell-Meyers. "Sheer Numbers: Critical Representation Thresholds and Women's Political Representation." *PS: Political Science and Politics* 5, no. 3 (2007): 553–565.

Beer, Janet, and Katherine Joslin. "Diseases of the Body Politic: White Slavery in Jane Addams' *A New Conscience and an Ancient Evil* and Selected Short Stories by Charlotte Perkins Gilman." *Journal of American Studies* 33, no. 1 (1999): 1–18.

Behr, Joshua. "Black and Female Municipal Employment: A Substantive Benefit of Minority Political Incorporation?" *Journal of Urban Affairs* 22, no. 3 (2000): 243–264.

Berg, Barbara J. *The Remembered Gate: Origins of American Feminism; The Woman and the City, 1800–1860.* New York: Oxford University Press, 1978.

Berman, David R. *Local Government and the States: Autonomy, Politics, and Policy.* Armonk, NY: M. E. Sharpe, 2003.

Berman, David R., and Lawrence L. Martin. "State-Local Relations: An Examination of Local Discretion." *Public Administration Review* 48, no. 2 (1988): 637–641.

Berry, Jeffrey M., Kent E. Portney, and Ken Thomson. *The Rebirth of Urban Democracy.* Washington, DC: Brookings Institution, 1993.

Billington, Monroe. "Susanna Madora Salter: First Woman Mayor." *Kansas Historical Quarterlies* 21, no. 3 (1954): 173–183.

Birmingham, Stephen. *The Grandes Dames.* New York: Simon and Schuster, 1982.

Blair, Karen J. *The Clubwoman as Feminist: True Womanhood Redefined, 1868–1914.* New York: Holmes and Meier, 1980.

Bledsoe, Timothy, and Susan Welch. "Patterns of Political Party Activity among U.S. Cities." *Urban Affairs Review* 23, no. 2 (1987): 249–269.

Bloch, Ruth H. "The Gendered Meanings of Virtue in Revolutionary America." *Signs* 13, no. 1 (1987): 37–58.

Boles, Janet. "Local Elected Women and Policy-Making: Movement Delegates or Feminist Trustees?" In *The Impact of Women in Public Office,* edited by Susan Carroll, 68–88. Bloomington: Indiana University, 2001.

———. "A Policy of Our Own: Local Feminist Networks and Social Services for Women and Children." *Review of Policy Research* 8, no. 3 (1989): 638–647.

Bondi, Liz. "Gender, Class, and Urban Space: Public and Private Space in Contemporary Urban Landscapes." *Urban Geography* 19, no. 2 (1998): 160–185.

Boris, Eileen. "Reconstructing the 'Family': Women, Progressive Reform, and the Problem of Social Control." In *Gender, Class, Race, and Reform in the Progressive Era,* edited by Noralee Frankel and Nancy Dye, 73–86. Lexington: University Press of Kentucky, 1991.

Bostrom, Meg. "Education, Gender and Race: A Review of Current Public Opinion." 2000. Available at http://www.buildinitiative.org/portals/0/uploads/documents/resource-center/educationgenderandrace.pdf.

Bowlker, Mrs. T. J. "Women's Home-Making Function Applied to the Municipality." *American City* 6 (1912): 863–869.

Boylan, Anne M. *The Origins of Women's Activism: New York and Boston, 1797–1840.* Chapel Hill: University of North Carolina Press, 2002.

Bratton, Kathleen, and Leonard Ray. "Descriptive Representation, Policy Outcomes, and Municipal Day-Care Coverage in Norway." *American Journal of Political Science* 46, no. 2 (2002): 428–437.

Brown, Michael P. "The Possibility of Local Autonomy." *Urban Geography* 13, no. 3 (1992): 257–279.

Brownill, Sue, and Susan Halford. "Understanding Women's Involvement in Local Politics: How Useful Is a Formal/Informal Dichotomy?" *Political Geography Quarterly* 9, no. 4 (1990): 396–414.

Browning, Rufus, Dale Marshall, and David Tabb. *Protest Is Not Enough.* Berkeley: University of California Press, 1984.

———. *Racial Politics in American Cities.* New York: Longman, 2003.

Buchanan, James M. "Principles of Urban Fiscal Strategy." *Public Choice* 11 (1971): 1–16.

Bullock, Charles. "The Election of Blacks in the South: Preconditions and Consequences." *American Journal of Political Science* 19, no. 4 (1975): 727–739.

Bureau of Justice Statistics. "Intimate Partner Violence, 1993–2010." November 2012. Available at http://www.bjs.gov/content/pub/pdf/ipv9310.pdf.

Burns, James M. *Leadership.* New York: Harper and Row, 1978.

———. *Transforming Leadership.* New York: Grove Press, 2004.

Burns, Nancy Elizabeth, and Paul Schumaker. "Gender Differences in Attitudes about the Role of Local Government." *Social Science Quarterly* 68, no. 1 (1987): 138–148.

Burns, Peter. *Electoral Politics Is Not Enough: Racial and Ethnic Minorities and Urban Politics.* New York: State University of New York Press, 2006.

Burns, Peter, and Matthew O. Thomas. "The Failure of the Nonregime." *Urban Affairs Review* 41, no. 4 (2006): 517–527.

Burrell, Barbara. *A Woman's Place in the House: Campaigning for Congress in the Feminist Era.* Ann Arbor: University of Michigan Press, 1994.

Button, James. *Blacks and Social Change: Impact of the Civil Rights Movement in Southern Communities.* Princeton, NJ: Princeton University Press, 1989.

Caporael, Linnda R., Robyn M. Dawes, John M. Orbell, and Alphons J. C. van de Kragt. "Selfishness Examined: Cooperation in the Absence of Egoistic Incentives." *Behavioral and Brain Sciences* 12, no. 4 (1989): 683–699.

Carroll, Susan J., ed. *The Impact of Women in Public Office.* Bloomington: University of Indiana Press, 2001.

———. "Woman Candidates and Support for Feminist Concerns: The Closet Feminist Syndrome." *Western Political Science Quarterly* 37, no. 2 (1984): 307–323.

Casper, Lynne M., Sara S. McLanahan, and Irwin Garfinkel. "The Gender-Poverty Gap: What We Can Learn from Other Countries." *American Sociological Review* 59, no. 4 (1994): 594–605.

Center for American Women and Politics. *Women Mayors in U.S. Cities 2007.* New Brunswick, NJ: CAWP, Eagleton Institute of Politics, 2007.

———. *Women Mayors in U.S. Cities 2011.* New Brunswick, NJ: CAWP, Eagleton Institute of Politics, 2011.

Centers for Medicare and Medicaid Services. "Medicaid Eligibles Demographics, Selected Fiscal Years." In *Data Compendium.* Washington, DC: Centers for Medicare and Medicaid Services, 2010. Available at http://www.cms .gov/Research-Statistics-Data-and-Systems/Statistics-Trends-and-Reports/ DataCompendium/14_2010_Data_Compendium.html.

Chamlin, Mitchell. "General Assistance among Cities: An Examination of the Need, Economic Threat, and Benign Neglect Hypotheses." *Social Science Quarterly* 68 (1987): 834–846.

Chattopadhyay, Raghabendra, and Esther Duflo. "Women as Policy Makers: Evidence from a Randomized Policy Experiment in India." *Econometrica* 72, no. 5 (2004): 1409–1443.

Checkoway, Barry. "The Politics of Public Meetings." *Journal of Applied Behavioral Science* 17, no. 4 (1981): 566–582.

Chess, Caron, and Kristen Purcell. "Public Participation and the Environment: Do We Know What Works?" *Environmental Science and Technology* 33, no. 16 (1999): 2685–2692.

Cochrane, Allan. "Redefining Urban Politics for the Twenty-First Century." In *The Urban Growth Machine: Critical Perspectives Two Decades Later*, edited by Andrew E. G. Jonas and David Wilson, 109–124. Albany: State University of New York Press, 1999.

Cole, Leonard. *Blacks in Power: A Comparative Study of Black and White Elected Officials.* Princeton, NJ: Princeton University Press, 1976.

Cole, Richard L., and David A. Caputo. "The Public Hearing as an Effective Citizen Participation Mechanism: A Case Study of the General Revenue Sharing Program." *American Political Science Review* 78, no. 2 (1984): 404–416.

Collins, Patricia. *Black Feminist Thought: Knowledge, Consciousness and the Politics of Empowerment.* New York: Routledge, 1990.

———. "Learning from the Outsider Within: The Sociological Significance of Black Feminist Thought." *Social Problems* 33, no. 1 (1986): 14–32.

Conover, Patricia Johnston. "Feminists and the Gender Gap." *Journal of Politics* 50, no. 4 (1988): 985–1010.

———. "The Role of Social Groups in Political Thinking." *British Journal of Political Science* 18, no. 1 (1988): 51–76.

Cott, Nancy. *The Bonds of Womanhood: "Woman's Sphere" in New England, 1785–1835.* New Haven, CT: Yale University Press, 1978.

Craw, Michael. "Deciding to Provide: Local Decisions on Providing Social Welfare." *American Journal of Political Science* 54, no. 4 (2010): 906–920.

———. "Overcoming City Limits: Vertical and Horizontal Models of Local Redistributive Policy Making." *Social Science Quarterly* 87, no. 2 (2006): 361–379.

Crenson, Matthew A. *Neighborhood Politics.* Cambridge, MA: Harvard University Press, 1983.

Crocker, Ruth. *Social Work and Social Order: The Settlement Movement in Two Industrial Cities, 1889–1930.* University of Illinois Press, 1992.

Croly, Jennie. *The History of the Woman's Club Movement in America.* New York: Henry G. Allen, 1898.

Crosby, Ned, Janet M. Kelly, and Paul Schaefer. "Citizens Panels: A New Approach to Citizen Participation." *Public Administration Review* 46, no. 2 (1986): 170–178.

Crowley, Jocelyn Elise. "When Tokens Matter." *Legislative Studies Quarterly* 29 (February 2004): 109–136.

Cutright, Phillips. "Measuring the Impact of Local Party Activity on the General Election Vote." *Public Opinion Quarterly* 27 (Fall 1963): 327–386.

Dahlerup, Drude. "From a Small to a Large Minority: Women in Scandinavian Politics." *Scandinavian Political Studies* 11, no. 4 (1988): 275–298.

———. "The Story of the Theory of Critical Mass." *Politics and Gender* 2, no. 4 (2006): 511–522.

Darcy, Robert, Susan Welch, and Janet Clark. *Women, Elections, and Representation.* Lincoln: University of Nebraska Press, 1994.

Deckman, Melissa Marie. "Gender Differences in the Decision to Run for School Board." *American Politics Research* 35, no. 4 (2007): 541–563.

———. "School Board Candidates and Gender: Ideology, Party, and Policy Concerns." *Journal of Women, Politics and Policy* 28, no. 1 (2007): 87–117.

DeLeon, Richard E. "The Urban Antiregime." *Urban Affairs Review* 27, no. 4 (1992): 555–579.

DeSena, Judith N. *Gender in an Urban World.* Research in Urban Sociology 9. Bingley, UK: Emerald Group, 2008.

———. "Local Gatekeeping Practices and Residential Segregation." *Sociological Inquiry* 64, no. 3 (1994): 307–321.

———. "Women: The Gatekeepers of Urban Neighborhoods." *Journal of Urban Affairs* 16, no. 3 (1994): 271–283.

Deyle, Robert E., and Richard A. Smith. "Local Government Compliance with State Planning Mandates: The Effects of State Implementation in Florida." *Journal of the American Planning Association* 64, no. 4 (1998): 457–469.

Diamond, Irene. *Sex Roles in the State House.* New Haven, CT: Yale University Press, 1977.

Dillman, Don A., Glenn Phelps, Robert Tortora, Karen Swift, Julie Kohrell, Jodi Berck, and Benjamin L. Messer. "Response Rate and Measurement Differences in Mixed-Mode Surveys Using Mail, Telephone, Interactive Voice Response (IVR) and the Internet." *Social Science Research* 38, no. 1 (2009): 1–18.

Dixit, Avinash, and John Londregan. "Fiscal Federalism and Redistributive Politics." *Journal of Public Economics* 68, no. 2 (1998): 153–180.

Dodson, Debra L., and Susan J. Carroll. *Reshaping the Agenda: Women in State Legislatures.* New Brunswick, NJ: Center for the American Woman and Politics, Eagleton Institute of Politics, 1991.

Dolan, Julie. "The Senior Executive Service: Gender, Attitudes, and Representative Bureaucracy." *Journal of Public Administration Research and Theory* 10, no. 3 (2000): 513–530.

———. "Support for Women's Interests in the 103rd Congress: The Distinct Impact of Congressional Women." *Women and Politics* 18, no. 1 (1997): 81–94.

Dolan, Kathleen, and Lynne Ford. "Change and Continuity among Women State Legislators: Evidence from Three Decades." *Political Research Quarterly* 50, no. 1 (1997): 137–151.

Domhoff, G. William. *Who Rules America? Power and Politics, and Social Change.* Boston: McGraw-Hill, 2006.

Donahue, Jesse. "It Doesn't Matter: Some Cautionary Findings about Sex and Representation from School Committee Conversations." *Policy Studies Journal* 25, no. 4 (1997): 630–647.

———. "The Non Representation of Gender." *Women and Politics* 20, no. 3 (1999): 65–81.

Dorr, Rheta Childe. *What Eight Million Women Want.* Boston: Small, Maynard, 1910.

Dovi, Suzanne. "Preferable Descriptive Representatives: Will Just Any Woman, Black, or Latino Do?" *American Political Science Review* 96, no. 4 (2002): 729–744.

Dryzek, John S. "Legitimacy and Economy in Deliberative Democracy." *Political Theory* 29, no. 5 (2001): 651–669.

Duerst-Lahti, Georgia, and Cathy Johnson. "Gender and Style in Bureaucracy." *Women and Politics* 10, no. 1 (1990): 67–120.

Dye, Thomas R., and James Renick. "Political Power and City Jobs: Determinants of Minority Employment." *Social Science Quarterly* 62, no. 4 (1981): 475–486.

Eagly, Alice H., Amanda B. Diekman, Mary C. Johannesen-Schmidt, and Anne M. Koenig. "Gender Gaps in Sociopolitical Attitudes: A Social Psychological Analysis." *Personality and Social Psychology* 87, no. 6 (2004): 796–816.

Eagly, Alice, and Mary Johannesen-Schmidt. "The Leadership Styles of Men and Women." *Journal of Social Issues* 57, no. 4 (2001): 781–797.

Eagly, Alice H., Mary C. Johannesen-Schmidt, and Marloes L. van Engen. "Transformational, Transactional, and Laissez-Faire Leadership Styles: A Meta-Analysis Comparing Women and Men." *Psychological Bulletin* 129, no. 4 (2003): 569–591.

Eagly, Alice, and Blair Johnson. "Gender and Leadership Style: A Meta Analysis." *Psychology Bulletin* 108, no. 2 (1990): 233–256.

Eduards, Maud. *Women's Representation and Women's Power.* Stockholm: Forskningsrapport, Stockholms Universitet, Statsvetenskapliga Institutionen, 1980.

Eisinger, Peter K. "Black Employment in Municipal Jobs: The Impact of Black Political Power." *American Political Science Review* 76, no. 2 (1982): 380–392.

Elkin, Stephen L. *City and Regime in the American Republic.* Chicago: University of Chicago Press, 1987.

Feder, Lynette. "Domestic Violence and Police Response in a Pro-Arrest Jurisdiction." *Women and Criminal Justice* 8, no. 4 (1997): 79–98.

Feiock, Richard C., and Jae-Hoon Kim. "Form of Government, Administrative Organization, and Local Economic Development Policy." *Journal of Public Administration Research and Theory* 11, no. 1 (2001): 29–50.

Felkenes, George T., and Jean Reith Schroedel. "A Case Study of Minority Women in Policing." *Women and Criminal Justice* 4, no. 2 (1993): 65–89.

Ferman, Barbara. *Challenging the Growth Machine: Neighborhood Politics in Chicago and Pittsburg.* Lawrence: University of Kansas Press, 1996.

Ferreira, Fernando V., and Joseph Gyourko. "Does Gender Matter for Political Leadership? The Case of U.S. Mayors." Working paper, Wharton School, University of Pennsylvania, 2011.

Fincher, Ruth. "Class and Gender Relations in the Local Labor Market and the Local State." In *The Power of Geography: How Territory Shapes Social Life*, edited by Jennifer Wolch and Michael Dear, 93–117. Boston: Unwin Hyman, 1989.

———. "Women in the City: Feminist Analyses of Urban Geography." *Australian Geographical Studies* 28, no. 1 (1990): 29–37.

Fincher, Ruth, and Jacinta McQuillen. "Women in Urban Social Movements." *Urban Geography* 10, no. 6 (1989): 604–613.

Fischel, William A. "Property Taxation and the Tiebout Model: Evidence for the Benefit View from Zoning and Voting." *Journal of Economic Literature* 30, no. 1 (1992): 171–177.

Flammang, Janet. "Female Officials in the Feminist Capital: The Case of Santa Clara County." *Western Political Science Quarterly* 38, no. 1 (1985): 94–118.

———. *Women's Political Voice: How Women Are Transforming the Practice and Study of Politics.* Philadelphia: Temple University Press, 1997.

Flexner, Eleanor. *Century of Struggle: The Women's Rights Movement in the United States.* Cambridge, MA: Harvard University Press, 1975.

Fox, Richard L., and Jennifer L. Lawless. "If Only They'd Ask: Gender, Recruitment, and Political Ambition." *Journal of Politics* 72, no. 2 (2010): 310–326.

———. "To Run or Not to Run for Office: Explaining Nascent Political Ambition." *American Journal of Political Science* 49, no. 3 (2005): 642–659.

Fox, Richard, and Robert Schuhmann. "Gender of Local Government: A Comparison of Women and Men City Managers." *Public Administration Review* 59, no. 3 (1999): 231–242.

Fridkin, Kim L., and Patrick J. Kenney. "The Role of Gender Stereotypes in U.S. Senate Campaigns." *Politics and Gender* 5, no. 3 (2009): 301–324.

Friedland, Roger, Frances Fox Piven, and Robert R. Alford. "Political Conflict, Urban Structure, and the Fiscal Crisis." *International Journal of Urban and Regional Research* 1, nos. 1–4 (1977): 447–471.

Fulton, Sarah A., Cherie D. Maestas, L. Sandy Maisel, and Walter J. Stone. "The Sense of a Woman: Gender, Ambition, and the Decision to Run for Congress." *Political Research Quarterly* 59, no. 2 (2006): 235–248.

Gangl, Markus, and Andrea Ziefle. "Motherhood, Labor Force Behavior, and Women's Careers: An Empirical Assessment of the Wage Penalty for Motherhood in Britain, Germany, and the United States." *Demography* 46, no. 2 (2009): 341–369.

Garber, Judith, and Robyne Turner. *Gender and Urban Research*. Urban Affairs Annual Review 42. Thousand Oaks, CA: Sage, 1995.

Gilligan, Carol. *In a Different Voice: Psychological Theory and Women's Development*. Cambridge, MA: Harvard University Press, 1982.

———. "In a Different Voice: Women's Conception of the Self and of Morality." *Harvard Educational Review* 47, no. 4 (1977): 481–517.

Gilman, Charlotte Perkins. *Women and Economics: A Study of the Economic Relation between Men and Women as a Factor in Social Evolution*. Boston: Small, Maynard, 1898.

Ginzberg, Lori D. *Women and the Work of Benevolence: Morality, Politics, and Class in the Nineteenth-Century United States*. New Haven, CT: Yale University Press, 1992.

Goldberg, Gertrude Schaffner, and Eleanor Kremen. *The Feminization of Poverty: Only in America?* New York: Praeger, 1990.

Goodwin, Joanne L. *Gender and the Politics of Welfare Reform: Mothers' Pensions in Chicago, 1911–1929*. Chicago: University of Chicago Press, 1997.

Gormley, William T. "The Representation Revolution: Reforming State Regulation through Public Representation." *Administration and Society* 18, no. 2 (1986): 179–196.

Grey, Sandra. "Numbers and Beyond: The Relevance of Critical Mass in Gender Research." *Gender and Politics* 2, no. 4 (2006): 492–502.

Guinier, Lani. *The Tyranny of the Majority: Fundamental Fairness in Representative Democracy*. New York: Free Press, 1994.

Gundry, Kathleen G., and Thomas A. Heberlein. "Research Report: Do Public Meetings Represent the Public?" *Journal of the American Planning Association* 50, no. 2 (1984): 175–182.

Guy, Mary Ellen, and Meredith A. Newman. "Women's Jobs, Men's Jobs: Sex Segregation and Emotional Labor." *Public Administration Review* 64, no. 3 (2004): 289–298.

Habermas, Jürgen. *Between Facts and Norms: Contributions to a Discourse Theory of Law and Democracy* Cambridge, MA: MIT Press, 1996.

Hafemeister, Thomas L. "If All You Have Is a Hammer: Society's Ineffective Response to Intimate Partner Violence." *Catholic University Law Review* 60, no. 1 (2010): 919–1002.

Hardy-Fanta, Carol, Christine Marie Sierra, Pei-te Lien, Dianne M. Pinderhughes, and Wartyna L. Davis. "Race, Gender, and Descriptive Representation: An Exploratory View of Multicultural Elected Leadership in the United States." Paper presented at the American Political Science Association annual meeting, September 2005.

Hart Research Associates and HousingWorksRI. "Affordable Housing in Rhode Island." 2010. Available at http://www.housingworksri.org/sites/default/files/SurveyResultsPresentation.pdf.

Harvey, Mark. "Welfare Reform and Household Survival: The Interaction of Structure and Network Strength in the Rio Grande Valley, Texas." *Journal of Poverty* 15, no. 1 (2011): 43–64.

Hawley, Willis D. *Nonpartisan Elections and the Case for Party Politics.* New York: Wiley Interscience, 1973.

Hayes, Kathy, and Chang Semoon. "The Relative Efficiency of City Manager and Mayor-Council Forms of Government." *Southern Economic Journal* 57, no. 1 (1990): 167–177.

Heidbreder, Brianne, and Katherine Felix Scheurer. "Gender and the Gubernatorial Agenda." *State and Local Government Review* 45, no. 1 (2013): 3–13.

Hero, Rodney E. "Latinos and Politics in Denver and Pueblo, Colorado: Differences, Explanations, and the "Steady-State" of the Struggle for Equality." In *Racial Politics in American Cities*, edited by Rufus Browning, Dale Marshall, and David Tabb, 247–258. New York: Longman, 1997.

Herrick, Rebekah, and Susan Welch. "The Impact of At-Large Elections on the Representation of Black and White Women." In *Ethnic Politics and Civil Liberties*, edited by Lucius Barker, 62–77. New Brunswick, NJ: Transaction, 1992.

Hewitt, Nancy. "Politicizing Domesticity: Anglo, Black, and Latin Women in Tampa's Progressive Movements." In *Gender, Class, Race, and Reform in the Progressive Era*, edited by Noralee Frankel and Nancy Dye. Lexington: University Press of Kentucky, 1991.

Hibbing, John R., and Elizabeth Theiss-Morse. *Stealth Democracy: Americans' Beliefs about How Government Should Work.* New York: Cambridge University Press, 2002.

Hildebrandt, Eugenie, and Patricia Stevens. "Impoverished Women with Children and No Welfare Benefits: The Urgency of Researching Failures of the Temporary Assistance for Needy Families Program." *American Journal of Public Health* 99, no. 5 (2009): 793–801.

Hirschman, Albert O. *Exit, Voice, and Loyalty: Responses to Decline in Firms, Organizations, and States.* Cambridge, MA: Harvard University Press, 1970.

Hooper, Agnes. *Women Journalists and the Municipal Housekeeping Movement, 1868–1914.* Lewiston, NY: Edwin Mellen, 2001.

Hough, Mazie. "Are You or Are You Not Your Sister's Keeper? A Radical Response to the Treatment of Unwed Mothers in Tennessee." In *Before the New Deal: Social Welfare in the South, 1830–1930*, edited by Elna C. Green, 100–119. Athens: University of Georgia Press, 1999.

Huddy, Leonie. "The Political Significance of Voters' Gender Stereotypes." *Research in Micropolitics* 4 (1994): 169–193.

Hunter, Floyd. *Community Power Structure.* Chapel Hill: University of North Carolina Press, 1953.

Inglehart, Ronald, and Pippa Norris. "The Developmental Theory of the Gender Gap: Women's and Men's Voting Behavior in Global Perspective." *International Political Science Review* 21, no. 4 (2000): 441–463.

Isaac, Larry, and William R. Kelly. "Racial Insurgency, the State, and Welfare Expansion: Local and National Level Evidence from the Postwar United States." *American Journal of Sociology* 86, no. 6 (1981): 1348–1386.

Jalalzai, Farida. "Women Rule: Shattering the Executive Glass Ceiling." *Politics and Gender* 4, no. 2 (2008): 205–231.

Jewell, Malcolm E., and Marcia Lynn Whicker. *Legislative Leadership in the American States.* Ann Arbor: University of Michigan Press, 1994.

Jezierski, Louise. "Class and Inequality in the City." In *Handbook of Research on Urban Politics and Policy in the United States,* edited by Ronald K. Vogel, 90–106. Westport, CT: Greenwood, 1997.

Jones, Bryan D., and Lynn Bachelor. *The Sustaining Hand: Community Leadership and Corporate Power.* Lawrence: University of Kansas Press, 1993.

Kanter, Rosabeth Moss. *Men and Women of the Corporation.* New York: Basic Books, 1977.

———. "Some Effects of Proportions on Group Life: Skewed Sex Ratios and Responses to Token Women." *American Journal of Sociology* 82, no. 5 (1977): 965–990.

Kantor, Paul. *The Dependent City Revisited: The Political Economy of Urban Development and Social Policy.* Boulder, CO: Westview, 1995.

Karnig, Albert K., and Susan Welch. *Black Representation and Urban Policy.* Chicago: University of Chicago Press, 1980.

Kathlene, Lyn. "Alternative Views of Crime: Legislative Policymaking in Gendered Terms." *Journal of Politics* 57, no. 3 (1995): 696–723.

———. "In a Different Voice: Women and the Policy Process." In *Women and Elective Office: Past, Present and Future,* edited by Sue Thomas and Clyde Wilcox, 188–202. New York: Oxford University Press, 1998.

———. "Position Power versus Gender Power: Who Holds the Floor?" In *Gender Power, Leadership, and Governance,* edited by Georgia Duerst-Lahti and Rita Mae Kelly, 167–194. Ann Arbor: University of Michigan Press, 1995.

———. "Power and Influence in State Legislative Policymaking: The Interaction of Gender and Position in Committee Hearing Debates." *American Political Science Review* 88, no. 3 (1994): 560–576.

———. "Uncovering the Political Impacts of Gender: An Exploratory Study." *Political Research Quarterly* 42, no. 3 (1989): 397–421.

Kaufmann, Karen. *The Urban Voter.* Ann Arbor: University of Michigan Press, 2004.

Kaufmann, Karen M., and John R. Petrocik. "The Changing Politics of American Men: Understanding the Sources of the Gender Gap." *American Journal of Political Science* 43, no. 3 (1999): 864–887.

Keiser, Lael R., Vicky M. Wilkins, Kenneth J. Meier, and Catherine A. Holland. "Lipstick and Logarithms: Gender, Institutional Context, and Representative Bureaucracy." *American Political Science Review* 96, no. 3 (2002): 553–564.

Keller, Edmond. "The Impact of Black Mayors on Urban Policy." *Annals of the American Academy of Political and Social Science* 439 (1978): 40–52.

Kelly, Florence. "Forbid Home Work and End Child Labor." *New York Globe*, December 7, 1912.

Kemp, Ray. "Planning, Public Meetings and the Politics of Discourse." In *Critical Theory and Public Life*, edited by John Forester, 177–201. Cambridge, MA: MIT Press, 1985.

Kerber, Linda. "The Republican Mother: Women and the Enlightenment—an American Perspective." *American Quarterly* 28, no. 2 (1976): 187–205.

Kerr, Brinck, Will Miller, and Margaret Reid. "Determinants of Female Employment Patterns in U.S. Cities." *Urban Affairs Review* 33, no. 4 (1998): 559–578.

Kittilson, Miki Caul. *Challenging Parties, Changing Parliaments: Women and Elected Office in Contemporary Western Europe*. Columbus: Ohio State University Press, 2006.

Klineberg, Stephen L. *Kinder Houston Area Survey, 1982–2010: Successive Samples of Harris County Residents*. Ann Arbor, MI: Inter-university Consortium for Political and Social Research, 2011.

Koch, Jeffery. "Candidate Gender and Women's Psychological Engagement in Politics." *American Politics Quarterly* 25, no. 1 (1997): 118–133.

———. "Do Citizens Apply Gender Stereotypes to Infer Candidates' Ideological Orientations?" *Journal of Politics* 62, no. 2 (2008): 414–429.

Korabik, Karen, Galen L. Baril, and Carol Watson. "Managers' Conflict Management Style and Leadership Effectiveness: The Moderating Effects of Gender." *Sex Roles* 29, nos. 5–6 (1993): 405–420.

Koven, Seth, and Sonya Michel, eds. *Mothers of a New World: Maternalist Politics and the Origins of Welfare States*. New York: Routledge, 1993.

———. "Womanly Duties: Maternalist Politics and the Origins of Welfare States in France, Germany, Great Britain, and the United States, 1880–1920." *American Historical Review* 95, no. 4 (1990): 1076–1108.

Krane, Dale, Planton Rigos, and Melvin Hill. *Home Rule in America: A Fifty-State Handbook*. Washington, DC: CQ Press, 2001.

Lang-Takac, Esther, and Zahava Osterweil. "Separateness and Connectedness: Differences between the Genders." *Sex Roles* 27, no. 1 (1992): 277–289.

Lawless, Jennifer L., and Richard L. Fox. *It Still Takes a Candidate: Why Women Don't Run for Office*. New York: Cambridge University Press, 2010.

———. *It Takes a Candidate: Why Women Don't Run for Office*. New York: Cambridge University Press, 2005.

Leighley, Jan E. *Strength in Numbers? The Political Mobilization of Racial and Ethnic Minorities.* Princeton, NJ: Princeton University Press, 2001.

Leloudis, James L., II. "School Reform in the New South: The Woman's Association for the Betterment of Public School Houses in North Carolina, 1902–1919." *Journal of American History* 69, no. 4 (1983): 886–909.

Lerner, Gerda. *The Creation of Patriarchy.* New York: Oxford University Press, 1986.

Lewis, Tiffany. "Municipal Housekeeping in the American West: Bertha Knight Landes's Entrance into Politics." *Rhetoric and Public Affairs* 14, no. 3 (2011): 465–491.

Lieske, Joel. "The Political Dynamics of Urban Voting Behavior." *American Journal of Political Science* 33, no. 1 (1989): 150–174.

Lijphart, Arend. "Unequal Participation: Democracy's Unresolved Dilemma." *American Political Science Review* 91, no. 1 (1997): 1–14.

Liu, Xinsheng, Eric Lindquist, Arnold Vedlitz, and Kenneth Vincent. "Understanding Local Policymaking: Policy Elites' Perceptions of Local Agenda Setting and Alternative Policy Selection." *Policy Studies Journal* 38, no. 1 (2010): 69–91.

Logan, John, and Harvey Molotch. *Urban Fortunes: The Political Economy of Place.* Los Angeles: University of California Press, 1987.

MacDonald, Jason A., and Erin E. O'Brien. "Quasi-experimental Design, Constituency, and Advancing Women's Interests: Reexamining the Influence of Gender on Substantive Representation." *Political Research Quarterly* 64, no. 2 (2011): 472–486.

Mansbridge, Jane. *Beyond Adversary Democracy.* Chicago: University of Chicago Press, 1983.

———. "Should Blacks Represent Blacks and Women Represent Women? A Contingent 'Yes.'" *Journal of Politics* 61, no. 3 (1999): 628–657.

Mathews, Joanna. *A Short History of the Orphan Asylum Society in the City of New York.* New York: Anson D. F. Randolph, 1893.

McCammon, Holly. "'Out of the Parlors and into the Streets': The Changing Tactical Repertoire of the U.S. Women's Suffrage Movements." *Social Forces* 81, no. 3 (2003): 787–818.

McCammon, Holly J., Karen E. Campbell, Ellen M. Granberg, and Christine Mowery. "How Movements Win: Gendered Opportunity Structures and U.S. Women's Suffrage Movements, 1866 to 1919." *American Sociological Review* 66, no. 1 (2001): 49–70.

McClain, Paula D. "The Changing Dynamics of Urban Politics: Black and Hispanic Municipal Employment—Is There Competition?" *Journal of Politics* 55, no. 2 (1993): 399–414.

McComas, Katherine. "Public Meetings about Local Waste Management Problems: Comparing Participants to Nonparticipants." *Environmental Management* 27, no. 1 (2001): 135–147.

———. "Theory and Practice of Public Meetings." *Communication Theory* 11, no. 1 (2001): 36–55.

McGerr, Michael. "Political Style and Women's Power, 1830–1930." *Journal of American History* 77, no. 3 (1990): 864–885.

McLanahan, Sara, and Erin Kelly. "The Feminization of Poverty: Past and Future." In *Handbook of the Sociology of Gender*, edited by J. Chafetz, 127–145. New York: Plenum, 2001.

Meier, Kenneth J., and Jill Nicholson-Crotty. "Gender, Representative Bureaucracy, and Law Enforcement: The Case of Sexual Assault." *Public Administration Review* 66, no. 6 (2006): 850–860.

Merritt, Sharyne. "Sex Differences in Role Behavior and Policy Orientations of Suburban Officeholders: The Effect of Women's Employment." In *Women in Local Politics*, edited by Debra Stewart, 115–129. London: Scarecrow, 1980.

Mezey, Susan Gluck. "Perceptions of Women's Role on Local Councils in Connecticut." In *Women in Local Politics*, edited by Debra Stewart, 61–85. London: Scarecrow, 1980.

———. "Women and Representation: The Case of Hawaii." *Journal of Politics* 40, no. 2 (1978): 369–385.

Mill, John Stuart. *Considerations on Representative Government*. Boston: Harper, 1862.

Morgan, David R., and Sheilah S. Watson. "The Effects of Mayoral Power on Urban Fiscal Policy." *Policy Studies Journal* 23, no. 2 (1995): 231–243.

Morone, James A. *The Democratic Wish: Popular Participation and the Limits of American Government*. New Haven, CT: Yale University Press, 1998.

Mossberger, Karen, and Gary Stoker. "The Evolution of Urban Regime Theory: The Challenges of Conceptualization." *Urban Affairs Review* 36 (2001): 810–835.

Mussen, Paul, Stephen Harris, Eldred Rutherford, and Charles B. Keasey. "Honesty and Altruism among Preadolescents." *Developmental Psychology* 3 (1970): 169–194.

Mutpfay, Patricia. "Domestic Violence Legislation and the Police." *Women and Politics* 18, no. 2 (1997): 27–53.

Nathan, Maud. *The Story of an Epoch-Making Movement*. New York: Doubleday, 1926.

Neighborhood Partnership Fund. "Talking about Housing: Developing Effective Messages." 2004. Available at http://housingtrustfundproject.org/campaigns/making-your-case/messages-that-work/public-opinion-research.

Nelson, William E. *Black Politics in Gary: Problems and Prospects*. Washington, DC: Joint Center for Political Studies, 1972.

Norris, Pippa, and Joni Lovenduski. *Political Recruitment: Gender, Race and Class in the British Parliament*. New York: Cambridge University Press, 1995.

North, Elizabeth Mason. *Consecrated Talents, or, the Life of Mrs. Mary W. Mason*. New York: Carlton and Lanahan, 1870.

Norton, Noelle. "Uncovering the Dimensionality of Gender Voting in Congress." *Legislative Studies Quarterly* 24, no. 1 (1999): 65–86.

Norton, Richard K. "More and Better Local Planning: State-Mandated Local Planning in Coastal North Carolina." *Journal of the American Planning Association* 71, no. 1 (2005): 55–71.

Oates, Wallace. "An Essay on Fiscal Federalism." *Journal of Economic Literature* 37, no. 3 (1999): 1120–1149.

———. *Fiscal Federalism*. New York: Harcourt Brace Jovanovich, 1972.

O'Brien, Erin. "The Double-Edged Sword of Women's Organizing." *Women and Politics* 26, nos. 3–4 (2004): 25–56.

Parkinson, John. "Legitimacy Problems in Deliberative Democracy." *Political Studies* 51, no. 1 (2003): 180–196

Pearce, Diane. "The Feminization of Poverty: Women, Work, and Welfare." *Urban and Social Change Review* 11, nos. 1–2 (1978): 28–36.

Pelissero, John, David Holian, and Laura Tomaka. "Does Political Incorporation Matter? The Impact of Minority Mayors over Time." *Urban Affairs Review* 36 (2000): 84–92.

Peterson, Paul. *City Limits*. Chicago: University of Chicago Press, 1981.

Phelps, Joseph, William Gonzenbach, and Edward Johnson. "Press Coverage and Public Perception of Direct Marketing and Consumer Privacy." *Journal of Direct Marketing* 8, no. 2 (1994): 9–22.

Phillips, Anne. *Feminism and Politics*. London: Oxford University Press, 1998.

———. *The Politics of Presence*. London: Oxford University Press, 1995.

Pitkin, Hanna Fenichel. *The Concept of Representation*. Berkeley: University of California Press, 1967.

Pleck, Elizabeth. *Domestic Tyranny: The Making of American Social Policy against Family Violence from Colonial Times to the Present*. New York: Oxford University Press, 2004.

Poggione, Sarah. "Exploring Gender Differences in State Legislators' Policy Preferences." *Political Research Quarterly* 57, no. 2 (2004): 305–314.

Porter, Georgia Pulsifer. *Maine Federation of Women's Clubs: Historical Sketches, 1892–1924*. Lewiston, ME: Lewiston Journal Printshop, 1925.

Powers, Jane Bernard. *The "Girl Question" in Education: Vocational Education for Young Women in the Progressive Era*. Studies in Curriculum History. New York: Routledge, 2012.

Preston, Michael. "Limitations on Black Urban Power: The Case of Black Mayors." In *The New Urban Politics*, edited by Louis Masotti and Robert Lineberry, 111–132. Cambridge, MA: Ballinger, 1976.

Rabrenovic, Gordana. *Community Builders: A Tale of Neighborhood Mobilization in Two Cities*. Philadelphia: Temple University Press, 1996.

Radford, Gail. *Modern Housing for America: Policy Struggles in the New Deal Era*. Chicago: University of Chicago Press, 2008.

Rast, Joel. "Governing the Regimeless City." *Urban Affairs Review* 42, no. 1 (2006): 81–112.

Reingold, Beth. *Representing Women: Sex, Gender, and Legislative Behavior in Arizona and California*. Chapel Hill: University of North Carolina Press, 2000.

———. "Women as Officeholders: Linking Descriptive and Substantive Representation." In *Political Women and American Democracy*, edited by Christina Wolbrecht, Karen Beckwith, and Lisa Baldez, 128–147. New York: Cambridge University Press, 2008.

Reingold, Beth, and Adrienne R. Smith. "Welfare Policymaking and Intersections of Race, Ethnicity, and Gender in U.S. State Legislatures." *American Journal of Political Science* 56, no. 1 (2012): 131–147.

Reingold, Beth, and Michele Swers. "An Endogenous Approach to Women's Interests: When Interests Are Interesting in and of Themselves." *Politics and Gender* 7, no. 3 (2011): 429–435.

Riis, Jacob August. *How the Other Half Lives: Studies among the Tenements of New York*. New York: Penguin, 1901.

Rose, Anne C. *Transcendentalism as a Social Movement, 1830–1850*. New Haven, CT: Yale University Press, 1981.

Rosener, Judy. "How Women Lead." *Harvard Business Review*, November–December 1990, pp. 119–125.

Rousseau, Jean Jacques. *The Social Contract*. New York: Penguin, 1968.

Rowe, Gene, and Lynn J. Frewer. "Public Participation Methods: A Framework for Evaluation." *Science, Technology and Human Values* 25, no. 1 (2000): 3–29.

Ryan, Mary P. *Womanhood in America: From Colonial Times to the Present*. New York: New Viewpoints, 1975.

Saidel, Judith R., and Karyn Loscocco. "Agency Leaders, Gendered Institutions, and Representative Bureaucracy." *Public Administration Review* 65, no. 2 (2005): 158–170.

Saiz, Martin, and Hans Geser. *Local Parties in Political and Organizational Perspective*. Boulder, CO: Westview, 1999.

Saltzstein, Grace Hall. "Female Mayors and Women in Municipal Jobs." *American Journal of Political Science* 30, no. 1 (1986): 140–164.

Sanbonmatsu, Kira. "Gender Stereotypes and Vote Choice." *American Journal of Political Science* 46, no. 1 (2002): 20–34.

———. "Political Parties and the Recruitment of Women to State Legislatures." *Journal of Politics* 64, no. 3 (2002): 791–809.

Sanbonmatsu, Kira, Susan Carroll, and Darcy Walsh. "Poised to Run: Women's Pathways to the State Legislatures." New Brunswick, NJ: Center for American Women and Politics, Eagleton Institute of Politics, 2009.

Sapiro, Virginia. "The Gender Basis of American Social Policy." In *Women, the State, and Welfare*, edited by Linda Gordon, 36–54. Madison: University of Wisconsin Press, 1990.

———. *The Political Integration of Women: Roles, Socialization, and Politics.* Urbana: University of Illinois Press, 1983.

———. "Research Frontier Essay: When Are Interests Interesting? The Problem of Political Representation of Women." *American Political Science Review* 75, no. 3 (1981): 701–716.

Schlesing, Mark, and Caroline Heldman. "Gender Gap or Gender Gaps? New Perspectives on Support for Government Action and Policies." *Journal of Politics* 63, no. 1 (2001): 59–92.

Schneider, Dorothy, and Carl J. Schneider. *American Women in the Progressive Era, 1900–1920.* New York: Facts on File, 1993.

Schumaker, Paul, and Nancy Elizabeth Burns. "Gender Cleavages and the Resolution of Local Policy Issues." *American Journal of Political Science* 32, no. 4 (1988): 1070–1095.

Schwindt-Bayer, Leslie. "Women Who Win: Social Backgrounds, Paths to Power, and Political Ambition in Latin American Legislatures." *Politics and Gender* 7, no. 1 (2011): 1–33.

Shapiro, Robert, and Harpreet Mahajan. "Gender Differences in Policy Preferences: A Summary of Trends from the 1960s to the 1980s." *Public Opinion Quarterly* 50, no. 1 (1986): 42–61.

Sharp, Elaine, and Steven Maynard-Moody. "Theories of the Local Welfare Role." *American Journal of Political Science* 35, no. 4 (1991): 934–950.

Shefter, Martin. *Political Crisis/Fiscal Crisis: The Collapse and Revival of New York City.* New York: Columbia University Press, 1992.

Sklar, Kathryn Kish. *Florence Kelley and the Nation's Work: The Rise of Women's Political Culture, 1830–1900.* New Haven, CT: Yale University Press, 1997.

Smith, Adrienne J. "'Cities Where Women Rule': Female Political Incorporation and the Allocation of Community Development Block Grant Funding." Paper presented at the American Political Science Association annual meeting, Washington, DC, September 2010.

Smith, Adrienne J., Beth Reingold, and Miles Owens. "The Political Determinants of Women's Descriptive Representation in Cities." *Political Research Quarterly* 64, no. 2 (2011): 315–329.

Smith, Daniel Scott. "Family Limitation, Sexual Control, and Domestic Feminism in Victorian America." In *Clio's Consciousness Raised*, edited by Mary Hartman and Lois Banner, 23–27. New York: Harper and Row, 1974.

Spain, Daphne. *How Women Saved the City.* Minneapolis: University of Minnesota Press, 2001.

Staeheli, Lynne A. "Gender Relations in Urban Growth Politics." In *Marginalized Places and Populations: A Structurationist Agenda*, edited by D. Wilson and J. O. Huff, 129–148. Westport, CT: Praeger, 1994.

Stansell, Christine. *City of Women: Sex and Class in New York, 1789–1860.* Urbana: University of Illinois Press, 1987.

Stead, William Thomas. *If Christ Came to Chicago!* New York: Larid and Lee, 1894.

Stein, Robert M. "Federal Categorical Aid: Equalization and the Application Process." *Western Political Science Quarterly* 32 (1979): 396–408.

———. "Municipal Public Employment: An Examination of Intergovernmental Influences." *American Journal of Political Science* 28, no. 4 (1984): 636–653.

Stephens, G. Ross. "State Centralization and the Erosion of Local Autonomy." *Journal of Politics* 36, no. 1 (1974): 44–76.

Stone, Clarence N. *Regime Politics: Governing Atlanta, 1946–1988.* Studies in Government and Public Policy. Lawrence: University Press of Kansas, 1989.

———. "Systemic Power in Community Decision Making: A Restatement of Stratification Theory." *American Political Science Review* 74, no. 4 (1980): 978–990.

———. "Urban Regimes and the Capacity to Govern: A Political Economy Approach." *Journal of Urban Affairs* 15, no. 1 (1993): 1–28.

Svara, James H. "Mayoral Leadership in Council-Manager Cities: Preconditions versus Preconceptions." *Journal of Politics* 49 (1987): 207–227.

———. "The Mayor in Council-Manager Cities: Recognizing Leadership Potential." *National Civic Review* 75 (1986): 271–305.

Sweet, Elizabeth L., and Sara Ortiz Escalante. "Planning Responds to Gender Violence: Evidence from Spain, Mexico and the United States." *Urban Studies* 47, no. 10 (2010): 2129–2147.

Swers, Michele. "Are Congresswomen More Likely to Vote for Women's Issue Bills than Their Male Colleagues?" *Legislative Studies Quarterly* 23, no. 4 (1998): 435–448.

———. *The Difference Women Make: The Policy Impact of Women in Congress.* Chicago: University of Chicago Press, 2002.

———. "Understanding the Policy Impact of Electing Women: Evidence from Research on Congress and State Legislatures." *PS: Political Science and Politics* 34, no. 2 (2001): 217–220.

Swers, Michele, and Carin Larson. "Women in Congress: Do They Act as Advocates for Women's Issues?" In *Women and Elective Office*, edited by Sue Thomas and Clyde Wilcox, 110–128. New York: Oxford University Press, 2005.

Theiss-Morse, Elizabeth, and John R. Hibbing. "Citizenship and Civic Engagement." *Annual Review of Political Science* 8 (2005): 227–249.

Thomas, Sue. "Effects of Race and Gender on Constituency Service." *Western Political Quarterly* 45, no. 1 (1992): 169–180.

———. *How Women Legislate.* London: Oxford University Press, 1994.

———. "The Impact of Women on State Legislative Policies." *Journal of Politics* 53, no. 4 (1991): 958–976.

Thomas, Sue, and Susan Welch. "The Impact of Gender on Activities and Priorities of State Legislators." *Western Political Quarterly* 44, no. 2 (1991): 445–456.

Thompson, J. Phillip, III. *Double Trouble: Black Mayors, Black Communities, and the Call for a Deep Democracy*. Transgressing Boundaries. Oxford: Oxford University Press, 2006.

Tiebout, Charles. "A Pure Theory of Local Expenditures." *Journal of Political Economy* 64 (1956): 416–424.

Tilly, Louise, and Patricia Gurin. *Women, Politics, and Change*. New York: Russell Sage Foundation, 1990.

Tolbert, Pamela S., and Lynne G. Zucker. "Institutional Sources of Change in the Formal Structure of Organizations: The Diffusion of Civil Service Reform, 1880–1935." *Administrative Science Quarterly* 28, no. 1 (1983): 22–39.

Tolleson-Rinehart, Sue. "Do Women Leaders Make a Difference: Substance, Style and Perception." In *The Impact of Women in Public Office*, edited by Susan Carroll, 149–165. Bloomington: University of Indiana Press, 2001.

Torgovnick, Kate. "The Cities Where Women Rule." *Time*, August 13, 2008. Available at http://content.time.com/time/nation/article/0,8599,1832490,00.html.

Tremblay, Manon. "The Substantive Representation of Women and PR: Some Reflections on the Role of Surrogate Representation and Critical Mass." *Politics and Gender* 2, no. 4 (2006): 502–511.

Trounstine, Jessica. "Dominant Regimes and the Demise of Urban Democracy." *Journal of Politics* 68, no. 4 (2006): 879–893.

Trounstine, Jessica, and Melody E. Valdini. "The Context Matters: The Effects of Single-Member versus At-Large Districts on City Council Diversity." *American Journal of Political Science* 52 (2008): 554–569.

Tyler, Tom R., and Andrew Caine. "The Influence of Outcomes and Procedures on Satisfaction with Formal Leaders." *Journal of Personality and Social Psychology* 41, no. 4 (1981): 642–655.

Tyler, Tom R., Kenneth A. Rasinski, and Kathleen M. McGraw. "The Influence of Perceived Injustice on the Endorsement of Political Leaders." *Journal of Applied Social Psychology* 15, no. 8 (1985): 700–725.

Ulbig, Stacy G. "Voice Is Not Enough: The Importance of Influence in Political Trust and Policy Assessments." *Public Opinion Quarterly* 72, no. 3 (2008): 523–539.

Underwood, Daniel, Heather Kim, and Michael Matier. "To Mail or to Web: Comparisons of Survey Response Rates and Respondent Characteristics." Paper presented at the Fortieth Annual Meeting of the Association for Institutional Research, Cincinnati, Ohio, May 2000.

U.S. Census Bureau. "Employed Civilians by Occupation, Sex, Race, and Hispanic Origin." In *U.S. Census 2010*. Washington, DC: U.S. Census Bureau, 2010.

———. "Homeownership Rates by Age of Householder and Household Type." In *U.S. Census 2010*. Washington, DC: U.S. Census Bureau, 2010.

———. "Industry by Sex." In *2011 American Community Survey*. Washington, DC: U.S. Census Bureau, 2011.

———. "Local Government Finances by Type of Government and State: 2006–07." In *2007 Census of Governments: Finance*. Washington, DC: U.S. Census Bureau, 2007.

———. "Own Children under 18 Years by Family Type and Age." In *2011 American Community Survey*. Washington, DC: U.S. Census Bureau, 2011.

———. "Select Population Profile in the United States." In *U.S. Census 2010*. Washington, DC: U.S. Census Bureau, 2010.

U.S. Department of Agriculture, Food and Nutrition Service. "Gender and SNAP Benefits of Participants by Selected Demographic Characteristic." In *Characteristics of Supplemental Nutrition Assistance Program Households: Fiscal Year 2010*. Alexandria, VA: U.S. Department of Agriculture, 2011. Available at http://www.fns.usda.gov/sites/default/files/2010Characteristics.pdf.

U.S. Department of Housing and Urban Development. "Picture of Subsidized Households for 2009." 2009. Available at http://www.huduser.org/portal/picture/picture2009.html.

Vanderleeuw, James M., Maria E. Sandovici, and Christopher A. Jarmon. "Women City Leaders and Postmaterialist Values: Gender Differences in Economic Development Priorities." *Journal of Women, Politics and Policy* 32, no. 3 (2011): 211–236.

Vega, Arturo, and Juanita M. Firestone. "The Effects of Gender on Congressional Behavior and the Substantive Representation of Women." *Legislative Studies Quarterly* 20, no. 2 (1995): 213–222.

Verba, Sidney, Nancy Burns, and Kay Lehman Schlozman. "Knowing and Caring about Politics: Gender and Political Engagement." *Journal of Politics* 59, no. 4 (1997): 1051–1072.

Webler, Thomas, Seth Tuler, and R.O.B. Krueger. "What Is a Good Public Participation Process? Five Perspectives from the Public." *Environmental Management* 27, no. 3 (2001): 435–450.

Weikart, Lynne A., Greg Chen, Daniel W. Williams, and Haris Hromic. "The Democratic Sex: Gender Differences and the Exercise of Power." *Journal of Women, Politics and Policy* 28, no. 1 (2007): 119–140.

Welch, Susan. "Are Women More Liberal than Men in the U.S. Congress?" *Legislative Studies Quarterly* 10, no. 1 (1985): 125–134.

———. "The Impact of Black Elected Officials on Urban Social Expenditures." *Policy Studies Journal* 7, no. 4 (1979): 707–714.

Welch, Susan, and Timothy Bledsoe. "The Partisan Consequences of Nonpartisan Elections and the Changing Nature of Urban Politics." *American Journal of Political Science* 30, no. 1 (1986): 128–139.

Welch, Susan, and Albert K. Karnig. "Correlates of Female Office Holding in City Politics." *Journal of Politics* 41, no. 2 (1979): 478–491.

Whitten, Robert H. "Political and Municipal Legislation in 1903." *Annals of the American Academy of Political and Social Science* 23 (March 1904): 128–145.

Willard, France. *Women and Temperance; Or, the Work and Workers of the Women's Christian Temperance Union.* Hartford, CT: Park, 1883.

Williams, Melissa. "The Uneasy Alliance of Group Representation and Deliberative Democracy." In *Citizenship in Diverse Societies,* edited by Will Kymlicka and Wayne Norman, 124–152. New York: Oxford University Press, 2000.

———. *Voice, Trust and Memory: Marginalized Groups and the Failings of Liberal Representation.* Princeton, NJ: Princeton University Press, 1998.

Wilson, Margaret Gibbons. *The American Woman in Transition: The Urban Influence, 1870–1920.* Westport, CT: Greenwood, 1979.

Winslow, Helen. *The President of Quex: A Women's Club Story.* Boston: Lothrop, Lee, and Shepard, 1906.

Wolbrecht, Christina. *The Politics of Women's Rights: Parties, Positions, and Change.* Princeton, NJ: Princeton University Press, 2000.

Wolfinger, Raymond E., and John Osgood Field. "Political Ethos and the Structure of City Government." *American Political Science Review* 60, no. 2 (1966): 306–326.

Wolman, Harold, John Strate, and Alan Melchior. "Does Changing Mayors Matter?" *Journal of Politics* 58, no. 1 (1996): 201–223.

Wong, Cara. *Group Closeness—1997 National Election Study Pilot Report.* Ann Arbor, MI: American National Elections Study, 1998.

Worden, Alissa Pollitz, and Bonnie E. Carlson. "Attitudes and Beliefs about Domestic Violence: Results of a Public Opinion Survey; II. Beliefs about Causes." *Journal of Interpersonal Violence* 20, no. 10 (2005): 1219–1243.

Wortman, Marlene Stein. "Domesticating the Nineteenth-Century American City." *Prospects* 3 (1977): 531–572.

Young, Iris Marion. "Gender as Seriality: Thinking about Women as a Social Collective." *Signs* 19, no. 3 (1994): 713–738.

Index

Abortion, 5. *See also* Reproductive rights
Addams, Jane, 8, 11. *See also* Settlement house movement
Affordable housing, 4, 5, 8, 10, 13, 97, 107, 108, 127; attitudes about, 13, 26, 29, 30; discussions of, 45, 46, 57, 58–59; expanding, 17, 42, 58, 59; use of, 15, 74. *See also* Public housing
African Americans, 21, 55, 139n17. *See also* Blacks; Race and ethnicity
American Association of Retired Persons (AARP), 78
American Association of University Women, 56, 105
American National Elections Studies, 12–13
Approval of leaders, 115–116. *See also* Representation
Asians, 23, 34, 53, 55. *See also* Race and ethnicity
At-large elections, 54–55
Authority, 17, 69, 94, 102
Autoregressive integrated moving average (ARIMA) model, 157n29

Autonomy, 18, 90, 92, 98, 102, 103, 114, 135. *See also* Fiscal federalism; Intergovernmental issues; Peterson, Paul; State control

Barber, Benjamin, 65
Beard, Mary, 11. *See also* Women's club movement
Blacks, 23, 34, 53, 54, 55. *See also* African Americans; Race and ethnicity
Browning, Rufus, 21
Budget, 22, 42, 85, 116, 134–135; decisions about, 17, 55, 59–60, 72; spending patterns in, 89, 91–92, 101–104, 113
Business associations, 56, 72, 74. *See also* Chamber of commerce; Downtown development associations

California, 45, 52, 54–55, 59–61, 68, 86
Canons of domesticity, 6
Chamber of commerce, 53, 56, 58, 72, 78, 106. *See also* Business associations
Child care, 5, 45, 100, 134. *See also* Day care

Sexual slavery, 10–11. *See also* Prostitution; Violence against women
Single parents, 13, 15
Social Security Administration, 5
Social services, 9, 12, 42, 54, 73, 74, 164n14, 165n17; attitudes about, 12–14; employment in, 100; funding for, 41, 101, 166n27; organizations relating to, 56, 57, 76, 78; use of, 13–16
Soroptimist International, 56, 76
State control, 4, 8, 18, 21, 33, 42, 88, 90, 94–95, 101–102. *See also* Autonomy; Intergovernmental issues
Supplemental Nutrition Assistance Program (SNAP), 15. *See also* Food

Tabb, David, 21
Taxes, 17–19, 42, 65, 70–73, 87, 88, 90, 101, 107, 117; attitudes about, 13–14, 66; revenue from, 113–114. *See also* Economic development; Property; Real Estate
Tenements, 10. *See also* Affordable housing; Public housing
Tone of discussions, 71, 76, 81–84, 162n41
Traditional women's issues, 4, 66, 138n8, 146n76
Transportation, 29, 31, 45, 46, 58, 128, 154n8. *See also* Economic development; Infrastructure; Zoning

Urban women's issues, 2–5, 8, 16, 21–22, 24, 69, 107–108, 128, 138–139n10,

164n14; attitudes about, 27, 29–31, 33, 39, 43, 106, 153n30; discussions of, 45–51, 58–60, 64, 75, 79, 83, 115; funding for, 89, 91–92, 117, 135, 164n12; groups active in, 75–76, 111, 115, 117; subjugation of, 17–18, 21–22, 104, 108, 115
U.S. census, 92, 150n104
U.S. Conference of Mayors, 28, 150n103

Violence against women, 4, 5, 10–12, 13, 57, 107; policies on, 60–62. *See also* Domestic violence; Intimate partner violence; Prostitution; Rape; Sexual assault

Whites, 6, 9, 11, 23, 34, 41, 52–53, 55, 86–88, 139n17
WIC (Special Supplemental Nutrition Program for Women, Infants and Children), 5, 89
Women's club movement, 7, 9–10. *See also* Beard, Mary
Women's Leadership Council, 78
Women's Leadership Forum, 56

YMCA, 56

Zoning, 17, 29, 45–46, 75, 128. *See also* Economic development; Infrastructure; Transportation

Mirya R. Holman is Assistant Professor of Political Science at Florida Atlantic University.